Vin Shanley was a headteacher for ten years before taking early retirement in 1995. Since then he has spent his time in Spain (outside the football season), and at home in Billingham, Stockton-on-Tees, where his daily routine includes: trying to keep fit in the gym; baby-sitting with his granddaughter; reading anything and everything on football; and writing. He is the author of two books on school assemblies, and *Classroom Clangers* (published by Arrow Books), a hilarious collection of anecdotes, howlers and misprints from the world of education.

Football
Shorts

The soccer book of anecdotes, quotes, gaffes and jokes

compiled by

Vin Shanley

ARROW

Published in the United Kingdom in 1997 by
Arrow Books

3 5 7 9 10 8 6 4

Illustrations by Paul Cemmick

First published in the United Kingdom in 1997 by Arrow Books

Arrow Books Limited
Random House UK Ltd
20 Vauxhall Bridge Road, London, SW1V 2SA

Random House Australia (Pty) Limited
20 Alfred Street, Milsons Point, Sydney, New South Wales 2061, Australia

Random House New Zealand Limited
18 Poland Road, Glenfield
Auckland 10, New Zealand

Random House South Africa (Pty) Limited
Endulini, 5a Jubilee Road, Parktown 2193, South Africa

Random House UK Limited Reg. No. 954009

A CIP catalogue record for this book is available from the British Library

Papers used by Random House UK Limited are natural, recyclable products
made from wood grown in sustainable forests. The manufacturing processes conform to the environmental regulations of the country of origin

Typeset by SX Composing DTP, Rayleigh, Essex
Printed and bound in the United Kingdom
by Mackays of Chatham PLC, Chatham, Kent

ISBN 0 09 925643 6

Contents

Introduction

For a kickoff . . . !

In which sport could you have an ex-sergeant major's son fired by the 'Gunners'? (Bruce Rioch at Arsenal); listen to a commentator declare: 'For those of you who are watching in black and white, Spurs are in the all-yellow strip'? (John Motson); hear fans chanting: 'Raymond, Raymond, show us your chest!'? (Ray Wilkins at QPR); read in a newspaper report: 'Bonner looked over his shoulder to see the ball skimming through his legs'?; and, in one match, a referee called, 'Ryan' and a linesman called 'Griggs' both officiate?

It is, of course, that national obsession, **FOOTBALL**: the sport which caused the streets of this land to be as deserted as the Antarctic when England played Germany in Euro '96, the nation to mourn at the outcome, and one bewildered and frustrated fan to exclaim:

'How the hell did we ever manage to beat this lot in two world wars?'

It is a game which transcends class but not always religion and politics, provides heroes, villains, community identity, a common interest, animated discussion, irrationality among the rational, bias, passion, unpredictability in a predictable world and, above all – the elixir of life – humour. This book is a compilation of some of the most amusing and comical stories, gaffes, and so on, from the modern game.

Acknowledgements

The 'Football Shorts Awards'

'*Medals*' for persistence and effort . . .

. . . to all **managers, players, officials, fans, stewards,** and all who strive to make match days memorable, and without whose wit, gaffes and comments this compilation would not have been possible.

'*Trophies*' for consistency and perseverance . . .

. . . to the array of **sports journalists** and **presenters**, too numerous to mention, in their tireless quest to report high quality and interesting news and views from the world of football.

And finally, '*Places in Europe*'. . .

. . . to my friends, in particular **Eddie Curran** and **Billy McNeil**, for their tactical advice; **Pat Wilmut**, for her logistical contribution; and members of my family – **Anne, Clare** and **Michael, Bernie** and **Simon, Vin** and **Jenny,** and **Katie** – for their stoical support.

I
Managers and Chairmen

Introduction

'When I got the job at Rangers, I said I was going to approach it in a laid-back manner. Laid back? I found myself screaming during games, shaking with nervousness on the touchline. I'd become like all the other half-witted managers.' (**Graeme Souness**)

If stress is the root cause of so many heart attacks and other terminal illnesses, it is a constant source of amazement that football managers aren't keeling over like ants sprayed with pesticide. Instead, with one or two notable casualties, they cling on and, like academic professors, never seem to fade away but only lose their faculties. **Lennie Lawrence**, who was the youngest player to win a full FA coaching badge at 17, and, in hindsight, it could be said that was his peak, typifies the nomadic determination of many managers who must constantly whistle to themselves '. . . Always look on the bright side. . .', as they trudge from one boot room to the next.

Such hope is reminiscent of the story of the little twins

at Christmas: one the pessimist, and the other the optimist. On Christmas morning the pessimist goes into his bedroom, and there, stacked high, are boxes wrapped in glistening paper. As he opens each, he is saying to himself: 'There won't be anything I really want in this.' Meanwhile his optimistic brother enters his room to find it full, from floor to ceiling, with horse manure. Undaunted, he grabs a shovel and digs away saying: 'With all this s***, there's got to be a pony in here somewhere.'

Kevin Keegan, the most celebrated victim of managerial pressure during the 1996-97 season, visually and emotionally wilted as the year came to an end. Emlyn Hughes, his one-time team-mate, commented:

'He's been different recently. He's aged 20 years in three months.'.

On 8 January, Keegan dramatically off-loaded the burden of the responsibility he could no longer endure. This was despite the fact that Newcastle had won their previous two league games, 7–1 and 3–0, stood fourth in the Premiership, and had qualified for the quarter-finals of the UEFA Cup. Kevin belongs to the increasing new breed of wealthy, and independent, Premiership managers, who can take football on their own terms, and his terms follow the path to death or glory. He subscribes to the type of philosophy behind Danny Blanchflower's axiom:

'Do things in style, and don't wait for the other lot to die of boredom', and for him, this particular journey led to under-achievement and capitulation echoed in the words:

'I have taken the club as far as I can.'

Alex Ferguson, in spite of his enviable success, and who, unlike Keegan, attained his elevated status after years of managerial stewardship, still reflects chronic match-anxiety in his popped-out eyes and intense gum-chewing. It was Alex who triggered the first signs of Keegan's advanced tension, when he himself revealed his own desperation and paranoia (infamy, ... infamy, ... they've all got it in for me!) in an April 1996 outburst, following a Manchester United *v* Leeds match.

To cynical observers, it was a blatant attempt to manipulate, and exploit, the media to gain psychological advantage at a critical stage of the championship race – and it worked! Keegan exploded live on Sky television and, in an almost uncontrollable frenzy, lambasted Ferguson for his slanderous insinuation that Newcastle had been party to a plot to ease their path to the title. Kevin, during less hysterical times, will have appreciated the implications of the jibe: 'Beaujolais is better than Alex Ferguson, because they only produce one good "whine" a year' but in the heat of that oft-repeated televised moment, he had presented the psychological advantage to Alex and Manchester United. In such ways stress, agitation, and inner-turbulence, is exhibited by the most successful of managers.

Kenny Dalglish, who has assumed the throne on Tyneside, and pioneered the poker-faced countenance, and woollen overcoat, was himself one of the most unexpected casualties to pressure. When he resigned from Liverpool in February 1991, an indication of what he had been going through was reflected in his statement:

'The pressure on match days is making my head explode. I can't go on.'

Later he explained:

'The biggest problem was the pressure I was putting myself under because of the desire to be successful. I had become unpleasant company at home. I was shouting at the kids. It became pretty obvious I had to get out.'

Added to this were the traumas of Heysel and, in particular, Hillsborough, and the subsequent heartache, which severely affected him, as he worked hard to help alleviate the anguish of grieving families.

Steve Coppell, having announced, on his appointment as Manchester City manager in October 1996:

'I really missed the buzz you get on a Saturday. . . . I can't tell you how much I'm pleased to be in the fray again,'

stepped down after only 32 days with the words:

'I have suffered from huge pressure . . . to the extent that I cannot function in the job in the way I would like.'

It also became too much for **Terry Cooper**, the former Leeds and England defender, who relinquished his post at Exeter in June 1995. He revealed:

'I'd felt under stress for some time, then it just hit me. I was driving home from watching a game, and I had to pull over to the side of the road, and phone for help. I couldn't drive another yard.'

And how times can change. In 1993, 'Big' **Ron Atkinson**, glittering and coasting along at Villa, had this to say: 'How can anybody call this work? People in this game don't realize how lucky they are. You drive to the ground, play a few five-a-sides, then have lunch. It's wonderful, enjoyable fun.'

In April and May 1996, as Coventry struggled against the 'big drop', only managing to secure Premiership safety in the last game, and then commencing the new 1996 season with dismal results, Ron was visibly suffering under the strain.

But who can out-do the cultivated, laid-back, coolness of ex-QPR manager, **Ray Wilkins**, who, come sun or shadow, clear sky or hurricane, always appears to have just put on his recently delivered dry-cleaning and be waiting for the bus. Just how would he react if he won the roll-over lottery? Perhaps a furrowed brow and 'We seem to have been very fortunate.' Carling Black Label should hire him. As one fan commented:

'He should be arrested for indecent composure.'

Managers cannot win. If they go berserk with excitement and show excessive emotion like **Barry Fry**, they are branded nutcases. If they remain impassive like **Bryan Robson**, who had the same demeanour when Middlesbrough were in the top five as he had when they were defeated in ten consecutive League games around Christmas and New Year 1996 and 1997, they are considered unfeeling and indifferent to the cause. It also makes you wonder, incidentally, how much time fans spend watching the manager at matches. No wonder some managers find solace in drink:

'Football is a game of two halves . . . then a pint, a few vodkas, and a bottle of whisky.'

The reality is likely to be, of course, as **Kenny Dalglish** has demonstrated, that: 'the mass of managers lead lives of quiet desperation', and such individuals as Bryan Robson and Ray Wilkins have the capacity to hide their feelings while the passion and tumult roar within them. The trouble is that fans want to see passion and boisterous commitment in their commanders.

Howard Wilkinson, the technical director of coaching, who some regard as having about as much public appeal as infected beef, once said:

'If I'm ever reincarnated, I'd like to return as a personality.'

He has tried, somewhat unsuccessfully, to rationalize his image:

'I cannot help the face that God has given me. People just look at my expression and categorize me as a bit of a miserable sod. They don't make the slightest attempt to get to know me. But that's the nature of the business. Half the problem with the people in this world is that they think they have a divine right to be happy all the time. I believe that you have to constantly earn that right.'

Given that philosophy, there are more than a few managers who should be leading lives of pitiable misery. Nor does Howard help his image with his demoralizing and depressing observations, which would make the Samaritans suicidal. When he was top of the League at Leeds for the first time in his managerial career in 1991, he enthused:

'Being top won't change too many things. It will probably rain tomorrow and the traffic lights will still be red.'

Did he ever take lessons from that well-known philosopher, Eric. . . ? Besides being pessimistic, Howard is also as prophetic, as if far more accurate than, Mystic Meg. As Leeds manager, 1995, he declared:

'There's only two types of manager: those who've been sacked, and those who will be sacked in the future.'

At the other end of the scale, there are those such as **Ian Branwell** and **Graham Taylor**, who persist in seeking their nirvana even though torrents of the brown matter cascade relentlessly down upon them. Managers of this ilk have made more comebacks than Lazarus or Joe Bugner ('. . .the man with the body of a Greek sculpture, but fewer moves'). The puzzling question is why these men, despite public vilification, abuse, jibes and, at times, sweat-ridden pyjamas, persist in seeking such employment. Perhaps more mysterious is why it is that clubs, and indeed the media, continue to hire them. On TV they appear as experts. Who was it who said that an 'expert' is a 'has-been' and a 'little drip' ('ex' and 'spurt')?

The truth of the matter is that the role of the football manager, particularly in the Premiership, has changed so much in recent years, it requires a plethora of qualities, skills and experience to which few can aspire. Shankley once said:

'Pressure is working down the pit. Pressure is having no work at all. Pressure is trying to escape relegation on fifty shillings a week. Pressure is not the European Cup, or the Championship, or the Cup Final. That's the reward.'

He was right – but as **Roy Evans** has said:

'If Shanks had come straight out of his era and tried to cope with things now, it would have driven him round the bend.'

But since then, thanks to the 1990 semi-final and a

weeping **Gazza** (Paul Gascoigne), football has become
trendy with a vast appeal among the nouveaux bimbos
and bimbesses, a mega-buck, City-controlled industry,
moving away from the fans and community; a touchline,
microphone-wielding, ambush of interlopers, and
Andy Gray ('measure-the-trajectory-and-velocity-of-
your-chewing-gum-expulsion'), a Foreign-Legion-cohort
influx of players, à la Ravanelli, and a society which
demands instant success, and the right to denounce, and
criticize, in return for astronomical wages.

A manager's task, never easy, has become more difficult, and while it is a serious business, it does, thank God,
have a lighter side. How managers deal with the stresses
and strains is the subject of this section, and for ease of
definition we have identified several categories into which
managers could be put.

The Manager As a Humorist

Before quitting Sheffield United, **Dave Bassett** said:

'The spirit at this club is the worst I've ever known, and
the tea's not much better either.'

Dave, known popularly throughout the game as
'Harry', reveals that his wife calls him by that nickname
and '. . . it's only when she calls me Dave that I know I'm
in the s***.'

Harry never had much money to spend at Sheffield, but
always asserted that the Board had been loyal to him.
'When I came, they said there would be no money, and
they've certainly kept their word.'

True to his word, though, Harry Bassett does keep his
promises:

'I told the chairman I would get them out of the
Division. I did, but the only thing was, we went down one
division instead of up!'

That was the year that he declared:

'Our strikers couldn't hit a donkey's arse with a frying pan'

and later:

'I've only ever thrown one cup of tea in a dressing room in temper – it went all over my suit.'

Often the voice of sanity, Dave advised:

'England can't always win 6–0. Bobby Charlton has retired.'

While at Sheffield United, Dave's goalkeeper, Simon Tracy, was sent off in the match against Spurs:

'He's got the brains of a rocking horse,' said the irate manager.

And just before his resignation from Sheffield United on 16 December 1995, Dave won the Blades' Revival Draw – £2,000 in travel vouchers!

When in November 1996 Dave was informed he was being linked with the Manchester City job, he quipped:

'I cannot stop people linking me with jobs. They can link me with Cindy Crawford if they like. I think my wife might have a laugh at that.'

Black humour, inspired by anxiety, and lack of resources, prompted Hamilton manager, Iain Munro, to say:

'I'd hang myself, but we can't afford the rope.'

Tommy Docherty handled his tensions by apparently putting them all down to experience and recording the better moments for after-dinner speeches. Tommy, who was Aston Villa chairman, Doug Ellis's, first of eight managerial victims, said in 1970:

'Doug once told me: "I'm right behind you, Tommy." I replied: "I'd rather have you in front of me, Mr Chairman. I feel safer that way."'

Later in his career, Tommy claimed that his doctor told him that he needed a complete break from football so he became manager of Wolves. It was at Wolves that Tommy touched on the point of silverware:

'I just opened the trophy cabinet. Two Japanese prisoners of war came out.'

He once said:

'Some teams are so negative they could be sponsored by Kodak.'

Tommy, now more in demand as an after-dinner speaker than a pundit, once informed Leighton James:

'Your pace is very deceptive. You are much slower than you appear.'

Poor Leighton came in for another onslaught when he made his Welsh debut at the age of 19 and, thanks to Peter Storey, he didn't get a kick. The Welsh manager told him after the match that he had been considering filing a Missing Persons report on him midway through the first half.

It was reported that Tommy, who had been fired by everyone but NASA, and had more clubs than a pack of cards, had once been considered as the 'manager of the month', but had not qualified, because he had not been long enough at any club.

He once quipped:

'I've always said there's a place for the Press, but they haven't dug it yet.'

As scathing was his observation:

'The ideal board of directors should be made up of three men – two dead and one dying.'

On the art of doing a good deal:

'A manager must buy cheap and sell dear. Another manager rings me to ask about a player. "He's great!" I say, "Super lad, goes to church twice a day, good in the air, two lovely feet, make a great son-in-law." You never tell them he couldn't trap a bag of cement.'

On the subject of his old club, Manchester United, buying a player:

'Half a million for Remi Moses? You could get the original Moses and the tablets for that price.'

The managerial spirit of hope and quiet desperation is reflected in this story from the Scottish League. **John Lambie**, formerly of Partick Thistle, was told by his coach during a match that one of his players, Colin McGloshan, had a head injury and didn't know who he was. 'For God's sake,' said Lambie, 'Tell him he's Pelé.'

John McGrath, the former Halifax manager, was another who relieved the stress through black humour. On receiving the sack from Halifax he commented:

'I left as I arrived – fired with enthusiasm.'

And again:

'Things got so bad I received a letter from Readers' Digest, saying I hadn't been included in their prize draw.'

Bobby Gould, while at West Brom, had a torrid time and, after one particularly virulent demonstration by supporters, cracked:

'That's not the worst reception I've ever had – did you ever see me as a player?'

Also while at West Brom, Bobby tried the psychological approach with his team to improve results. He once brought into the dressing room a 23-stone supporter to heap invective upon the players after their dismal 2–1 defeat against Bournemouth. The fan was scathing in his comments generally, then turned to one player and told him:

'And you – you should f*** off back to f****** London!'

Bobby once said:

'That's thrown a spanner in the fire!'

Gould has named the team he would like to represent Wales in the qualifying rounds for the next World Cup – it's Borussia Dortmund.

Kevin Keegan caused palpitations – delayed until January 1997 – among Newcastle fans when, at the most crucial part of the championship race in 1996, he announced on the local Century Radio:

'I don't want to stay in football. I have no inclination at all, and a career in politics really interests me. In fact, I would like to be Prime Minister.'

The broadcast brought in a deluge of worried calls, none of them realizing it was 1 April!

Still, even if Newcastle United failed to win the Premier title in 1996, they did win the title of 'the sexiest of squads' – an accolade presented by London Agency, STORM. Les Ferdinand and David Ginola won top marks, but what clinched it was Kevin Keegan, who out-sexed the doleful Alex Ferguson. Newcastle can thank God it all didn't rest on Peter Beardsley, the player who, it has been suggested, has 'a face made for radio'.

While on the subjects of fashion and 'the manager as a humorist', it seems appropriate to quote Alex Ferguson on the occasion of Manchester United's 3–1 defeat at Southampton in April 1996.

Question: 'What went wrong?'

Ferguson: 'Simple – the shirts we wore. The players couldn't pick each other out.'

But could it have just been a case of the team feeling a bit off colour? Whatever, Southampton fans would not let the matter drop. Their chant on 20 October 1996, during their 6–3 thumping of United, enquired: 'Have you got another strip?'

Kenny Dalglish, the manager with a better track-record than Linford Christie, possesses a rare sense of humour. As director of coaching at Blackburn, the story is told of the occasion when he entered a London Restaurant, where Sir John Hall's son, Douglas, was dining. Newcastle, at that time during the 1995-96 season, would have sold the Tyne Bridge to get Alan Shearer. Kenny received a note, from Hall Jnr as he settled down to his meal, which read: 'Subject to contract, Newcastle United bid £10 million for Alan Shearer.'

Kenny wrote back: 'Get in touch again when you're sober.'

So another £5 million is the cost of sobriety!

Fate works in mysterious ways. A year later, on 14 January 1997, Kenny became Newcastle manager, and sat at Sir John's left hand at the introductory press conference.

Question from one of the assembled journalists: 'Kenny, will you be moving to the North-East?'

Kenny: 'Yes, as soon as the chairman has moved out of his small house.'

Sir John lives in Wynyard Hall, a mansion in 100 acres of woodland and landscaped gardens.

Kenny's accent is hard to understand even for the Geordies who live within striking distance of the border, so it came as no surprise when it was suggested that an interpreter might be appointed for him as well as Asprilla.

This theme of disorder on the part of Barry was upheld by Mark McGhee, the Wolves manager: 'His management style seems to be based on the chaos theory.'

Some made the cutting remark that Barry thought tactics were tiny sweets in plastic boxes.

Then there was another foreign player, José Domingues, who played for Birmingham, and of whom Barry said:

'José? I love him. Everybody loves him. But when you analyse what he does, his first ball is crap.'

Even on the day of his dismissal Barry was irrepressible. The message on his answerphone was:

'Kristine's gone shopping as usual, and I've gone to the Job Centre looking for new employment. Funny old game, innit?'

Continental chairmen might insist that pre-season preparation take the form of a monastic-like retreat where the body and mind is honed to perfection for the onslaught of the ardours of the approaching season. Not Barry, who took over at Peterborough in the close season of 1996, then promised his players a refreshing break from pre-season training so that they could all 'get a bird, get p****d and play 18 holes of golf'.

Peter Boizot, founder of the Pizza Express chain. became president and major shareholder at Peterborou~ in January 1996 and confirmed Barry Fry's mana~ position. He commented ominously: 'Barry assu~ . . . that we have a nucleus of players with whi~ make progress.' To most people a 'nucle~ 'small core', but to Barry . . .

The Manager As England's Su~

A waitress at the England hotel be~
Switzerland in November 1995 ~

It is a problem fans, and those who have had to listen to Kenny, have lived with for years. In 1986 a letter appeared in the *Evening Standard*:

'For the benefit of Anglo-Saxon viewers, I wonder if the TV sports presenters would consider using subtitles when interviewing Kenny Dalglish.'

On Kevin Keegan's first public appearance after his resignation from Newcastle, at Catterick Races on 31 January 1997, hacks were quick to point out that his horse, 'Matching Colours', failed to finish the course.

And on Kenny Dalglish's first interview on Sky after returning to management, he met up with his old adversary, Nick Collins, in the post-match interview. Newcastle had won 4–3 in added-time after Leicester City were leading 3–1 with 12 minutes to go.

Nick Collins: 'Is it the excitement of afternoons like that which you missed, Kenny?'

Kenny Dalglish: 'It was your interviews I missed, Nick! You can see now why Kevin went grey, Terry Mc is white, and I've got the Grecian 2000 ready.'

Another Scotsman who can exhibit a droll sense of humour is the National manager, **Craig Brown**. Speaking to a football gathering, he noticed in the audience Billy Kirkwood, the Dundee manager. 'I hear,' said Craig, 'that Dundee United have approached Duncan Ferguson in prison with a £4 million bid to bring him back to the club, but that Duncan prefers it where he is.'

Question: 'What is the difference between Bill Clinton and Ken Bates?'
Answer: 'Bill accepts that he can't hold on to Chelsea for ever.'

On the subject of chairmen, when **Mike Bateson** of Torquay appointed as manager the former Southampton and Yugoslavian full back **Ivan Golac**, he commented: 'We made him an offer he should have refused.'

Frank Clark, while manager of Nottingham Forest, managed to smile throughout his trials and tribulations as his team failed to win a game in almost four months. On his resignation in December 1996, he said:

'I felt like a turkey waiting for Christmas. As soon as the club got new owners I was going to be out like a shot.'

In other words, like a turkey, he, like his team, would be well-stuffed.

George Graham, manager of Leeds, announced:

'My teams play like Brazil. They won the last World Cup from defence, whatever anyone says.'

Indeed they did, George – but Brazil also scored goals!

Jimmy Quinn, manager of Reading, commenting on his injury-prone goalkeeper, Bulgarian Bobby Mihaylor:

'The only thing he hasn't had is mad cow disease.'

Lawrie McMenemy, whose record at Sunderland matched Linford Christie's in the Atlanta 100 metres final, and who in that north-eastern city is remembered with as much fondness as mustard gas, survived the catastrophes of his stewardship as Graham Taylor's right-hand man to serve Southampton once again. The football club, he reports:

'. . . is a very well run outfit from Monday to Friday. It's Saturdays we've got a problem with.'

Ian St John, the Liverpool legend, and one-time soccer presenter and pundit, commenting on his experience as a football manager:

'I gave it up out of sickness and fatigue – I was sick tired of the players.'

The Manager As an Eccentric

At one stage in 1996, **Barry Fry**, it is claimed, had more his squad at Birmingham than the American Olymp team.

Barry abandoned his squad numbering system while at Birmingham. He said:

'The players have enough problems without carrying such big numbers around.'

When Terry Venables, the man who has had enough books written by him, or about him, to rival the Bible, said he was going to resign, Barry Fry decided he would apply for the job. Always the optimist, he said:

'For a start, the fans would love me because I'd pick everybody. We'd start with a squad of 300 and sort it out from there.'

Even before the advent of 'rent-a-crowd' Barry, it is interesting to note, from the start of the 1990-91 season to the end of 1993, Birmingham used 85 different players i the First Team.

Poor old Barry didn't get much support from Ste Claridge, who moved in March 1996 from Birmingha to Leicester, and scored that amazing goal in the last seconds in the play-off against Crystal Palace, wh ecured Premiership football, and their winner in the oca-Cola Cup Final:

In pre-season training, all we did was run over a h like a scene from *Zulu*.' He goes on: 'In one ga d with a Swedish player, and we didn't even ther's names. He was called Sigurd Rushfeld ught he was a ball-boy; then Fry sent him

cup of tea and, according to the two English physios who
were with him at the time, asked him if he cared for sugar.
Apparently the response was: 'Sugar! Are you serious?'

While on the subject of Terry on foreign soil, just
before he was dismissed by Barcelona in 1987, he said:

'I can still go out as long as it's after midnight, I'm
wearing dark glasses and it's a dimly-lit restaurant.'

'Terry Venables likes neat passing and triangles. The
way some of his players go missing, he can only be talking about the Bermuda Triangle.' (Letter.)

When born-again Christian, **Glen Hoddle**, was appointed
to succeed Venables after the European Championships,
1996, one sports writer wrote: 'The FA have found a
Christian to throw to the lions.' Hoddle will need the
entire world supply of fortitude and perseverance if, in
the effluxion of time, he has to put up with the type of
jibes directed at previous managers.

Apparently it is not easy for footballers to share with
their team-mates that they have discovered religion, and
have found Christ. Justin Fashanu claimed it was as difficult as admitting you are gay. Fashanu goes on: 'John
Robertson (who played with him at Nottingham) started
calling me "Brother Justin".'

To return to Glen Hoddle, it would seem that his laid-
back, come-what-may disposition is eminently suitable
for the pressures of the England job. It is not true that he
has more life in him after taking a dose of valium, but
what some say is true surrounds an occasion when he
played for Monaco. Apparently, in a match against
Auxerre, one of the opposition was injured and there was
a delay while physios and doctors fussed around. It was a
balmy Mediterranean evening, so Glen lay down while
the problem was sorted out. Minutes later play was ready

to resume but, before it could do so, Monsieur Hoddle, who had been busy taking forty winks, had to be woken from his slumbers.

When Glen Hoddle, (once known as 'Glenda', reveals his No. 2 at Chelsea, Peter Shreeves), was appointed England's coach, according to a US journalist, Americans thought 'Glen Hoddle' was a malt whisky.

Written on **Graham Taylor**'s car after the film which showed him to be hesitant, unsure, insecure, edgy . . . : 'I used to be indecisive, but now I'm not so sure.'

The comment that: 'In the case of Taylor, never has mediocrity been as well rewarded since the time Caligula made his horse a Consul', was only reasonable in hindsight.

Taylor's statement, and indeed utilization of the obvious, did not help his cause: 'Footballers are no different from human beings.'

And was it Graham Taylor who said: 'Nothing ever seems to go right for me. I have a canary that hums.' . . . ?

He could be right. On his re-appointment to Watford in February 1996, his close friend, Elton John, made it clear that continued reference to the 'turnip' tag should finally come to an end: 'It needs to be buried,' he commented. Thank you, Elton. With friends like that . . .

At least Taylor never had to put up with an official protest movement specifically set up against him. The Italian manager had the 'Anti-Sacchi Club', which very droll-ly, he promised he would join himself.

One difficulty, which national coaches often refer to, is the need to relieve the boredom of players during tournaments when squads can be together for up to six weeks. It is a problem exacerbated by limited contact with families and only partially mitigated by the plushest and most 'gastronomique' of hotels where players are cosseted and provided with everything from golf courses to sight-seeing trips. It is a predicament the average fan, strapped for cash with ten days in Tossa de Mar or Galashiels, probably does not appreciate. But managers do face the problem of the 'Give a man a Toyota and he wants a Mercedes' genre – and different members of the profession have addressed this in a variety of interesting and illuminating ways:

Alf Ramsey insisted that players handed in their passports so that a check could be kept on their where-abouts.

Don Revie increased the tedium by organizing bingo, skittles and the chipping of golf balls à la Butlins.

Ron Greenwood made the mistake of relying on players' professionalism and treated them like adults. Moore and Greaves, amongst others, broke the curfew and the trust put in them.

Graham Taylor's *pièce de résistance* was 'football golf', which most players went along with but not Chris Waddle. On one occasion Chris, who wanted to discuss and practise tactics, refused to leave the coach and watched the Rugby Cup Final.

Some have said **Terry Venables** never disciplined any-one. Hence the clubbing in Hong Kong, the 'bash' on board Cathay Pacific, and the mischievous back-drop of prancing prima donnas in the gloom during his TV inter-view before the Switzerland match in Euro '96 began.

Perhaps Terry's judgement of what is acceptable is sus-pect. How can this observation from November 1996 be explained? 'Tony Adams . . . has always led by example.'

– By getting his round in!?

Glen Hoddle, in the effluxion of time and in keeping with his Christian commitment, might get the lads into the right mental frame of mind by singing such hymns as 'Fight the Good Fight', 'Do Not Be Afraid' or 'Onward, Christian Soldiers'. Up until now he has demonstrated a man-management style which is fair and firm and eminently sensible, as when he gave Paul Merson a day off before the match against Poland on 9 October 1996 to attend an AA meeting: 'These things come before football. Paul still needs to go to these things, and it's fine by me.'

Hoddle could have done with some divine intervention at the press conference in Moldova when dealing with this type of question from one of that country's reporters:

'Can you tell us the height and weight of the players in the England team?' (Pause as Hoddle tries not to wince – he recovers quickly.)

'I'll have to get back to you on that one.'

Bobby Gould, the Wales Manager, passed some of the time with his players prior to the Holland World Cup match in November 1996 in the team's Eindhoven hotel, voting for a captain. Vinnie Jones triumphed and in another vote – this time of confidence in Vinnie and himself, Bobby revealed: 'By rights he shouldn't be here in terms of technical ability, but then neither should I. We've both taken our chances.' His logic got no better. 'If Wimbledon can beat Arsenal, Tottenham and Liverpool, Wales can beat the likes of Holland.' Wales lost 7–1. Guus Hiddink, the Dutch coach, commented: 'For five or six minutes Wales were a threat.'

Then there was the manager who justified his choice of captain by saying: 'The players will follow him anywhere, if only out of curiosity.'

It is interesting to hear the names of some past captains of England:

Charles Alcock; Hubert Heron; Francis Sparks; Billy Moon; Harry Daft; Cunliffe Gosling; Charles Wreford-Brown; Ernest 'Nudger' Needham; Reginald 'Tip' Foster; Steve Bloomer; Billy Walker; Alf Strange; Tommy Cooper.

The Manager – Bobbing and Weaving

When asked to comment on David Batty's and Graham Le Saux's skirmish in the UEFA Cup match in November 1995, the suggestion is that **Kenny Dalglish**'s comment should have been: 'I thought Graham's left jab to the head was quick and accurate, but David needs to spend more time on his defensive footwork.'

As a player, **Bryan Robson** was not the most popular. Opposing fans often used to chant: 'Robson, Robson man of the match', in recognition of the award they felt was always made to him – even when he hadn't been playing.

At the present time Bryan is serving his apprenticeship in management and clearly he is following in the path of other successful and pioneering leaders of the trade by proclaiming: 'When I say that I listen to players, that doesn't necessarily mean that I take any notice of them.'

But how times change. When Fabrizio Ravanelli, the star who rejects most things including overseas pronouncements, telephone charges and team-mates who don't pass the ball, criticized 'Boro's training methods, lack of facilities and fitness-training, Bryan declared: 'A lot of things he said were noted because we are always open to things which can improve us.' Fair enough, but worrying when the criticisms are so fundamental to basic soccer coaching and a club-player voices publicly recurrent complaints. It was Edmund Burke who said: 'There is a limit at which forbearance ceases to be a virtue.'

Bryan Robson might well claim that he was about as lucky as Job while Middlesbrough was in the Premiership – as fortunate as the man who confessed to murder on his death-bed, then made a recovery. Plagued by two seasons of injuries, near-miss transfer deals and a star who went missing, his side managed only six League wins throughout 1996 and was ultimately relegated. Nevertheless, he did energize Middlesbrough as a club, attracted world-class players and produced unprecedented interest on Teesside. His day will come again.

While at the Riverside, mention should be made of the occasion when Middlesbrough first made a bid for Barmby, now with Everton, and Tottenham chairman, Alan Sugar, sneered: 'We don't know what is meant by money in Middlesbrough but in London it's the stuff you put in the bank.'

And do we perhaps detect a further note of southern jealousy in *Evening Standard* writer, Michael Herd's, acidic comment on Juninho's decision to join Middlesbrough. Herd said he would be going to 'one of the most ravaged industrial landscapes on earth'. A pathetic attempt at a put-down by someone who clearly didn't know the area, and who lost all credibility through his ignorance.

Even further north at Partick Thistle, when **Bertie Auld** was manager, he used to indulge in post-match drinking sessions, in his office, with his chairman, Miller Reid, friends and pressmen. They often lost track of time. After one such session, there was a knock at the door at two o'clock in the morning, and there stood two constables.

They were invited in for a drink. 'No, it's all right, Mr Auld,' one of them said. 'We just wanted to let you know you've left your floodlights on.'

Alan Buckley, who has gained a reputation for getting teams promoted on a shoestring, commented on taking over at West Brom: 'The chairman said we had no money and he's been as good as his word.'

Apropos of finance, the crack going round the Midlands in February, 1996, was: 'Alan Buckley, the West Brom boss, has been arrested for trying to get ten players out of a cigarette machine.'

Sometimes the problem for managers is not a shortage of players, but of players of the right calibre. **Brian Little**, now of Aston Villa, talking of when he took over at Darlington, gave this insight:

'Within five minutes of my first day, one of the players walked in and said: "By the way, I'm not training today. I don't train very much, but if you want me to play at the weekend, I will." ' When the Club was relegated to the Conference at the end of that season, Little got rid of 20 players in an hour . . . and Darlington blossomed.

The Manager As a Foreign Body
When one examines the vitriol and sarcasm which exist in some foreign clubs, then British clubs look like millponds in the eye of the hurricane.

As can be imagined, there is little love lost between the fans, players and officials of Madrid and Barcelona. The intense and bitter rivalry stems from political history and traditions as well as common footballing hatred. You can imagine how Saint **Gary Lineker**, playing at the time for Barcelona, increased his popularity in and around the city

It is a problem fans, and those who have had to listen to Kenny, have lived with for years. In 1986 a letter appeared in the *Evening Standard*:

'For the benefit of Anglo-Saxon viewers, I wonder if the TV sports presenters would consider using subtitles when interviewing Kenny Dalglish.'

On Kevin Keegan's first public appearance after his resignation from Newcastle, at Catterick Races on 31 January 1997, hacks were quick to point out that his horse, 'Matching Colours', failed to finish the course.

And on Kenny Dalglish's first interview on Sky after returning to management, he met up with his old adversary, Nick Collins, in the post-match interview. Newcastle had won 4–3 in added-time after Leicester City were leading 3–1 with 12 minutes to go.

Nick Collins: 'Is it the excitement of afternoons like that which you missed, Kenny?'

Kenny Dalglish: 'It was your interviews I missed, Nick! You can see now why Kevin went grey, Terry Mc is white, and I've got the Grecian 2000 ready.'

Another Scotsman who can exhibit a droll sense of humour is the National manager, **Craig Brown**. Speaking to a football gathering, he noticed in the audience Billy Kirkwood, the Dundee manager. 'I hear,' said Craig, 'that Dundee United have approached Duncan Ferguson in prison with a £4 million bid to bring him back to the club, but that Duncan prefers it where he is.'

Question: 'What is the difference between Bill Clinton and Ken Bates?'
Answer: 'Bill accepts that he can't hold on to Chelsea for ever.'

On the subject of chairmen, when **Mike Bateson** of Torquay appointed as manager the former Southampton and Yugoslavian full back **Ivan Golac**, he commented: 'We made him an offer he should have refused.'

Frank Clark, while manager of Nottingham Forest, managed to smile throughout his trials and tribulations as his team failed to win a game in almost four months. On his resignation in December 1996, he said:

'I felt like a turkey waiting for Christmas. As soon as the club got new owners I was going to be out like a shot.'

In other words, like a turkey, he, like his team, would be well-stuffed.

George Graham, manager of Leeds, announced:

'My teams play like Brazil. They won the last World Cup from defence, whatever anyone says.'

Indeed they did, George – but Brazil also scored goals!

Jimmy Quinn, manager of Reading, commenting on his injury-prone goalkeeper, Bulgarian Bobby Mihaylor:

'The only thing he hasn't had is mad cow disease.'

Lawrie McMenemy, whose record at Sunderland matched Linford Christie's in the Atlanta 100 metres final, and who in that north-eastern city is remembered with as much fondness as mustard gas, survived the catastrophes of his stewardship as Graham Taylor's right-hand man to serve Southampton once again. The football club, he reports:

'. . . is a very well run outfit from Monday to Friday. It's Saturdays we've got a problem with.'

Ian St John, the Liverpool legend, and one-time soccer presenter and pundit, commenting on his experience as a football manager:

'I gave it up out of sickness and fatigue – I was sick and tired of the players.'

The Manager As an Eccentric

At one stage in 1996, **Barry Fry**, it is claimed, had more in his squad at Birmingham than the American Olympic team.

Barry abandoned his squad numbering system while at Birmingham. He said:

'The players have enough problems without carrying such big numbers around.'

When Terry Venables, the man who has had enough books written by him, or about him, to rival the Bible, said he was going to resign, Barry Fry decided he would apply for the job. Always the optimist, he said:

'For a start, the fans would love me because I'd pick everybody. We'd start with a squad of 300 and sort it out from there.'

Even before the advent of 'rent-a-crowd' Barry, it is interesting to note, from the start of the 1990-91 season to the end of 1993, Birmingham used 85 different players in the First Team.

Poor old Barry didn't get much support from Steve Claridge, who moved in March 1996 from Birmingham to Leicester, and scored that amazing goal in the last 20 seconds in the play-off against Crystal Palace, which secured Premiership football, and their winner in the 1997 Coca-Cola Cup Final:

'In pre-season training, all we did was run over a hill. It was like a scene from *Zulu*.' He goes on: 'In one game, I played with a Swedish player, and we didn't even know each other's names. He was called Sigurd Rushfeldt, and we thought he was a ball-boy; then Fry sent him on to play.'

This theme of disorder on the part of Barry was upheld by Mark McGhee, the Wolves manager: 'His management style seems to be based on the chaos theory.'

Some made the cutting remark that Barry thought tactics were tiny sweets in plastic boxes.

Then there was another foreign player, José Domingues, who played for Birmingham, and of whom Barry said:

'José? I love him. Everybody loves him. But when you analyse what he does, his first ball is crap.'

Even on the day of his dismissal Barry was irrepressible. The message on his answerphone was:

'Kristine's gone shopping as usual, and I've gone to the Job Centre looking for new employment. Funny old game, innit?'

Continental chairmen might insist that pre-season preparation take the form of a monastic-like retreat where the body and mind is honed to perfection for the onslaught of the ardours of the approaching season. Not Barry, who took over at Peterborough in the close season of 1996, then promised his players a refreshing break from pre-season training so that they could all 'get a bird, get p****d and play 18 holes of golf'.

Peter Boizot, founder of the Pizza Express chain, became president and major shareholder at Peterborough in January 1996 and confirmed Barry Fry's managerial position. He commented ominously: 'Barry assures me . . . that we have a nucleus of players with which we can make progress.' To most people a 'nucleus' means a 'small core', but to Barry . . .

The Manager As England's Supremo

A waitress at the England hotel before the match against Switzerland in November 1995 brought **Terry Venables** a

cup of tea and, according to the two English physios who were with him at the time, asked him if he cared for sugar. Apparently the response was: 'Sugar! Are you serious?'

While on the subject of Terry on foreign soil, just before he was dismissed by Barcelona in 1987, he said:

'I can still go out as long as it's after midnight, I'm wearing dark glasses and it's a dimly-lit restaurant.'

'Terry Venables likes neat passing and triangles. The way some of his players go missing, he can only be talking about the Bermuda Triangle.' (Letter.)

When born-again Christian, **Glen Hoddle**, was appointed to succeed Venables after the European Championships, 1996, one sports writer wrote: 'The FA have found a Christian to throw to the lions.' Hoddle will need the entire world supply of fortitude and perseverance if, in the effluxion of time, he has to put up with the type of jibes directed at previous managers.

Apparently it is not easy for footballers to share with their team-mates that they have discovered religion, and have found Christ. Justin Fashanu claimed it was as difficult as admitting you are gay. Fashanu goes on: 'John Robertson (who played with him at Nottingham) started calling me "Brother Justin".'

To return to Glen Hoddle, it would seem that his laid-back, come-what-may disposition is eminently suitable for the pressures of the England job. It is not true that he has more life in him after taking a dose of valium, but what some say is true surrounds an occasion when he played for Monaco. Apparently, in a match against Auxerre, one of the opposition was injured and there was a delay while physios and doctors fussed around. It was a balmy Mediterranean evening, so Glen lay down while the problem was sorted out. Minutes later play was ready to resume but, before it could do so, Monsieur Hoddle, who had been busy taking forty winks, had to be woken from his slumbers.

When Glen Hoddle, (once known as 'Glenda', reveals his No. 2 at Chelsea, Peter Shreeves), was appointed England's coach, according to a US journalist, Americans thought 'Glen Hoddle' was a malt whisky.

Written on **Graham Taylor**'s car after the film which showed him to be hesitant, unsure, insecure, edgy . . . : 'I used to be indecisive, but now I'm not so sure.'

The comment that: 'In the case of Taylor, never has mediocrity been as well rewarded since the time Caligula made his horse a Consul', was only reasonable in hindsight.

Taylor's statement, and indeed utilization of the obvious, did not help his cause: 'Footballers are no different from human beings.'

And was it Graham Taylor who said: 'Nothing ever seems to go right for me. I have a canary that hums.' . . . ?

He could be right. On his re-appointment to Watford in February 1996, his close friend, Elton John, made it clear that continued reference to the 'turnip' tag should finally come to an end: 'It needs to be buried,' he commented. Thank you, Elton. With friends like that . . .

At least Taylor never had to put up with an official protest movement specifically set up against him. The Italian manager had the 'Anti-Sacchi Club', which very droll-ly, he promised he would join himself.

One difficulty, which national coaches often refer to, is the need to relieve the boredom of players during

tournaments when squads can be together for up to six
weeks. It is a problem exacerbated by limited contact with
families and only partially mitigated by the plushest and
most 'gastronomique' of hotels where players are
cosseted and provided with everything from golf courses
to sight-seeing trips. It is a predicament the average fan,
strapped for cash with ten days in Tossa de Mar or
Galashiels, probably does not appreciate. But managers
do face the problem of the 'Give a man a Toyota and he
wants a Mercedes' genre – and different members of the
profession have addressed this in a variety of interesting
and illuminating ways:

Alf Ramsey insisted that players handed in their
passports so that a check could be kept on their where-
abouts.

Don Revie increased the tedium by organizing bingo,
skittles and the chipping of golf balls à la Butlins.

Ron Greenwood made the mistake of relying on players'
professionalism and treated them like adults. Moore and
Greaves, amongst others, broke the curfew and the trust
put in them.

Graham Taylor's *pièce de résistance* was 'football golf',
which most players went along with but not Chris
Waddle. On one occasion Chris, who wanted to discuss
and practise tactics, refused to leave the coach and
watched the Rugby Cup Final.

Some have said **Terry Venables** never disciplined anyone. Hence the clubbing in Hong Kong, the 'bash' on
board Cathay Pacific, and the mischievous back-drop of
prancing prima donnas in the gloom during his TV interview before the Switzerland match in Euro '96 began.

Perhaps Terry's judgement of what is acceptable is sus-
pect. How can this observation from November 1996 be
explained? 'Tony Adams . . . has always led by example.'

– By getting his round in!?

Glen Hoddle, in the effluxion of time and in keeping with his Christian commitment, might get the lads into the right mental frame of mind by singing such hymns as 'Fight the Good Fight', 'Do Not Be Afraid' or 'Onward, Christian Soldiers'. Up until now he has demonstrated a man-management style which is fair and firm and eminently sensible, as when he gave Paul Merson a day off before the match against Poland on 9 October 1996 to attend an AA meeting: 'These things come before football. Paul still needs to go to these things, and it's fine by me.'

Hoddle could have done with some divine intervention at the press conference in Moldova when dealing with this type of question from one of that country's reporters:

'Can you tell us the height and weight of the players in the England team?' (Pause as Hoddle tries not to wince – he recovers quickly.)

'I'll have to get back to you on that one.'

Bobby Gould, the Wales Manager, passed some of the time with his players prior to the Holland World Cup match in November 1996 in the team's Eindhoven hotel, voting for a captain. Vinnie Jones triumphed and in another vote – this time of confidence in Vinnie and himself, Bobby revealed: 'By rights he shouldn't be here in terms of technical ability, but then neither should I. We've both taken our chances.' His logic got no better. 'If Wimbledon can beat Arsenal, Tottenham and Liverpool, Wales can beat the likes of Holland.' Wales lost 7–1. Guus Hiddink, the Dutch coach, commented: 'For five or six minutes Wales were a threat.'

Then there was the manager who justified his choice of captain by saying: 'The players will follow him anywhere, if only out of curiosity.'

It is interesting to hear the names of some past captains of England:

Charles Alcock; Hubert Heron; Francis Sparks; Billy Moon; Harry Daft; Cunliffe Gosling; Charles Wreford-Brown; Ernest 'Nudger' Needham; Reginald 'Tip' Foster; Steve Bloomer; Billy Walker; Alf Strange; Tommy Cooper.

The Manager – Bobbing and Weaving

When asked to comment on David Batty's and Graham Le Saux's skirmish in the UEFA Cup match in November 1995, the suggestion is that **Kenny Dalglish**'s comment should have been: 'I thought Graham's left jab to the head was quick and accurate, but David needs to spend more time on his defensive footwork.'

As a player, **Bryan Robson** was not the most popular. Opposing fans often used to chant: 'Robson, Robson man of the match', in recognition of the award they felt was always made to him – even when he hadn't been playing.

At the present time Bryan is serving his apprenticeship in management and clearly he is following in the path of other successful and pioneering leaders of the trade by proclaiming: 'When I say that I listen to players, that doesn't necessarily mean that I take any notice of them.'

But how times change. When Fabrizio Ravanelli, the star who rejects most things including overseas pronouncements, telephone charges and team-mates who don't pass the ball, criticized 'Boro's training methods, lack of facilities and fitness-training, Bryan declared: 'A lot of things he said were noted because we are always open to things which can improve us.' Fair enough, but worrying when the criticisms are so fundamental to basic soccer coaching and a club-player voices publicly recurrent complaints. It was Edmund Burke who said: 'There is a limit at which forbearance ceases to be a virtue.'

Bryan Robson might well claim that he was about as lucky as Job while Middlesbrough was in the Premiership – as fortunate as the man who confessed to murder on his death-bed, then made a recovery. Plagued by two seasons of injuries, near-miss transfer deals and a star who went missing, his side managed only six League wins throughout 1996 and was ultimately relegated. Nevertheless, he did energize Middlesbrough as a club, attracted world-class players and produced unprecedented interest on Teesside. His day will come again.

While at the Riverside, mention should be made of the occasion when Middlesbrough first made a bid for Barmby, now with Everton, and Tottenham chairman, Alan Sugar, sneered: 'We don't know what is meant by money in Middlesbrough but in London it's the stuff you put in the bank.'

And do we perhaps detect a further note of southern jealousy in *Evening Standard* writer, Michael Herd's, acidic comment on Juninho's decision to join Middlesbrough. Herd said he would be going to 'one of the most ravaged industrial landscapes on earth'. A pathetic attempt at a put-down by someone who clearly didn't know the area, and who lost all credibility through his ignorance.

Even further north at Partick Thistle, when **Bertie Auld** was manager, he used to indulge in post-match drinking sessions, in his office, with his chairman, Miller Reid, friends and pressmen. They often lost track of time. After one such session, there was a knock at the door at two o'clock in the morning, and there stood two constables.

They were invited in for a drink. 'No, it's all right, Mr Auld,' one of them said. 'We just wanted to let you know you've left your floodlights on.'

Alan Buckley, who has gained a reputation for getting teams promoted on a shoestring, commented on taking over at West Brom: 'The chairman said we had no money and he's been as good as his word.'

Apropos of finance, the crack going round the Midlands in February, 1996, was: 'Alan Buckley, the West Brom boss, has been arrested for trying to get ten players out of a cigarette machine.'

Sometimes the problem for managers is not a shortage of players, but of players of the right calibre. **Brian Little**, now of Aston Villa, talking of when he took over at Darlington, gave this insight:

'Within five minutes of my first day, one of the players walked in and said: "By the way, I'm not training today. I don't train very much, but if you want me to play at the weekend, I will."' When the Club was relegated to the Conference at the end of that season, Little got rid of 20 players in an hour . . . and Darlington blossomed.

The Manager As a Foreign Body
When one examines the vitriol and sarcasm which exist in some foreign clubs, then British clubs look like millponds in the eye of the hurricane.

As can be imagined, there is little love lost between the fans, players and officials of Madrid and Barcelona. The intense and bitter rivalry stems from political history and traditions as well as common footballing hatred. You can imagine how Saint **Gary Lineker**, playing at the time for Barcelona, increased his popularity in and around the city

when asked, after scoring goals for England against the Spanish national side: 'How does it feel scoring against Spain when you play for a Spanish team?' Gary, aware no doubt that he was performing the next day at the Nou Camp, responded: 'I do not play for a Spanish team, I play for a Catalan team.' Nice one, Gary!

After a recent match, Madrid's top man, **Ramon Mendoza**, described his counterpart at Barcelona, **Luis Nunez**, as a 'miserable dwarf'. Nunez, not to be outdone, called Mendoza a 'senile old man'.

Another Madrid president, but this time of Atletico Madrid, **Jesus Gil**, who makes Ken Bates seem like Mother Teresa, can be as perceptive as he can be ruthless. Talking of Hugo Sanchez, he comments: 'He is a very dangerous man, as welcome as a piranha fish in a bidet.'

Gil, who said, in 1996: 'Whoever doesn't like Atletico winning ought to die!' could have been speaking about himself, and not Sanchez. He has sacked 29 managers in the last eight years, and recently he called the president of Compostela, José María Caneda, 'a son of a bitch and a b*****d', because he had said Marbella's citizens were stupid for electing Gil mayor. The insults degenerated to a level you would be pushed to find among the vilest misfits of Madrid, before Gil concluded: 'I'm a real man with two balls, and I told Caneda he was the son of a bitch of the biggest slag I've ever seen in my life!' In retrospect, the hostility between Sugar and Venables looks distinctly tearoomish.

Another European chairman who exudes ruthless power, though in a more cultured yet ruthless manner, is **Gianni Agnelli**, the real dictator behind the throne of Juventus.

David Platt, who had a difficult year there, tells of the occasion when Juventus had been beaten 5–1 by Pescara. Agnelli decided to fine the whole squad £10,000 each. Platt had been on international duty in Norway, but was still included in the fine on the basis that if Juventus had won, as a member of the squad, he would have enjoyed the bonus. Gianni then told Baggio, the club captain, that, if they beat Lazio in their next game, then he would forget about the fine; but lose or draw, then the fine was to go up to £15,000. It was the last game of the season, and the Lazio players could not understand the effort of the Juventus players, when there was nothing at stake. Gazza apparently spluttered: 'What the hell's going on?' The final result was: Juventus 4, Lazio 1.

Meanwhile in Bologna, the two bastions of Italian life, the Church and football, have come into conflict. According to the club's chaplain, Don Libero Nanni, the players approached him to resolve discord between themselves and Bologna's coach, **Renzo Ulivieri**. According to Don Libero: 'The players say he is a tyrant. They're over-stressed and sick of the ball.'

'If he represents Heaven, I don't want to go. Imagine what the women will be like – old and ugly,' responded Ulivieri. Surely the red card of excommunication, and an early baptism of fire and brimstone for that!

And foreign national managers do have their problems – even if self-inflicted. Manager of Argentina, **Daniel Passarella**, dropped long-haired Fernando Redondo and Claudio Carniggia from the squad because they refused to conform to his rule of short hair. One might have thought the reason for this imposition might be neatness or discipline – but no! 'It impedes vision,' says Passarella.

Terry Yorath, coach of the Lebanese national side, and

based in that war-torn city, Beirut, flirts with danger on a daily basis. He recalls the occasion when his players were warming up before the kickoff when Israeli helicopter gunships appeared above the stadium. 'The players strolled off the pitch as if to let the Israelis know that they weren't frightened of them,' says Terry.

And from the threat of violence to the actuality.

Carlos Alberto Oliveira, director of the Brazilian FA, was on a radio programme with **Marcia Braga**, the Flamengo club's president, and traded insults with him. **Silvio Guimaraes**, Vice-President of the Pernambuco State FA, threw a chair at Braga and Oliveira threatened to fetch a gun and shoot Braga.

And it's worse on the pitch, as can be seen from this comment by **Leo Beenhakker**, then coach of Real Madrid, after his side's defeat by Osasuna:

'We offer no excuses, though the shower of cans, eggs, nuts and bolts throughout the match did not help my team.'

In Brazil there seems to be a tradition for managers to return to the club from which they were sacked, and . . . sacked, and . . . **Jair Pereira** in September 1996 began his fifth period in charge at Riccardo Barreto. Meanwhile **Alcir Portela**, who is nicknamed 'The Fireman', because he is conscripted to coach teams when there is a crisis, is on his fourth 999 call-out.

The Manager As an Object of Scorn
Poor old Fulham, on top of everything else, had as chairman and manager, two individuals who have been about as popular as *Eldorado* – **Ian Branfoot** and **Jimmy Hill**. While at Southampton, Ian Branfoot, in football terms

performed the equivalent of hari-kari, dropping Le Tissier and then bringing him back for the match against Newcastle, when he scored two astonishing goals. At the time it was suggested that Le Tissier was sending a message to Branfoot – one goal for each finger.

One thing that can be said about Jimmy Hill, the Fulham chairman, is that he can laugh at himself. He tells the tale of when he returned to Craven Cottage to play the then current Fulham side. A thunderous shot from Bobby Robson was saved by the goalkeeper's foot and, the ball spinning viciously, at speed and at an angle, came to Hill. He volleyed it, and it screamed into the net from 15 yards. A voice bellowed from the Cottage: 'Pity you didn't play like that when you were here, Hill!'

When, in June 1993, it was agreed that Shearer should go to Blackburn for £3.3 million, Branfoot asked him if he would stay until he had found a replacement. 'I told him I had him by the bollocks because he was on a four year contract,' said Branfoot. To which Shearer, according to Branfoot, retorted: 'I've got *you* by the bollocks, because if you don't let me go, I'll start messing you about, and I'll talk to the press.' He did. 'He slaughtered me,' says Branfoot. A little scenario which, if true, says much about our top striker – win on and off the pitch!

Few can have been so reviled as the unfortunate Ian Branfoot while at Southampton, where at times he was convinced that he was being followed, and received one threat that he would be kidnapped and taken to a zoo. As the clouds gathered he could at last raise a smile. In 1994 he was asked at a press conference:

'Are funds available for new players?'

Answer: 'Oh yes. About £2.54.'

The Manager As Cock o' the Walk

Jackie Charlton is a hero, not only in Ireland, but in his native North-East, despite the fact that he resigned after a very short time as manager of Newcastle in 1985 after being jeered by the crowd. It was an occasion which prompted Stan Seymour, then Newcastle chairman, to claim: 'I told him not to be such a great big baby.'

In 1966, after the World Cup, Jackie and 'our kid', Bobby, did well by their home town of Ashington by playing in a game there to raise funds for the club. The story is that the Mayor of Ashington started the game before the assembled thousands by declaring: 'It gives me great pleasure the day ti come and kick yi bahl off. If A wus tharty years younger, A'd kick ahl yi bahls off.'

Big Jack's inclination to resolve disputes physically rather than verbally could be pretty basic as his notorious 'Little Black Book' and his own words will testify. Commenting on the incident in the 1990 World Cup Finals when Voller spat upon Rijkaard, the Republic of Ireland manager said: 'If he'd done it to me, I'd have chinned him.'

Jack's propensity to resort to more vigorous solutions was witnessed when he commented upon the *Sun*'s 'turnip' taunt at Graham Taylor: 'If a journalist wrote that about me he'd have to go into hiding.'

Jack's style as a player and a manager was also pretty direct and basic. In 1988, as manager of the Republic of Ireland, he explained: 'My philosophy is to play in their half of the field. Get the ball behind them – get the buggers turning, turning, turning. When you've done that enough times, holes are going to open up, and one of our fellas, whoever's nearest, gets to the ball first, and all the rest pile in.'

Jack's Republic of Ireland teams were notable for including players who had the most tenuous of connections with the country through their antecedents. On one occasion, when Jack was heavily into FAI, ('Find An Irishman'), James Traynor of the *Glasgow Herald*, speculated that Jack may have been keeping an eye on Motherwell's Nick Cusack, 'who has an Irish grandparent or perhaps owns an Irish Setter'.

Jack did eventually cap Bernie Slaven when he played for Middlesbrough after there had been a campaign to get Bernie capped for Scotland (Bernie was half Scottish and half Irish. Half of him wanted to get drunk while the other half didn't want to pay for it!). It's a good joke, but in fact Bernie is a teetotaller! Part of the campaign included 'Boro supporters wearing tee shirts with 'Bernie Slaven for Scotland', emblazoned upon them. The tee shirts were ready for sale when Jack picked Bernie for Ireland. If anyone wants any tee shirts . . . !

On one of his popular after-dinner dates, organized at the Billingham Arms Hotel by the then chairman of Billingham Town, Tony Maxwell, Jack completed his highly amusing address, having sunk deeper and deeper into his Geordie accent as the drink, and the applause, relaxed him. Questions were called for from the floor and a southern gentleman, perhaps from the *Evening Standard* (see story on Juninho – 'Bobbing and weaving'), and from the rear of the huge dining room, asked: 'Would you mind repeating the last 20 minutes, please, Jack, because I couldn't understand a bloody word you said.'

If it was the drink which affected him, its cost would not have come out of Jack's pocket. He's well known for being slow to put his hand into it to extract money. As someone said of Jack: 'If you can get a drink out of him, you can plait sawdust.' Or the alternative is . . . Question: 'What's the difference between Big Jack and a coconut?' Answer: 'You can get a drink out of a coconut.'

SPOT THE DIFFERENCE!

I'M NOT SHY!

One quip is that on one of his first visits to a Dublin pub, Jack went in and bought a round of beer. 'Will an English tenner be all right?' asked Jack. 'No problem,' said the barman, and with that, Jack broke into a chorus of 'The Blaydon Races'.

'Always borrow from a pessimist,' Jack might advise. 'He never expects it back anyway.'

What is fact is that on another occasion in Ireland, Jack was suffering from head pains:

'I had my ears checked out at a clinic in Dublin, and the doctors gave me a brain scan at the same time. There was nothing in it.'

Obviously Jack's 'kid' brother, Bobby, has got a lot of sense – or has he?

'Every time I fly long distances, I religiously put brown paper over my feet. Works every time – never suffer from jet lag.'

Not everybody finds Big Jack as amusing. In fact, for such a popular and jovial character, he has managed to attract quite a band of inveterate enemies. Liam Brady could not forgive Jack for bringing him off in the friendly against Germany. Brady only gained one more cap, and the antagonistic parties vented their spleen in the tabloids. The relationship was not helped because Jack, who can never remember names, persisted in calling him 'Ian' (Ian Brady has been serving the last 30 years in prison for his part in the Moors Murders). Nothing is better designed to get up a person's nose more than not remembering his name whether or not he is a personality. How Tony Cascarino must have resented being referred to by Jack as 'that ice-cream lad!'

When the World Cup was held in Italy in 1990, Jack and his players went to meet Pope Paul II. When the Pope shook hands with Jack he said: 'Yes, Mr Charlton, I know you. You're the Boss.'

It was a situation everybody, apparently even God's representative, clearly understood. As Liam Brady pointed out: 'You play Jack Charlton's way or not at all.'

On another occasion when Jack was outlining his theories to the Irish side, David O'Leary interjected: 'But Jack . . .' He was brought up short by the Big Man who, pulling his World Cup medal from his pocket, said: 'When you've got one of these, Bonny Lad, then you can argue with me.'

The sentiment of that rebuff, if not the logic, can be understood – which is more than can be said for this explanation of Jack's on becoming manager of the Republic: 'I've appointed Maurice Setters as my assistant. He's well placed, living in Doncaster.'

But back to Jack's lack of facility with names, and witness this exchange at a press conference during the 1990 World Cup:

Question: 'Jack, which of the Egyptians has impressed you?'

Answer: 'I couldn't tell you, I don't know their names. There was the boy with the beard, the dark lad in mid-field, the 'keeper, the little dark lad who played centre-midfield, the very coloured boy, and the boy who played up front – Hassan, Hussain?'

But if Jack couldn't remember names, he never quite became quite as forgetful as the late and great **Bob Paisley** who called every footballer 'Doings'. It is recorded that he once announced a back four made up of 'Doings, Doings, Doings and, what's his name, Doings.'

Paisley clearly had problems trying to remember other details. Graeme Souness says: 'Bob would start a sentence, and one of the players would finish it for him.' What Souness could have meant, of course, was that there were so many 'know-alls' like himself – Phil Thompson, Dalglish and McDermott – in the dressing room, poor Bob couldn't get a word in edgeways.

Tommy Smith ('he should have lived in the Dark Ages – 'cos he looks terrible in the light') tells of the occasion Liverpool were playing Barcelona in a UEFA semi-final and Bob told the team: 'That right back, don't worry about him, he's not fast but he's quick.'

Tommy, whose photograph they say mothers in Liverpool put on the mantelpiece to keep the kids away from the fire, once allowed Graeme Souness, on his arrival from Middlesbrough, to borrow his hair-dryer, but when he tried it again, told him in no uncertain terms

what he should do. It is may be surprising that Souness –
described by admirers as 'Renoir with a razor', and by
opponents as more like 'Rolf Harris with a rapier' – did
not have his own hair-dryer (Kenny Dalglish shared a
room with him for six years and remembers his extended
mirror-preening sessions.) But more surprising, surely, is
that Tommy used a hair-dryer. It damages the image a
tadge – bit like Vinnie having a weekly facial and mani-
cure.

Paisley, from time to time, could show flashes of humour.
When Avi Cohen, the Israeli defender, joined Liverpool,
he was asked by a reporter:

'Is he Orthodox?'

'What if he is?' asked Bob.

'Well, he won't be able to play on Saturdays,' said the
reporter.

'That's all right, then,' quipped Bob. 'I've got ten
others just like him.'

On another occasion it was reported that Bob, frustrated beyond measure by John Barnes' propensity to
hang on to the ball, had a quiet word with him after training one day: 'Look, John. I'm fat and over 50. Now you
run with the ball and I'll pass it, and let's see who reaches
the target first.'

The Manager As a Malfunctioning Mouthpiece

Bobby Robson, unlike Bob Paisley, remembered names
well but he was not above 'wishing he'd never said that'.
Asked on one occasion what he would have liked to have
been if not involved in football, he replied: 'I would have
given my right arm to have been a concert pianist.'

And again after the 3–2 win over Cameroon in the 1990
World Cup Finals: 'We didn't underestimate them. They

were a lot better than we thought.'

And . . .

'Ray Wilkins' day will come one night.'

'I'm here to say goodbye. Maybe not goodbye, but farewell.'

'. . . home advantage gives you an advantage . . .'

'Eighteen months ago they (Sweden) were arguably one of the best three teams in Europe, and that would include the Germans, Holland and Russia and anybody else if you like.'

Besides having difficulties with words and adding-up, Bobby can be a bit absent-minded. In an early game with Barcelona, he put Pizzi on – then substituted him five minutes later.

It's good to see that Bobby has not only conquered cancer, but gone on to manage Barcelona. (Just how is he coping with Catalan when he has such difficulty making himself understood in English?) There had been a suggestion that the Portuguese club, Porto, would be his last as a manager. 'The president said I would die at Porto, and I nearly did,' said Bobby enigmatically.

To give Bobby credit, he could, at times, hit the nail right on the head with a brief comment.

Speaking about the mood in the dressing room after the penalty shoot-out against Germany in Turin in the 1990 World Cup, he said: 'It was like a morgue – utter desolation and despair.'

Gary Lineker, on the morning after the defeat, made a papal-like appearance on the balcony of his hotel room, and uttered these infallible words to the assembled company of down-hearted hacks below in the forecourt:

'All you have to remember is that it's only a game.'

That rousing and irresistible rallying-call must have snapped them out of their depression!

... *A Small Diversion by Way of Wimbledon* ...

Gary, as wholesome as fresh fruit, and whiter than newly-revealed coconut, had the play, *An Evening With Gary Lineker*, written about him, when the irreverent question was asked: 'Do your farts smell of perfume, Gary?'

Gary Lineker met his match when he took on **Joe Kinnear**, Wimbledon's manager. When Gary, the 'Queen Mother', as he is referred to in the aforementioned play, suggested that the Wimbledon *v* Aston Villa Cup Tie of February 1993 was so dull, that: 'you'd have been better off watching it on Ceefax,' Joe's response was:

'He's an arse-hole – he's two bob. You don't mock the afflicted – you don't watch a blind man walking down the street and then kick him in the bollocks, but that's what he did to us on television.'

The feud, on the part of the 'Crazy Gang', continued when, in a Dublin hotel in 1995, **Vinnie Jones** threw some toast at Gary and taunted him with chants of 'Big Ears'.

And then in September 1996, Gary, in an astonishing attack in the *Radio Times*, rubbished Vinnie with such comments as: 'Football does not need Vinnie', and accusing him of being 'a self-hyped personality'. Sentiments which, he must have known, would have roughly the same effect as sticking a sharp stick up a 16-stone Rottweiler's backside. It was too much for the 'Crazy Gang' who, under the leadership of Mr Kinnear, sent a fax, accusing him of being unprofessional, and then warming to the task, called him a

> 'wimp . . . with the charisma of a jellyfish without a
> sting,'

and how

'. . . in a war he would have been first behind Vinnie and the first to run for cover.'

The fax continued:

'. . . the BBC would do better marketing him as a cure for insomnia.'

The weekend after this altercation, *Football Focus* technicians floated an animated jellyfish across the screen as Gary was making his presentation.

And still Vinnie wouldn't let it drop: 'Tart is a four letter word, so I wouldn't call him (Gary) that.'

Gary, of whom David Elleray once remarked:

'. . . neither provokes nor reacts – rather like a British diplomat', must really be sensitive about those ears . . . or was it as simple as the fact that he hates toast?!

But wait! – Perhaps there is a side to Gary that hitherto has not emerged. International hockey player, Jane Sixsmith, appeared on *They Think It's All Over* as the guest to be identified by a blind-folded Gary. '. . . he had to feel me, which was great fun. He is very down-to-earth, and not the goody-two-shoes that everyone thinks he is . . .'

At times, Gary can be as riveting as the horse racing results and does drop the odd clanger. On being invited to comment on the pitch for a Manchester United *v* Montpellier European tie, he remarked: '. . . most of the players will be wearing rubbers tonight.'

. . . And Returning to the Category of 'Ouch! Can I Say That Again?'

One manager – and it was not Bobby Robson – on being informed that his next European tie was away to Bayern Munich, responded: 'That's OK. It's somewhere I've never been, Bayern.'

Even the apparently cultured and faultless **Sir Alf Ramsey** could make the odd cock-up. It is reported that Alf had thought the great success of the team was due to the 'harmonium in the dressing room'.

The cock-up made by Sir Alf in the vital World Cup game against Poland at Wembley in 1973 was not of a verbal nature. Requiring a victory to qualify and the score standing at 1–1, Alf decided to make a substitution. It was only then that he realized that his watch had stopped, and, instead of 15 minutes remaining as he thought, there were only two. 'Kevin, get stripped!' he ordered. Kevin Keegan took off his track-suit. 'Not that Kevin – the other one!' he yelled, meaning Kevin Hector. Kevin duly appeared for 120 seconds, and headed inches wide with the best chance of the night. And the watch? 'When I got home, and what happened sunk in, I took it off and never wore it again,' said Alf.

And now to the incident between ex-Grimsby manager, **Brian Laws**, and the Italian import, **Ivano Bonetti**. To recap on what did actually take place – Bonetti began to tuck into a plateful of food after Grimsby had lost 2–1 to Luton. Laws, who perceived this on entering the dressing room, considered it an inappropriate response to defeat and told the Italian in no uncertain terms to put down the food. Bonetti responded by throwing a chicken leg at his manager, who belted him, causing a fracture of the cheekbone. And the chairman's response? 'It has been blown up out of all proportion.' But wait – after peace had been re-established, a picture of the two protagonists appeared in a newspaper shaking hands, and the caption underneath read: 'Laws and Bonetti bury the hatchet.' Brian Laws has since had to pay damages for assault and battery. On the subject of Bonettis, wasn't there another one in a World Cup match who was delivered a sucker punch?

And to think that assistant manager, Kenny Swain, had said of Ivano in December: 'He's a hell of a weapon to have in your side.'

Manager of Ipswich, **George Burley**, on his teenage goal-keeper, Richard Wright: 'He could go on to be an international player but he has to keep his feet on the ground.'

'No one hands you cups on a plate.' (**Terry McDermott**.)

'There are 0–0 draws and 0–0 draws – and this was a 0–0 draw.' (**John Sillett** at Coventry, 1989.)

'. . . when Gary Flitcroft played for the "A" team, he had "footballer" written all over his forehead.' (**Colin Bell**.)

'Chester made it very hard for us by having two men sent off.' (**John Docherty** at Bradford City.)

'St Mirren had been under the rack.' (**Chick Murray**.)

Swindon FC brought in the police when a suspicious package was found. **John Gorman**, manager at the time, said: 'It's been blown up out of all proportion.'

When **Terry Venables** was made England manager, the *Birmingham Sports Argus* clearly thought it had been divinely inspired: 'It's a god appointment,' it proclaimed.

Jim Rosenthal interviewed **Kasey Keller** for LWT's London Match:

'So what's an American doing playing in goal for Millwall?'

'Trying to keep the ball out,' replied Keller.

Post-match interviews:

Reporter to **Kenny Dalglish**: 'How did you see the

goal?'

Kenny: 'From the dug-out.'

Reporter to **Trevor Francis**: 'Did that win give you pleasure?'

Trevor Francis: 'Do you get paid for asking questions like that?'

Steve Coppell, when manager of QPR: 'Geoff Thomas has got a couple of broken bones in his wrist. He can't even wipe his own arse.'

Reporter: 'Is that why you signed Steve Harrison?'

Newspapers can make pretty bewildering cock-ups. The *Daily Express* reported:

McMenemy was shattered. After locking his team away for a real talking to, he came out of the dressing room to say: 'It was our worst performance and our worst result. I blame myself. When you are 4–0 up, you should never lose 7–1.'

And . . .

'In most associations, half the committee does all the work, while the other half does nothing. I am pleased to put on record that in this football club it is just the reverse.' (*Liverpool Echo.*)

Ceefax makes its fair share of gaffes. It claimed that **Kenny Dalglish** missed Blackburn's game against Liverpool because – 'he was at a weeding'.

In the match between Chelsea and Everton, 13 January 1996, Mark Hughes was sent off for allegedly stamping on Dean Unsworth when he claimed he was attempting to avoid him. Commenting on the incident, **Glen Hoddle**, Chelsea's manager said: 'If anyone is found guilty, I will step on them.'

When Paul Warhurst was sent off against Notts

County in 1990, **Joe Royle**, then Oldham manager, said:
'The lad was sent off for foul and abusive language, but
he swears blind he didn't say a word.'

The Manager With a Team Fit For a Joke

After making a substitution in a vital relegation match in
April 1996, which resulted in a 1–0 win, **Alan Ball**, then
manager of Manchester City, said: 'I thought if we were
going to lose it, we might as well lose it by trying to win
it.'

> Question: 'Did Nick Leeson arrive in Singapore
> sporting a Manchester City shirt because he knew he
> was going down?'
> OR ... Was he aware that football teams, like
> investments, can go down as well as up?

Why not get all the cracks about Manchester City's
unfortunate 1995-96 season out of the way ... ?

> Question: 'What is the difference between
> Manchester City and a lift?'
> Answer: 'A lift doesn't take nine months to go
> down.'

And ...

> Question: 'What's the difference between
> Manchester City's Squad and a puddle?'
> Answer: 'A puddle has more depth.'

And ...

The Stockport fanzine, *The Tea Party*, carried this bit
of information: '**Tony Book**, Manchester City Coach and
1960s captain, has been presented with a £3,000 bill from
the Electricity Board.' Francis Lee explained to him:
'You were the last one in the Maine Road trophy room 19
years ago and forgot to turn out the lights.'

Heard the one about Manchester City's new Chinese manager? – 'Win One Soon.'

It was amazing that City didn't sign Scunthorpe's Alan Knill at the time. Man. City's Knill had the right ring about it.

A man repeatedly goes into this shop and asks again and again for a packet of condoms. Eventually the assistant says: 'Hey, what are you up to?' 'Look,' says the man. 'I'm really sorry. I'm too embarrassed to ask for a Manchester City strip.'

'I went over to the Bury fans and said: "Look on the bright side. You could be supporting Manchester City."' (Richie Bond, after scoring the goal for Blyth Spartans which knocked Bury out of the FA Cup.)

Sometimes you can understand why Manchester City do become the target of ridicule. **Jimmy Frizzell**, Stadium manager at Main Road, gave a sound engineer a ticket to be present in case the PA system broke down. It did – then Jimmy realized that he hadn't made a note of the engineer's seat number. He had told him that, if he was needed, he would be contacted through the PA system.

And from 1997: ... 'Manchester City have as much chance of coming up as the *Titanic*.'

Even caretaker, **Phil Neal**, realized at City you had to have a sense of humour: 'Watching Manchester City is probably the best laxative you can take.'

... *And More Cock-Ups*

Writer, Glen Moore, reviewing **George Graham**'s book in the *Independent*, referred to him as 'The boy from Barlinnie' – when in fact George is from Bargeddie and has never spent time, as has Duncan Ferguson of

Everton, as a guest of Her Majesty at the Glasgow prison.

Not all footballers receive the same type of sympathy as Duncan did at Everton. Heard at the Peterborough *v* Swansea match, 14 October 1995, emanating from manager, **John Stills**, as Danny Carter got up and hobbled back into play: 'Danny, Danny. You all right?' Danny nodded. 'Well stop f*****g limping then.'

'I'm definitely maybe going to play Sturrock.' (Dundee manager, **Jim McLean**.)

Jimmy Hill always has a lot to say so it comes as no surprise that at times his comments can be bewildering. On **Fowler**'s performance against Croatia, 24 April 1996: 'It wasn't a bad performance, but you can't tell whether it was good or bad.'

Not quite as bewildering, perhaps, is an observation from **Colin Murphy**, ex-Notts County General Manager, who, while manager of Lincoln City, wrote this piece of advice on how to break down opposing defences: 'Of the keys on the ring at the moment, we should be selecting more correctly to unlock opposing mechanisms. However, there is not a lock that cannot be unlocked so we shall continue to endeavour to unlock the lock, but in doing so, we must not get locked out.'

And on 'Being Your Own Man': 'While it may therefore be argued that constant pressures, criticism and barrages we are subject to wittingly or unwittingly manifest themselves by the development of irrational immunities and personal eccentricities, this is, however, better than listening or willing to people other than yourself or the rare, trusted competent aide. It is better than weakening to the less informed, those of devious motive or media buffoonery.'

No wonder Colin won the Golden Bull Award from the Plain English Campaign – for doing to the English Language what the Common Market did for British cows. We are informed: 'Colin listens to Radio 4 and keeps a dictionary in the loo.'

A close second for the accolade must have been the former manager of Crystal Palace, **Alan Smith**, who not only went into extremely intricate calculations to demonstrate what might have been but never was:

'Seven games we've lost 1–0, another seven we've drawn 0–0. If we'd drawn the 1–0 games we lost, we'd have another seven points. If the seven goal-less draws had been 1–0 to us we would have 28 points more and be third in the Premiership.'

Ah, if only autumn leaves were £5 notes!

The Manager As a Straight Talker

Howard Wilkinson commented on his team's mental capacity after the Leeds *v* West Ham match (13 January 1996): 'I've never had any doubt about the character and spirit of our lot – I have about their intelligence.'

If his team lacked intelligence, then it must have been to them that he addressed this world-shattering piece of information: 'If you score one goal, the other team has to score two to win.'

Perhaps Howard got his direct-speak approach from his own time as a player at Sheffield Wednesday: 'I knocked on the manager's door and said: "Could I have a little bit of your time – I don't know whether I'm coming or going." He said: "Wilkinson, I can tell you – you're definitely going."'

In January 1997 Howard was appointed Technical Director of Football after 'going' from Leeds. They say he was head-hunted – Henry VIII style? Time will tell.

Ruud Gullit quickly set his stall out on becoming Chelsea manager:

'The trouble with some players,' he said, 'is they want to be cuddled every day – but I don't have the time. I pick certain players for certain games . . . if they don't like what I'm doing, then they know what they can do.' So bye-bye, John Spencer.

In fact Gullit is a generous man, as Terry Phelan will declare despite his short stay at Chelsea before moving on to Everton. He dedicated his 1987 'Footballer of the Year Award' to Nelson Mandela, once gave half of his salary to a children's charity and, through his reggae group, 'Revelation Time', raises money for projects in South Africa.

Ron Atkinson has never had any doubts about his own capacity. Bumping into one of his ex-players, Cyrille Regis, a born-again Christian, Big Ron gibed: 'What's all this crap about you finding God? You worked with him at West Brom for four years.'

He has always had that superior belief in himself. While acting as an analyst for ITV during Euro '96, Ron insisted he be ferried hither and thither in a chauffeur-driven limousine. Meanwhile, fellow-panelist, Jack Charlton, went by train. 'I'm a man of the people,' said Big Jack. 'It wouldn't do for me to be seen being driven around.'

On the other hand, Ron has always enjoyed, and made no secret of it, the finer things in life. Even when his contract was terminated with Manchester United, he answered in response to how he was coping: 'I've had to swap my Merc for a BMW, I'm down to my last 37 suits, and I'm drinking non-vintage champagne.'

Ron has also shown the odd burst of humour. He was so sick of one journalist who kept turning up late for press conferences, he decided to teach him a lesson. As the reporter entered, late yet again, Big Ron began: '. . . So there you are, gentlemen – our new signing who will be joining us on Monday.'

'Sorry, Ron,' said the latecomer. 'Could you repeat? I missed that.'

'Yes,' said Ron. 'We've signed a Dutch player. He's called Vakenning, first name Ruudi.'

The reporter scribbled all this down. 'And where's he from?'

'It's a small club – called Vastasleep,' replied Ron.

Ron still enjoys tormenting reporters – in an interview for *Football Focus*, at the end of September 1996, when he was manager of Coventry. . .

> Reporter: 'You've spent a lot of money but not had a lot of success. Are you worried?'
> Ron: 'I'm disappointed.'
> Reporter: 'Are you worried?'
> Ron: 'I'm disappointed – are you listening?'
> Reporter: 'Why do you still want to be a manager?'
> Ron: 'I don't want to get a proper job.'
> Reporter: 'Why do you do it?'
> Ron: 'I like winning – though it's that long since I have won, I've forgotten how it feels.'

Soon after this, Ron made way for Gordon Strachan. When Aston Villa manager, Ron was once in conversation before a match, with a highly-placed woman in the football hierarchy who remarked casually: 'I see your son's playing today.' She was referring to Dalian Atkinson – no wonder Ron doesn't think there's a place for women in football: 'I think women should be in the kitchen, in the discotheque or in a boutique.'

Big Ron tells the story of how one of the reserves approached him and told him he was having difficulties because he had never been dropped before and was taking it badly. Ron advised him to be like Nick Faldo and work hard at his game. 'The next thing I know,' reveals Ron, 'he's doing exactly what Nick Faldo does. He's taken up golf.'

Even the confident Ron could in his anger come out with the odd *non-sequitur*: 'I never comment on referees,' he said after the West Brom match with Red Star Belgrade in 1979, 'and I'm not going to break the habit of a life-time for that prat.'

It is true that, when he was at Sheffield Wednesday, Ron supported the referee. George Courtney awarded a goal and Les Sealey, the Sheffield goalie, had to be restrained by his team-mates. Ron castigated his goalkeeper: 'If they've (the FA) any sense, they'll hang him.'

But . . .

The Midlands Soccer Annual of 1969 shows a photograph with the original caption, which reads: 'Oxford's Ron Atkinson is restrained by brother Graham from punching the referee.'

Sometimes players are entitled to question the faculties of their managers. It was **Eddie Turnbull**, manager of Hibernian in the 1970s, who informed university-educated Alan Gordon: 'The problem with ye is all ye brains are in ye heed.'

Ronnie Moran of Liverpool has a saying before Liverpool play less talented sides which they are expected to beat: 'Don't go out with your Big Heads on.'

The Manager As a Champion
Alex Ferguson didn't attain his status as the most able and successful of existing British managers without long and arduous experience.

A raw talent, with principles of discipline and justice formulated in his apprenticeship at the Govan shipyard, has gradually evolved to the point where he is consulted on man-management by Sir Richard Greenbury, the chairman of Marks and Spencer. His dedication to the game is total – he cancelled his honeymoon to sit his SFA coaching examination. His expectations of players' standards of behaviour are high. (At Aberdeen he forced four players to recite nursery rhymes after they had damaged their landlady's airing cupboard – 'If they act like children, I'll treat them like children'; and following on from Ron Atkinson at Manchester United, he laid down strict rules regarding drinking and club-life – Bye-bye, John McGrath!) His sense of justice is finely tuned, stemming from an occasion when playing for Rangers against Celtic he was accused by the manager, Derek White, of not trying. Hence support of Cantona, who he believed had suffered enough, and his policy of no public criticism of players.

All in all Alex is a manager with all the necessary attributes save a soupçon of paranoia – but as they say: 'Just because you are paranoid, it doesn't mean they aren't out to get you!' Then again one is reminded of the man who went to the psychiatrist:

Patient: 'I do believe everyone hates me.'

Psychiatrist: 'Don't be silly! Not everybody has met you yet!'

And Alex has learned from his mistakes. Gordon Strachan remembers one of his foul-ups when he was manager at East Stirling: 'One time Alex sent out a side including two wingers. The only problem was he forgot to pick a centre forward. So these two blokes had instructions to put in plenty of crosses – but there was nobody in the middle to get on the end of them.'

Alex Ferguson's plain speaking post-match observations on 'Match of the Day' provoked another ex-Liverpool player, besides Kevin Keegan, to a retaliatory counterblast. When Kenny Dalglish managed Liverpool, Alex Ferguson commented:

'The provocation and intimidation at Anfield is incredible. I can understand how teams come away from here choking on their own vomit, and biting their tongues, knowing that they had been done by the referee. When you lose, it sounds like sour grapes, but we got a result and I am saying it.'

Kenny Dalglish (interrupting Ferguson): 'You might as well talk to my six-week-old daughter – you'll get more sense out of her.'

After this confrontation it is surprising to find a few years later, in 1996, that Alex wrote the foreword for Kenny's new autobiography: *Dalglish: My Autobiography*. One of his comments might be honest – but not of the endearing variety. After mentioning that Kenny had probably only a few true friends, he continues: 'There's nothing wrong with that because, at the end of the day, you only need six people to carry your coffin.'

Alex might not equate sour grapes with bitterness but where does that leave his chairman, Martin Edwards, when he failed to lure Alan Shearer to Manchester United:

'Alan would have been delighted to come to Manchester United, only Blackburn didn't want him to join us. I'm sure the people at Blackburn thought if Shearer came here, they and the rest of football would have to forget it for the next few years.'

A stamping foot, a trembling lip and, 'He was a man of strong passions, and the green-eyed monster ran up his leg, and bit him to the bone.' (P. G. Wodehouse, *Full Moon*.)

The Manager As an Inspiration

Peter Taylor told the tale of once being on the top deck of a double-decker bus with **Brian Clough** when the bus driver decided to leave people standing at the bus-stop because he wanted to get home quickly. Cloughie bounded down the stairs and berated the man and made him turn around and pick up those he had left.

'To be a successful manager, young man, what you need is circumspection', it is alleged Cloughie advised **Stuart Pearce**. 'In that case, I should be all right,' responded Stuart. 'I had it done as a lad.'

This was the same Stuart Pearce who, according to John Motson in 1991, 'has got the taste of Wembley in his nostrils'. Not as big a gaffe as commentator, John Helm, who informed the nation that: 'Viv Anderson has pissed a fatness test'.

Stuart – 'Psycho' to one and all, though his international disciplinary record shows that he has been booked only twice in 60-odd games – had great respect for Cloughie and a grudging admiration for his brash style.

'Clough was the only manager who would take you on holiday in the middle of the season and arrive back on Saturday just in time for the game. I remember the lads once carrying their duty free into the ground.'

Before **Nigel Clough**'s ill-fated move from Nottingham Forest to Liverpool, there was some talk of him being transferred to a foreign club. A reporter asked Dad Clough what he thought of their Nigel – always referred to by the manager as 'The Number 9' – going abroad. 'It could be a very good move for our Nigel,' said Brian. 'There will be new opportunities, new experiences, and he could learn new skills. Yes, it's up to the lad – he's a big lad now, he has to make up his own mind and it's up to him. Mind you, he'd better ask his Mam first.'

'At the time I had seen him spouting off on the box and I thought: "What a big-headed bastard." Then, when I got talking to him, I still thought "What a big-headed bastard,"' said Larry Lloyd, commenting on the time he signed for Clough. Larry also tells of the time, the night before the Forest's League Cup Final against Southampton in 1979, when Cloughie called a team-meeting at 10.00 p.m.:

'Four waiters came in with twelve bottles of champagne and Cloughie says: "Come on lads, let's get tucked in." John O'Hare had a strange look on his face so Cloughie said: "What's the matter with you?" John said: "I'm a pint man, boss." So then the waiter comes in with fifteen pints and Cloughie says: "No one is going to leave until all this has gone." Archie Gemmell was doing his nut because he's an in-bed-by-nine o'clock man. We didn't finish drinking until about two o'clock. I had to carry Tony Woodcock to bed. We won 3–2. I think we were still getting the drink out of our system.'

Larry also tells the story of the time he played for England in a very poor game, when England was defeated 4–1 against Wales at Wrexham in 1980. Cloughie said to him:

'You're good at quizzes. Here, I've got one for you. Which player won two England caps on the same day?'

Lloyd confessed he didn't know.

'You, you Anglo-Saxon b******. Your first and your last.'

Duncan McKenzie recalls the time he signed for Clough

in 1974.

'How many ball players do you think are left in the game?' he asked his new manager.

'Probably one less than you think, young man,' replied Clough.

Cloughie never suffered from self-modesty, which helps explain his huge success as a player, manager and personality – and he always made sure his players kept their feet on the ground, as Teddy Sheringham reports:

'I went eleven games without scoring and Mr Clough told me: "It's a difficult game, Edward. I once went four games without a goal myself."'

And . . .

When Ian Woan was transferred from Runcorn to Nottingham Forest, he tells of the first day he arrived at the ground. 'I turned up with a beard and Clough said: "Next time I see you, young man, I want you clean shaven. When you're a player you can have a beard and not until I say so." He never told me I was a player either . . . the b******.'

Ian wasn't the only one who wasn't close to Cloughie. Clough could recognize flair and he would encourage it – on the field. What he found hard to accept was emerging talent which expressed itself loquaciously on tactics and systems in the dressing room. Hence the reason he would inform Martin O'Neill, manager of Leicester, and motivator on a par with himself: 'The trouble with you, son, is you're a smartarse!'

At the Football Managers' Association meeting in December 1992, the protection of visiting managers was discussed after incidents of fans hammering on dug-outs.

'Any other problems at away games?' asked chairman, Howard Wilkinson.

'Yes,' said Cloughie. 'We can't win!'

On another occasion it is alleged that Cloughie insisted on cracking a bottle of champagne with Peter Taylor. 'What shall we drink to?' asked Taylor. 'What about three in the morning?' suggested Cloughie.

Cloughie had the habit of kissing anybody who suddenly took his fancy, man or woman. It was something few others could have got away with without salacious media comment. In much the same way he could say things which for others would be unacceptable because everyone knew it was only 'Old Big Mouth' spouting 'orf'. Witness his remark in 1991 when he was thinking of buying Neil Webb back from Manchester United: 'He's not actually a very good player but he's got a lovely smile which brightens up Monday mornings.'

Cloughie was bitterly disappointed by his sacking from
Leeds in 1984, but it had its compensations in the shape
of a £90,000 'Golden Handshake': 'When Leeds sacked
me, all my worries about pensions and bringing up three
kids were gone, and I became a better manager.'

Seventeen years later, Cloughie commented: 'Leeds are
a big club these days, and a successful one too. I'm also
glad to see they've recovered financially since paying me
off a few years ago.' A little insight into how much the
sacking still wrankled.

The Leeds episode in no way dinted Brian's confidence
and self-belief. In 1985 he asserted his interest in replac-
ing Eoin Hand, the Republic of Ireland's manager: 'It's
easy enough to get to Ireland. Just a straight walk across
the Irish Sea as far as I'm concerned.'

Brian was the man everyone wanted to listen to on television and he did come out with some gems. On the pundit
panel for the 1986 World Cup Finals, Mike Channon
said: 'We've got to get bodies in the box. The French do
it, the Italians do it, the Brazilians do it . . .' and Cloughie
responded: 'Yes, even educated bees do it.'

After three and a half years away from Nottingham
Forest, Cloughie went to see the team play Coventry City
(0–1), 29 January 1997. Cloughie received a rapturous
welcome as he took his seat in the Directors' box, a loca-
tion he doesn't like, because, as he says: 'You're trying to
concentrate on the football, and you have to put up with
these inane comments which have nothing to do with the
game. You hear some twit behind you asking his wife if
she is warm enough. But I behaved myself, and I didn't
try and coach from there.' As garrulous and honest as
ever – nothing changes!

One of the best Cloughie stories which Brian himself enjoys telling occurred when he was at Nottingham Forest. He telephoned the boot room and ordered one of the apprentices to bring him a cup of tea.

'Hey, young man, you do know who I am, don't you?'

'Of course, Mr Clough, but do you know who I am?' asked the voice at the other end.

'Do I buggery!' roared Cloughie.

'Then get your own bloody cup of tea – I'm busy cleaning the boots!' replied the apprentice.

Apparently Cloughie gave the lad a rise . . . three feet off the ground with a right-upper-cut!

Cloughie's brash style might have caused antipathy amongst some, but in Hartlepool, and especially among a generation of pupils and teachers of The English Martyrs' School, he will retain an admiration and affection which will long be remembered. In 1983, at the height of his fame, he came to present prizes at an Awards Night, and for three hours he unstintingly signed autographs and chatted with pupils. David Relton, then headteacher, recalls:

'I asked him what his fee was, and he replied: "Nothing!" I then asked him what his expenses were, and he said: "Listen – I've got more bloody money than you'll ever have! B***** off!"'

The Manager As a Legend

On becoming manager of Liverpool, **Bill Shankley** said: 'I want to build Liverpool into a bastion of invincibility which will conquer the world.' He almost did it, with passion, emotion, a ruthless determination and, very often, with humour.

Bill Shankley once telephoned Tommy Docherty and said to him: 'Tommy, boy, about this laddie Tony

Hateley?' Tommy, always on the look-out for a good deal, decided on playing it cool: 'Right Shanks – a great talent. A hundred thousand wouldn't buy him.' 'You're right there, Tommy, and I'm one of those hundred thousand,' said Shanks.

Tony Hateley's skills were so concentrated in his head that Shankley once referred to him as 'the Douglas Bader of Football'.

After Shankley had signed the huge Ron Yeats from Dundee United, he announced to the press: 'Come and meet the new laddie. I'll take you for a walk around him.'

Yeats was a Scots player, and Shankley valued them – at least some of them: 'If you've got three Scots in your side, you've got a chance of winning something. If you've got any more, you're in trouble.'

Shankley included Roy Evans in the first team 11 times at Liverpool, one of them against George Best – 'I probably marked him out of the game,' says Roy. Roy, for the most part, played at left back in the reserves, and, at 26, Shankley told him: 'Hang up your boots, son. You'll make a much better coach.'

On another occasion, Shankley commented that there were only two teams in Liverpool – 'Liverpool and Liverpool Reserves'.

To gain the psychological advantage before a game, Shankley was not averse to rubbishing the opposing team's players. On one occasion it is recounted that he came into Liverpool's dressing room and stated: 'I've just seen Bobby Moore. What a wreck! He's got bags under his eyes, he's limping and he's got dandruff.' Another time: 'One of them's got a dicky knee, one's too old and the other's a drunkard,' he told the team. Liverpool were about to play Manchester United, and Shankley was referring to Law, Charlton and Best.

In fact, there are still many Newcastle supporters who believe that the reason their team failed miserably in the 1974 Liverpool *v* Newcastle Cup Final was the way Shankley demolished the manager, Joe Harvey, in a pre-match TV interview. Joe disintegrated in the face of Shanks's psychological pressure and transferred his anxiety to the team. The result, as reported by David Coleman: 'Keegan two, Heighway one, Liverpool three, Newcastle none.'

Joe Mercer managed to preserve his reputation as a very competent manager, but it must have been down to something more than his inspirational patter before he sent his team out for a match. Apparently, he would often enthuse: 'The grass is green, the paint is fresh – now go out there and play.'

Shankley expected total devotion and courage. When asked why he had transferred one of his players, he said: 'He's got the heart of a caraway seed.'

To another player, he advised: 'Look, if you're in the penalty area and aren't quite sure what to do with the ball, just stick it in the net and we'll discuss your options afterwards.'

Shankley was totally absorbed with football, and, curiously, had a fascination for gangsters. TV film shows the Liverpool team, before the 1974 Cup Final, sauntering around the Wembley pitch, dressed in black shirts, white ties, sharp suits and black and white shoes – gear 'à la mob'. Was it a legacy from the Shankley era which caused them to appear at the final in 1996 dressed in white suits?

The attraction did not stop there. Tommy Smith recalls:

'Before one big match Shankley entered the dressing room and put a brown envelope on the table. We waited for him to tell us about the opposition, but he just told me to open the envelope. When I did, in it there were pictures of Al Capone, Bugsy Malone, and other American mobsters. Shanks said: "You think you've got a hard game today. I just want you to think how hard it would be if you were up against this lot." . . . and that was it!'

It was once rumoured that, during the football season, Shankley had taken his wife out to celebrate their wedding anniversary. Some of the lads at the club couldn't believe that Bill deviated from his total seven days of football ritual and could not resist asking him where he had taken her.

'Ay, I gave the wee woman a good night out,' said Shanks. 'I took her to see Tranmere Rovers Reserves . . . but it was nay our wedding anniversary, it was her birthday . . . Can you see me getting married in the football season?'

Clearly, for Shanks, a honeymoon without football would be like a honeymoon without a wife.

That grand old man of soccer, and adversary of Shankley, **Sir Matt Busby**, like so many of that generation, lost a chunk of his playing career when war broke out in 1939. The story is told of Matt joining up. He had signed for Liverpool from Manchester City to finish his career. When he went for his medical and gave his details, a clerk, who clearly knew nothing about football or Matt, asked him his civilian occupation. 'Footballer,' replied Matt. When he arrived at his first unit, the fiercely proud Scotsman, Matt, whose accent could be very strong, found that he had been classified as a 'food boiler'.

The Manager As a Dietician

More often than not managers ensure that players are well-prepared physically, with the right food and drink to carry them through. This is not always the case. In Liberia, in 1980, the national side was threatened with death by firing squad if they lost. They managed a draw.

Incentives of a different nature were aimed at encouraging the Kuwait national team. In 1982, they were promised, and received, for reaching the World Cup Finals, a luxury car, a house and the equivalent of £50,000.

What to feed players before a match varies from country to country and continent to continent. It might be pasta in Europe but Ian Porterfield, who was, for a time, coach of the Zambian side, reveals an interesting pre-match cuisine for the national footballers of Zaire: 'In the 1970s Zaire players were eating monkeys' hearts.'

Unfortunately, when the cook ran out of ingredients, the team started losing matches.

It is interesting to note that **Major Frank Buckley**, the legendary manager of Wolves in the 1930s, who literally flooded the pitch at Molyneux because he believed his team played better on a heavy surface, encouraged other teams to believe he fed his players 'monkey-gland' pills. He had, in fact, organized his players to have an anti-flu jab but, to have the psychological advantage, promoted the deception. It worked on Everton, who were hammered 7–1, and later claimed that the Wolves players were detached from reality, and almost superhuman.

Chris Waddle had a word to say about diet when comparing the stars of the 1970s with the present time: 'Players are much fitter these days. In Hudson's day they'd probably eat chip-butties before the game and go out to play at 2.55 p.m. We all eat tagliatelle, and are out warming up at least 20 minutes before kickoff.' (Alan Hudson had commented that Cantona would not have got into Chelsea's 1970s side.)

'Alcohol,' we are informed by **Graeme Souness**, 'isn't part of the lifestyle in Italy. They work on the principle that your body's a machine; you drain that machine, now you've got to put back into your system whatever is good for that machine. And the one thing you don't fill it with is alcohol.'

> 'Our players don't bloody drink for a start. There are no 12-pint-a-night-men here. They go straight home to their families, and they always behave like responsible athletes.' (**Bobby Robson**, then Porto manager, on why Portuguese clubs are doing so much better than English ones in European competition.)

Twelve pints? Kids' stuff, Bobby! The *Ealing Gazette* asked QPR striker, **Kevin Gallen**:

> 'What is your greatest achievement away from football?'
>
> Answer: 'Downing 20 pints in a row.'

Now there speaks a dedicated athlete with a fine sense of accomplishment. And what is more, he also seems to have the right qualifications for his second choice of a career. Next Question:

> 'What would you do if you weren't a footballer?'
>
> Answer: 'I've no idea. But I'd quite like to be a doctor.'

Kevin's not the only one pre-occupied with alcohol. **Ian Walker**, the Spurs goalkeeper, described his chief ambition in 1993: 'To be marooned on a desert island with an endless supply of lager, women and Sky TV.' And his favourite aroma: 'A woman's perfume and the smell of a Big Mac.'

So **Karren Brady**, managing director of Birmingham City, was only partially correct when she said: 'Footballers are only interested in drinking, clothes and the size of their willies.'

Not surprisingly, **Gazza** has something to say on the matter. According to him, you can tell when things are going well at Rangers when the squad goes on the booze for 48 hours after a match. A case of: 'The club that drinks together wins together.'

Some take their problems abroad. The ex-Spurs and Everton fullback, **Pat Van den Hauwe**, was released from the South African Premier side, Hellenic, in October 1996: 'Pat needs to have expert counselling over his drinking habits . . . He had to leave here. He was setting the worst possible example to the team. He just wanted to party and he let himself go completely. He went missing half the time,' said Chris Gie, the Hellenic manager.

Some don't seem to realize that there is a problem. In 1983, **Charlie Nicholas** said: 'On a boys' night out after a game, the most I'll have is seven or eight pints of lager. That to me isn't being drunk.'

It was the ex-Liverpool player, **Jan Molby**, well-known for his penchant for lager, who in 1993 was described by Brian Glanville as appearing '. . . corpulent enough to be playing darts for Denmark.' One is reminded of an observation by the commentator, Tony Green, at the height of the British Open Darts Championships: 'You've gotta be fit to play this game.' (Mind you – Jocky Wilson once said: 'I've been described as fat, boozy and toothless. That's pretty accurate.')

It emerges that ex-Wimbledon midfielder, **Oyvind Leonardsen**, quite remarkably, is almost teetotal. 'It's not that I don't like drinking beer, but I couldn't drink like they do (*that is, his team-mates*). Not during the season anyway.'

> (A Wimbledon player: 'Someone who would trample over 11 naked women for a pint of lager – but wouldn't leave the scene.')

In this context, one is reminded of the player who goes to the doctor's because he was not feeling well. After examining him the doctor says: 'I can't find anything the matter with you – it must be the drink.' To which the player replies: 'No, problem, Doc. I'll come back when you're sober.'

But this preoccupation with drink among British professional players must give cause for concern when an experienced manager like **Lou Macari** believes that booze is a bigger problem than drugs.

After some of the England players had made the infamous foray into a nightclub and had a bit of a booze after that disappointing match against Switzerland in Euro '96, **Graham Taylor**'s opinion on the matter was canvassed and he concurred with Macari:

'I have felt for a long time that drink is the worst problem affecting the game in our country,' he commented. 'The thing most players do after the match is dive into a hospitality lounge and start supping beer . . . they will go out later, and start drinking some more. It doesn't seem to happen with players in the rest of Europe.'

He went on to cite the occasion when, as a club manager, a player was injured during a match and the physio went on to treat him. The physio discovered he could hardly stand up because he was so full of drink. This gives a whole new meaning to: 'He's lost his bottle.'

In Britain, unlike on the continent, there is the pub culture which is inbred from early days and which some players find difficult to resist. There is a possibility that this practice might change as players realize that excessive drinking does not equate with an extended career and the influence of those dedicated and moderate foreign players has its effect. However, the attraction of post-match alcohol for relaxation will be difficult to root out – as this example will serve to demonstrate . . .

After the draw between Brentford and Blackpool on Saturday 14 September 1996, it was reported that **Gary Brabin**, the Blackpool defender, was arrested. His detention was the result of an altercation after the game, with Brentford's **Jamie Bates**. Bates had been wheeled out from the dressing room with an oxygen mask over his face and taken to the West Middlesex Hospital. Pretty dramatic and startling – but a rapid reversion to the norm when Roy Johnson, the club's physio, phoned from the hospital with the news: 'Jamie has recovered. He has asked for a lager.' The following week in the Blackpool *v* Chelsea programme, Brabin was described as 'a midfielder who likes to get involved'.

But as the Bible might say: 'Let him who is without sin cast the first can of Stones. . . .' For football, from its earliest years, has been sponsored by pubs and taverns. Referees are merely enforcing rules – tablets of 'Stones'! – which trace their origins back to the 'Men Only' bar, and the inebriated and officious Graham Kellys of yesteryear.

How things have changed from those innocent days of the late 1940s and 1950s. In 1949, in *Stanley Matthews' Football Album*, appeared the following: 'Billy Wright is a model professional. He is a teetotaller, does not smoke, goes to bed early, and lives modestly in lodgings. After home games he goes to the theatre, and on two evenings a week to the technical college. He likes to spend the other evenings quietly at home, listening to his collection of gramophone records of opera and classical music, and making rugs.'

The Manager As Custodian of the 'Crazy Gang'

Alan Cork, talking about Wimbledon: 'The club were staying in an army camp in Krefeld in Germany, when an announcement came over the tannoy. It said something like: "In the event of the nuclear warning alarm sounding, please put on the gas-mask provided and leave the building immediately." We were all in on it except Fash. Anyway, the alarm goes off at about five o'clock in the morning, and we're all pretending to be asleep and Fash dives out of bed, puts his gas mask on and runs out. We all got up and looked out of the window, and there was Fash disappearing into the distance. The most frightening thing was when John Leslie hid in my wardrobe for about 25 minutes once. Eventually, he jumped out and yelled "BOO!". It frightened the f****** life out of me.'

Clearly, life with the 'Crazy Gang' did have its surprises and at the centre of them seems to have been **Wally Downes**. Incidents of his changing-room sense of fun, some might say the 'devil having work for idle hands', show no respect for persons. 'Jokes' ranged from (*see above*) to Andy Thorn, as an apprentice, being asked on the coach journey from Luton to get as much lager as he could carry. He humped the booze on to the mini-bus, and just as he was about to re-board, Wally shoved him out, slammed the doors, and the mini-bus drove off. 'It took me two hours to get home, the b*****ds. I had to phone my Mum.'

It is hardly surprising that the Wimbledon players lack a degree of finesse and refinement when you learn of the incentives to performance which their leader, **Sam Hammam**, offers. In the case of **Dean Holdsworth**, one-time hero, Sam offered the following:

1. If he scored 15 goals in his first season, a gold bust of the scorer (he got 19). 'Reg' got his sculptured bust.
2. The next season Sam promised to kiss his backside if he scored 15 – and he did. He reached the target at Newcastle and the others couldn't wait to get into the dressing room. 'They were all trying to put Vaseline on my bum,' said Dean. Again, Sam was as good as his word.
3. The next season, Sam said he would give him a camel which he was going to donate to London Zoo – but Holdsworth never made 15, suffering recurrent injuries.
4. In the 1995-96 season, Dean asked for a Ferrari, but never reached the required target.

'I have to hand it to Manchester United. They have the best players in the League – and the best referees.' (Sam Hammam, Wimbledon owner, after United's win at Selhurst Park when Alan Kimble was sent off.)

Sam's comment is reminiscent of **Jimmy Hagan**'s post-match comment when he managed Portugal's Vittoria Setobal: 'I shouldn't be so upset at losing to Benfica. After all, they have the best players, the best referees, and the best linesmen.'

Joe Kinnear's problems were more numerical in the 1995-96 season: 'I can count on the fingers of one hand ten games when we've caused our own downfall.'

Joe can also be paranoid: 'I mean, 'oddle plays a long

ball and you lot all go: "Ooh, aah, what a beautiful pass!" If we do the same thing: "Oh, it's Wimbledon, playing route one as usual." Yeah, I know we got enemies, people that 'ate the club and 'ate me.'

Paranoia must be a complex which comes with the job because back in 1987 **Dave Bassett**, then manager, was moaning: 'Arsenal keep hitting that 6ft 4in Irishman (Niall Quinn) with high balls, and it's quality football. We hit a 6ft 3in black fella (John Fashanu) on the head, and it's violence.'

But Joe normally does show his sense of humour when he isn't feeling persecuted. At the start of the 1996 season and after the transfer of Shearer to Newcastle, Joe revealed that Sam Hammam asked him if he had his choice, which two would be at the top of his list. Joe replied: 'Sir John Hall and Jack Walker.'

And when, on Sunday 12 January 1997, Joe received the prized award of the 'Managers' Manager' from Sky Television, presented by Engelbert Humperdink, he quipped: 'With a name like that you should be in the "Crazy Gang".'

And the reason for his team's impressive run from the start of the 1996-97 season?: 'We've been drinking much more, and kicking the ball in the sky much more.'

The zenith of Wimbledon's achievements, and in recent years there have been many high spots, much to the dismay of many in the media and certain pundits, was the 1988 Cup Final victory over Liverpool. Then, as now, Liverpool symbolized all that was good and wholesome in British football. They represented the nobility, the blue-blood of the League with a pedigree Cruft's champions would die for. Wimbledon represented the upstarts, the back-street lads with no money but plenty of kamikaze aggression who liked nothing better than rattling and cocking a snook at the establishment. In John Motson's words, it was 'The "Crazy Gang" versus "The Culture Club"', and the comment was made that, if Wimbledon won, 'it would be the worst thing that could happen for English football'.

While Liverpool, before that final, followed their usual routine of a Friday evening meal of pies and peas, an early night and the sleeping-pill attendance of Ronnie Moran, **Bobby Gould**, à la Cloughie, gave his squad £200 and told them to relax in the local. Laurie Sanchez, whose car tyres had been let down by Wise, recalls how it broke Bobby's heart to hand over the money.

The psyching out of Liverpool, which had begun the week before when it was reported that **Vinnie** was going 'to tear Kenny Dalglish's ear off and spit in the hole', continued in the tunnel. Much to Kenny's distaste, the Wimbledon players chanted: 'In the hole, in the hole, in the hole . . .' as the teams were led out.

Within five minutes Vinnie had upended McMahon, who they saw as the 'leader' and driving force. The pattern had been set, and the underdogs felt they had drawn first blood. Sanchez's headed goal and Aldridge's missed penalty ensured that the aristocrats had fallen and the commoners had triumphed. Jimmy Hill, who had intoned the hymns of praise for Liverpool since first transmission, looked abashed, yet still had the gall to attend Wimbledon's victory celebrations, much to Vinnie's disgust 'Get 'im out!' he roared.

The Manager As Negotiator

On top of everything else, managers have agents to deal with.

Jon Holmes, representative for such greats as Lineker,

Gower and Carling, comments: 'My wife tells people I'm a Kwik-Fit Fitter when they ask her what I do.'

Nor is it surprising when he pours scorn on the traditions of the game. 'Can you think of any other trade in the latter part of the twentieth century where they call their superiors "gaffer" or "boss"? I think that's pathetic,' he caustically remarks. Well, yes, isn't it the practice among an abundance of occupations and particularly 'Kwik-Fit Fitters'?

It was Holmes who had to parley with **Brian Clough** when he was investigating the possibility of signing Gary McAllister, then at Leicester. At one point, Cloughie said to McAllister: 'I'm talking to you, not your bimbo.'

'When I try to speak to him about his future, he tells me to talk to his agent. Well, it's not his agent he rings when the car won't start or the baby has ear ache. It's me or my wife at two in the morning.' (**Alan Smith**, when he was manager at Crystal Palace, on Chris Armstrong.)

If Alan Smith does not appear to have any time for agents, **Joe Kinnear** makes his feelings pretty obvious. Joe refers to them as 'Dogs, worms, and vermin,' while **Graham Taylor** suggested: 'Agents do nothing for the good of football. I'd like to see them lined up against a wall and machine-gunned.'

Another manager who would concur with Joe is **John McClelland**, formerly manager of St Johnstone. Lying in a hospital bed on a drip, he was visited by a player and his agent who he thought had come to see how he was. They had arrived to discuss the player's contract!

Even that FA epitome of politeness, **Graham Kelly**, had this to say: 'I wouldn't cross the road to talk to an agent.'

And what of agent, **Eric Hall**, once voted the fourth most hated man in the game. Dan Davies, who writes in *Goal*, the publication which has helped to do for the football fan what Delia Smith has done for home-cook-ing, says simply:

'He is nothing less than an horrific, walking, breathing Viz character – a mutant hybrid of Cockney w***** and spoilt b******.'

The Manager In the Age of Tolerance

Perhaps the most obtuse bit of partisanship of the 1995-96 season came from ex-Rangers' **Terry Butcher**, who asked his chef at his Stirling Hotel to change the price of the Christmas dinner from £16.95 to £16.90 since it was on 12 July 1690 that the Protestant, King Billy (William of Orange), defeated the Catholic-inclined James II at the Battle of the Boyne.

Butcher has shown periodically a remarkable lack of judgement in making public his bias. In 1990 he wrote: 'I don't like U2, that's rebel music, southern Irish, and Simple Minds – I found out that Jim Kerr was a Celtic supporter, so all my Simple Minds tapes, they went out of the window. Celtic, you hate 'em so much . . .' – and it was of this man that Bobby Robson intoned: 'What character, what stature, what a patriot, what a player!'

Mind you, it's not only Rangers' or Celtic's fans who continue to show old loyalties. Linfield, the Manchester United of Northern Ireland, who are based at Windsor Park, draw their support from the Protestant community, and until relatively recently a Catholic would have been about as welcome as a pre-match beefburger. Things are changing, however, but still the fans' prejudices humor-ously shine through. The Catholic, Pat Fenlon, is referred to as 'Billy', the name equated with Protestantism after King William of Orange.

If Butcher won't attract much Celtic custom at his hotel,

Mike Bateson, the sharp-tongued chairman of Torquay, seems determined to alienate the few supporters his club has. Perhaps that explains their position in the League. 'The vocal minority, depending upon the time of year, want the manager out, the chairman out, the players out, or even the bleedin' programme-sellers out. God knows what sort of lives these people live during the week. These supporters are complete and utter dickheads. ... God unhinges their heads, scoops their brains out, and then issues them to a football club.'

Mark McGhee, who pledged his troth to Leicester, then abandoned them for Wolves, has given an interesting and cynical view of his conception of management: 'Loyalty isn't for players or managers. It's for those people who watch their team every week.'

McGhee might have a point. Bobby Robson, offered the Newcastle position in January 1997, turned it down because of a sense of loyalty to Barcelona – and this from a man whose commitment to the England and Sporting Lisbon jobs was so ruthlessly terminated. Mickey Duff, the boxing manager, has a favourite expression: 'In the end loyalty is what they shaft you with.'

'Let's go and sort this out down the tunnel.' **Terry McDermott** to **Bruce Rioch** during the managerial contre-temps after the sending off of David Ginola during the quarter finals of the Coca-Cola Cup match (10 January 1996) between Arsenal and Newcastle.

Talking of possible fisticuffs among club officials, what is to be made of this item from the *Sheffield Telegraph* following an incident of assault in Hackenthorpe: 'The two suspects were both wearing dark-coloured three-quarter-length coats of the type sometimes worn by football managers.' Could they have been referring to 'Donkey' jackets?

Violence of a more sinister nature is becoming more prevalent in modern-day football. True, extreme demonstrations of opposition did occur, for example, in 1885, after Preston had won 5–1 at Aston Villa. The winning team was attacked by home fans: 'Thicker and faster came the stones, and showers of spittle covered us,' reported one of the Preston players.

But managers are coming in, more and more, for serious threats. In the early 1970s, fans at Reading made their displeasure felt towards **Jack Mansell** merely by tying abusive messages to his son's bicycle.

In 1996, **Jimmy Mullen**, manager at Burnley for over four years, was accosted at a Take-Away restaurant by savage supporters, who then tried to set fire to his wife's dress.

In the same season, leaflets containing death threats against **Ian Branfoot** of Fulham were circulated at Craven Cottage.

Managerial Snippets — 'Things They Never Said'

Barry Fry: 'I'm happy with the squad I've got.'

Alex Ferguson: 'We deserved to lose. I have no complaints.'

George Graham: 'I'm interested in the game – not the money.'

Mark McGhee: 'I think the manager as well as the players and fans should demonstrate loyalty.'

Ron Atkinson: 'All that glistens is not gold.'

Jack Charlton: 'Here – let me buy this round!' or 'Would you like a cigarette?'

Kevin Keegan: 'Defence is the name of the game.'

Peter Reid: 'The Board has said: "Spend, spend, spend!"'

Brian Clough: 'I don't really have an opinion on that.'

Howard Wilkinson: 'I always look on the bright side.'

Joe Kinnear: 'Gary Lineker is an excellent TV presenter.'

Lawrie McMenemy: 'We'll be looking for a small retirement home in Sunderland.'

Harry Redknapp: 'Foreign players have been the answer to my prayers.'

Martin O'Neill: 'I'm lost for words.'

'Manager-Speak' . . .

Those aspiring to lead clubs would be well-advised to familiarize themselves with managerial 'Footy-Speak', a vocabulary which is essential to achieve credibility.

Players are referred to as 'Lads'. (If you are Scottish or a disciple of Shankley, then an individual player can be referred to as 'The boy' – as in 'The boy done well'.)

Wherever possible, add a '-y' to the surname – e.g. Giggs-y, Platt-y, Clarke-y. (Careful if called Fuchs, Jess, Horne, Fann, Will, Lune, Nodd, or Babs.)

Teams give 110 per cent and 'You can't ask for more than that'.

'Early-doors' – an Atkinsonism, meaning 'early on in the game before patterns have developed'.

'At the end of the day . . .' – phrase to use when no other comes to mind.

'Despite defeat, I thought the lads were magnificent.' = effort, great/skill, crap.

'It would be unfair to single out only one player here.' – if I do the rest will sulk.

'Great vision' – does not always make the obvious five-yard pass.

'A real work-horse with a great engine' – runs around like a madman for 90 minutes, but never settles in any direction.

'He's more of a striker' – a prima donna who's too idle to help out in defence.

'Reckless challenge' – Vinnie Jones would have been ashamed of it.

'A bit of a lad' – a pain in the backside.

'Good for the dressing room' – perpetrates childish pranks.

'Temperamental' – sulky and immature.

'Has picked up a virus' – dropped.

'He'll be hard to replace' – thank God we've managed to off-load him.

'I have the full backing of the Board' – they've told me if I don't win the next five games, I'm out.

'There is money to spend' – what we get back off the bottles.

'An articulate lad' – can say 'over the moon' without stammering.

'He's still learning' – at the moment he's crap, but there is hope.

'A true veteran' – we have the oxygen cylinders standing by.

'Shrewd' – devious.

'Ambitious' – ruthless.

'Prediction' – guess.

'Frank discussion' – wholesale argument.

'Very frank discussion' – punch-up

'Urgency' – panic.

'Extreme urgency' – blind panic.

'The referee seemed to miss that'/'The linesman's flag went up very late' – the b****** has bottled out.

'Unfortunately he wasn't able to finish it off' – you pay

the s*d £15,000 a week and he can't get the ball between the sticks.

'A very ambitious shot' – greedy and wasteful.

'That is why it's such a wonderful game' – once again my pre-match forecast has been totally inaccurate.

(Cup game against Lower Division Team) 'It will be a hard game for us' – unless we have five sent off, we'll wipe them off the park.

'A mountain to climb after that goal' – as much chance as a Manchester United supporter in the Kop.

'Seems a bit short of match practice' – looks slower than Cyril Smith.

'Comfortable victory' – opposition slaughtered; a walk in the park.

'And that's for sure' – a Hoddle-ism used as emphasis.

Managers At a Club Awards Night Out

'Friends, when I came here this evening, only God and myself knew what I was going to say – now only God knows.'

'As a speaker, I really enjoy being with smart, knowledgeable, exciting and decent people – I don't even mind being with people like you.'

'Thank you, Mr Chairman. The trouble with many speakers is you can't hear what they're saying. The trouble with him is that you can.'

'Can I now introduce you to our chairman. When he speaks, he will add something extra to the evening . . . about 45 minutes.'

'The timing of this award is perfect, even though while the last speech was being made, I thought I might have to award it posthumously.'

'I spent the best years of my life in the arms of another woman – me mother's.'

'As a child, I felt very insecure. When I was four I was kidnapped – and they only asked for expenses.'

'When you finish your playing career, become a manager and grow old, three things happen. First, you lose your eyesight; second, you lose your memory; and the third is . . . I can't remember the third!' (Or, in the case of some managers . . . your temper!)

'. . . But at the End of the Day'

'If you can keep your head while all around are losing theirs, then you clearly don't understand the situation.'

'Be thankful for your problems, for if they were fewer, someone with less ability would have your job.'

'If you are not big enough to stand criticism, then you're too small to be praised.'

'No matter what goes wrong, there is always somebody who knew it would.'

'Forgive your enemies, but never forget their names.'

'The most knocking is done by those who can't ring the bell.'

'Speak when you're angry and you'll make the best speech you'll ever regret.'

'A manager laughs at his chairman's jokes not because they are clever, but because he is.'

'A chairman who can smile when things go wrong has found someone to blame it on.'

'Knowledge is power if you know it about the right people.'

'When someone says he is laying all his cards on the table – count them!'

'A man would do nothing if he waited until he could do it so well that no one could find fault with it.'

'The more you say, the less people remember.' (Apropos of which it is interesting to hear Big Jack's philosophy: 'You have got to get a system that everybody understands very quickly. The more complicated it becomes, the less likely they are to succeed – and everyone must know their responsibilities.')

'No one is indispensable – but some are irreplaceable.'

'And never go to bed angry – stay up and fight!'

'Live every day as if it's your last – and one day . . . you'll be right!'

And finally . . .

'Now I want you players to tell me what you think and put forward your suggestions, even if it means you're put on the transfer list.' (Ashley J. Roy – ex-manager.)

2
Players

Introduction

To so many, football is the elixir of life and can be the most beautiful of games. Players are heroes who have survived a rigorous and intense process of selection to attain, through skill and commitment, what many would have loved to achieve. We like to know about their views, strengths, foibles and personalities in the mysterious world of varied relationships within clubs which form the backdrop to Saturday afternoon's glory spot.

There are those who would say that footballers, though subject to greater pressures and, at the highest level, greater rewards than the majority of professions, are as clever, or as daft, as any other. Three factors, however, conspire to challenge this observation and deposit them into a special educational needs category. One of them is that, because they are in the public eye, few incidents or quotes escape media attention. If a bricklayer responded that Hitler's first name was 'Heil', it would not merit attention – but it would become newsworthy if it were a Premiership football player.

A second reason is that the system of recruitment into

the sport at the age of 16 cuts short a general education which often has already been marginalized in the single-minded quest to achieve footballing ambition. As Julian Dicks of West Ham proclaims: 'I'm not the brainiest person. I ain't got no O-levels, nothing. I didn't go back for my results because all I ever wanted to do was play football.' The result is that basic deficiencies in knowledge are highlighted. For example, Mark Draper of Aston Villa expressed the wish that, at a future date, he would play abroad for 'an Italian club like Barcelona'.

The third factor is that professional footballers do not help themselves by their pronouncements about colleagues. Steve McManaman revealed that fullback, Rob Jones, is nicknamed 'Trig' after the intellectually challenged character in 'Only Fools and Horses'. He goes on to say that Liverpool right back, Jason McAteer, is called 'Dick' because 'you can't have two people called "Trig" in your side, can you?' It was further revealed that when McAteer had been in America for the World Cup, he had been asked by a waitress if he wanted his pizza cut into four or eight pieces. 'Four,' replied Jason. 'I'm not that hungry.'

Further gossip emerged from a Liverpool player – this time anonymously, but nevertheless funny. A particular Liverpool player, at the suggestion of a colleague who had seen him pay a hotel bill with a wad of notes, applied for a credit card. He was filling in the application on the way to a match and asked a team-mate:

'What do I put for "Company"?'

'Just put "Liverpool FC",' he advised.

A little later, as he progressed through the form, he was looking puzzled.

'Now what's the matter?' he was asked.

'I'm not sure what to put here for "Position". They're playing me at the back, but I prefer the wing.'

And just to emphasize the disservice colleagues can do, Gavin Peacock, formerly of Chelsea, revealed that his then team-mate, Frank Sinclair, '. . . thought the brain was on the left side of the head – so he always put penalties to the goalkeeper's right, because he said it took longer for the messages to get down to the right side of the keeper's body.' Apparently, when it was explained to him that indeed this was not the case, Sinclair sighed in exasperated realization: 'Oh no! It's the heart that's on the left, isn't it?'

The truth of the matter is that, among the ranks of professional footballers, there is frequently a wealth of intelligence, rapidity of wit and a mischievousness which can be very entertaining.

Malcolm Allison
Malcolm still recalls a full-blooded clash with Derek Dooley, following which he said: 'I thought I was dying. It came into my mind that I was going to die and I still had £200 in the dressing room that I hadn't spent.'

Clive Allen
Clive, now a Sky-Armchair-Pundit (SAP) had this to say on joining Arsenal from QPR in June 1980, two months before a second £1 million transfer, to Crystal Palace: 'A move like this only happens once in a lifetime.'

Dalian Atkinson
'If I was still at Ipswich, I wouldn't be where I am today.'

Alan Ball
The story goes that Alan Ball turned out hippie fashion in 1972 for Arsenal against Leeds wearing a string of beads which someone had given him in the Bahamas during his

summer holiday. At one point he was flattened by Bremner and in attempting to get to his feet said to Bremner: 'Give me a hand then.' Bremner looked at him, clapped his hands and said: 'Crazy man, crazy.'

Tessi Balogun

In the 1956 season Peterborough United had on their books a Nigerian called Tessi Balogun. One Saturday, playing for the reserves, it began to snow, and Tessi, who had never ever seen snow before, was so completely thrown and disorientated by the experience, he ran off the pitch and could only be coaxed back when the snow had stopped.

On the subject of playing in extreme weather conditions, Peter Clynes from Moor Green FC, Birmingham, recounts a tale from his club's involvement in an FA Amateur Cup played on 31 January 1948. The match was away to East Tanfield, a club from a pit-village up in the bleak windswept hills of south-west Durham. In winter it can be so cold the breath crackles. The local players, miners from the local colliery, found the conditions – a raging blizzard and zero temperatures – barely tolerable. The visitors from the leafy Midland middle-class suburb of Hall Green found it unbearable. The match kicked off, but within a short time six Moor Green players were forced to seek refuge in the clubhouse's hot bath and tots of whisky. East Tanfield were down to nine men and Moore Green to five when the ref abandoned the game. Geordie hospitality was extended to a roaring fire and more whisky (despite the fact that East Tanfield had been 2–0 up). The Midlanders, pleasantly inebriated, made their hazardous way home, to win 3–2 at a later date and in more clement weather.

John Barnes

Nowadays a stockier John Barnes flourishes in the midfield, having adapted his silky skills to spray consistently accurate passes and bring balance and maturity to a rejuvenated Liverpool. What is significant is that he seems to have lost that injury-prone reputation which brought the comment that he suffered physical impairment appearing on 'A Question of Sport'. At least he didn't attain the nickname of 'Sicknote', which belongs to his ex-Liverpool team-mate, Stan Collymore.

Warren Barton

One footballer with an eye for the catwalk is Warren Barton. His team-mate at Newcastle, Robert Lee, commented: 'Warren's the best-dressed footballer I've ever seen. Even in training we're all in track suits and he arrives in shirt, trousers and shoes – and his hair lovely. We all call him "The Dogs", as in "The Dog's Bollocks".'

Jim Baxter

Jim Baxter, that elegant and legendary ex-Raith Rovers, Rangers, Sunderland, Nottingham and Scotland genius, was once considered by Don Revie as a signing for his Leeds machine. 'I'm told,' said Revie, 'you drink everything brewed and distilled around here, there aren't enough women for you to chase, and you're not averse to the odd brawl.' Baxter responded: 'Aye, you're very well informed.' 'Well, Jimmy,' said Revie, 'I'd love to have you in my team – but then, I want to sleep at nights.'

Baxter's glorious career and skills were destroyed before time as a result of his lifestyle which Jimmy himself sums up in these words: 'Friday night was Saturday night to me, and when they said you shouldn't have sex for two days before a game, I said sex an hour before made me a better player.'

When on international duty in Ireland, the story is that the Scottish team were taken on a tour of Dublin. 'We are now passing the biggest pub in Ireland.' Jimmy's voice was heard to boom out from the back of the bus: 'Why?'

Sports journalist, Robert Philip, has said of Jim, who is now teetotal and has raised thousands to finance liver transplants, two of which he has undergone himself: 'If Gascoigne is worth £5 million, Slim Jim was worth £10 million . . . to see Baxter play football was to hear Caruso sing, to see Van Gogh paint . . .'

Chris Beaumont
Chris was sent off in the 1994 season play-off match when playing for Stockport County against Burnley. His manager at the time, Danny Bergera, raged: 'He crazy . . . crazy, I don't know why he do it. Chris, he such a pussy-cat, my sister could punch him out.'

George Berry

A few years ago, just before kickoff at Stoke, on a wet Saturday, George Berry went on to the pitch to test various boots. From the terraces came the voice: 'Try a left and a right this week, George!'

George Best

George Best has probably prospered more in recent years by being prepared to laugh at himself, and has come out with some witty one-liners from what he can remember. Here are some of them:

> Reflecting on his attempts to reform he said: 'In 1969 I gave up drinking and sex. It was the worst f****** 20 minutes of my life.' George, it is said, kept fit 'by wrestling with his conscience'.

Rodney Marsh once asked George Best how he felt when Matt Busby phoned his home in Belfast to tell him that Manchester United wanted to sign him. 'F****** astounded,' said Best. 'We didn't have a f****** telephone.'

> 'Have you ever had any ambition to manage a club?' George Best was once asked. 'I'd love to,' replied Best. 'Stringfellows.'

'I've always had a reputation for going missing – Miss England, Miss United Kingdom, Miss World . . .'

> On the Mrs Merton Show:
>
> 'George, you achieved every schoolboy's dream.'
>
> George: 'I did – I married Miss World.'

'They keep saying that Bobby Charlton and me didn't get on well. I sent my lad to his Soccer School of Excellence – he came back bald.'

> 'I spent a lot of my money on booze, birds and fast cars. The rest I just squandered.'

George, who once, it is said, revealed that he 'drank to

forget, but never forgot to drink', claimed he was thinking of writing his autobiography and would appreciate receiving any information as to what he was doing between 1972 and 1983.

He tells the story of his last game against Ajax for Manchester United. He nutmegged Neeskins half-a-dozen times, took off his ties, and threw them at him. 'There,' said Best, 'use them to tie your legs together.'

George isn't the only one in the Best family with a sense of humour. His Dad, Dickie Best, recalls the night Manchester United won the 1965 Championship. At the post-match celebrations, Dickie was approached by a director's wife who asked: 'Mr Best, how did you come to sire such a marvellous son?' In his most refined accent Dickie replied: 'Madam, if I was to show you here, both of us would be thrown out.'

George gets a lot of satisfaction recounting the occasion when he returned to a five-star Birmingham Hotel, having won £25,000 on the gambling-tables. The porter, with sandwiches, entered the bedroom where he was staying with a former Miss World. The bundles of notes were scattered all over the room, and a scantily clad Miss World was perched on the bed.

'Can I ask you a question, please, Mr Best?' said the Porter.

'Of course,' replied George.

'Where did it all go wrong?'

George: 'I don't get involved in politics. Only once – someone threw a petrol bomb at me.'

Reporter: 'What did you do?'

George: 'I drank it!'

Danny Blanchflower

Bill Nicholson's captain, Danny Blanchflower, had a reputation as an intelligent and far-sighted individual. When the players were being presented to the Duchess of Kent at the Leicester *v* Spurs 1961 FA Cup Final, she asked Danny why it was that Leicester players had their names printed on the back of their tracksuits when his team did not. 'We don't need them, Ma'am,' he replied. 'We know each other.'

There is the story of a Tottenham star, during the days of Nicholson, arriving at Heathrow to take his family on holiday and not being able to travel because he had not realized he needed a passport. Though he had travelled to the Continent many times to play in matches, everything had been organized by the club.

Speaking of foreign travel, one is reminded of the joke about the footballer who was standing at Heathrow with an abundance of luggage, which mostly belonged to his wife, for their two-week holiday. 'We should have brought the piano as well,' said the resolute star. 'There's no need to be sarcastic,' said the wife. 'I wasn't being sarcastic,' he said. 'I left the tickets on top of it.'

Luther Blisset

It was widely rumoured that when AC Milan bought Luther Blisset from Watford in 1983, they thought they had bought John Barnes until Luther turned up at the San Siro Stadium.

Billy Bonds

West Ham player, Billy Bonds, spent 27 years at the club, and the joke was that Japanese prisoners-of-war, who had hidden in the jungle since 1945 had as their first question on emerging: 'Is Billy Bonds still playing for

West Ham?' When he did finally resign from the manager's job, in 1994, he said: 'It's going to be strange not going into training at Chadwell Heath every day. I think my car will go there by itself in the morning.'

Zbigniew Boniek

The introductory sentence of Sue Mott's book, *Girl's Guide to Ball Games*, begins: 'The only professional footballer I have ever slept with was Zbigniew Boniek of Poland.' Not as lustful as it might first appear, unfortunately, since the circumstance occurred only because of an accommodation problem.

Marco Boogers

The register of West Ham's recent overseas players Bilic, Dumitrescu, Lazaridis, Mautone, Miklosko, Raducioiu and Rieper, which reads like a Colditz roll call, includes individuals who, to a greater or lesser extent, have already enjoyed success in the claret and blue. Few could accomplish less than the unfortunate Marco Boogers, the Dutch striker, bought for £800,000 and destined to play only 88 minutes for the club. After being sent off in the first week of the season after a foul on Manchester United's Gary Neville, he went missing by September. He was discovered living in a caravan in the Dutch countryside and, it was said, had suffered a breakdown. In February he was loaned to Groningen.

Mark Bright

When Mark Bright left Leicester City, because of racial taunts, and went to Crystal Palace, Steve Coppell assured him: 'Come down to our Club and you won't get that type of abuse.' Later, Ron Noades said: 'That's one of the problems with black players. Not many of them can read the game. When you're getting into midwinter, you need a few of the white hard men to carry the artistic black players through.'

Trevor Brooking
When Trevor retired from the professional game, he played Sunday morning football with Havering NALGO. His reaction: 'You drop your shoulder and move round a defender, only to discover he didn't read your first dummy. So you crash straight into him and he comes away with the ball.'

Perhaps the same thing happened when Trevor represented the media against Georgian journalists before England's World Cup qualifier in November 1996, in Tbilisi. After clattering into a burly hack he needed four stitches after a punch-up with him. Trevor's response: 'Where was Bonzo (Billy Bonds) when I needed him?' Later it was reported Trevor was suffering from shock, not from the right-upper-cut, but from the sight of Graham Kelly running on to replace him.

Steve Bruce
When commenting upon his club's popularity, or lack of it, on the eve of the March 1996 crunch-match with Newcastle at St James's Park, Steve Bruce said:

'With this club, it's black or white – you either love Manchester United or you hate them.' Colour blind as well as having the best nose in the business!

Eric Cantona
It could be argued that any one of Ardiles, Klinsmann, Gullit or Schmeichel has been the most successful import into English football. However, not one of them achieved as much or had the same impact (or should that be the

clout?) of Eric Cantona. Having won one Championship for Leeds (1992), he went on to win Manchester United four (1993, 1994, 1996 and 1997), and thanks to his infamous indiscretion, lost them another. But how Trevor Francis, and above all the fans, must lament his lack of foresight when, as manager of Sheffield Wednesday, he rejected the Frenchman. And how difficult Alex Ferguson must have found it to believe his luck as he hastened to hand over the paltry sum of £1.2 million to secure the Frenchman. It was the equivalent of finding a Goya at the local car boot sale.

It is a scenario slightly reminiscent of the Alan Shearer debacle at Newcastle, who went there on trial as a 12-year-old. Shearer's comment: 'I told them I was a centre forward, but they played me in goal for two days.'

To think he need not have gone home at a cost of £15 million, but could have stayed there for nothing!

The incident involving Eric at Selhurst Park brought with it justifiable condemnation and hypocrisy in equal measure – but would-be wit surfaces quickly.

The speed of humour was almost as fast as the kick itself. Next day there was the question:

> 'What have Cantona and Camilla Parker-Bowles got in common?'
> Answer: 'They've both had their leg over at the Palace.'

Is Eric's 'stamping ground' Selhurst Park?

> And at the 'Dog and Partridge' pub in Didsbury you could buy a pint called 'Cantona' – 'a beer with a kick in it' . . . and presumably one that was bitter and left you with a hell of a hangover.

A French journalist commented ruefully: 'You wouldn't expect him to do that to a fan. A player, yes, but not a fan.'

> Nobody could have been more surprised than Alex
> Ferguson: 'Eric is not a tackler. I've told him not to
> tackle, because he can't!'

Cloughie had little sympathy over the incident: 'I'd have
cut his balls off,' he said.

Eric narrowly avoided a custodial sentence, thanks in
the main to the efforts of Alex Ferguson who showed
great loyalty and deserves much credit in sticking with
him through thick and thin (or should it be 'kick and
sin'?). Is it true that Eric showed his thanks in true Gallic
fashion by giving Alex a kiss on both cheeks – the only
problem being that Alex was fastening his shoelaces at the
time?

It would seem that: 'Eric jumped in with two feet at
being given a second chance.'

Isn't it amazing that, just over a year after Eric's
'Hokey-Kokey', he had a wine named after him which
has been priced at £4.99 for distribution through super-
markets. The producers described it as 'gutsy red', and
could perhaps have added: 'with a deceptive kick in it' –
or perhaps: 'smooth with a sudden explosion'.

We were constantly appraised of the fact that Eric
Cantona, – 'Captain Conceited' – once described as the
most perfectly balanced footballer – (*une frite* on each
shoulder!), is a cultured, refined Frenchman, who reads
and cogitates deeply – hence the respect with which the
following profound statement was greeted: 'When the
seagulls follow the trawler, it is because they think sardines will be thrown into the sea.' The statement was so
vague, and obtuse, people thought there must be something in it. A little bit like laughing at a joke when you
haven't a clue what it's about. If Eric considered himself
to be the trawler, and the seagulls the scavengers of the
press, waiting for the juicy tit-bits to be dropped over the
side, it might perhaps have been more appropriate to use
the metaphor of wolves tracking a wounded animal.

It seems that only Gordon Strachan at the PFA
Awards emerged with the voice of sanity: 'If a Frenchman
goes on about seagulls, trawlers and sardines, he's called
a philosopher. I'd just be called a short Scottish bum talking crap.'

It is interesting to hear Eric's mother saying that:
'When he was a small boy at school, he could not stand
the slightest injustice. He was different from other children.' Things often don't change.

A closer examination of some of the thoughts of Eric
might cause many to challenge the epithet of philosopher.

'I paint psychedelic works. Everything that comes

into my head. It's very black. A real can of worms.'
'The eye, this is an interesting subject . . . the eye
means vision and precision. Like seagulls. Look how
precise their vision is.'

Later Eric changed his fixation with the seagull when
he shared this thought with the world: 'I'd come back as
an eagle. I love the way eagles move, the way they soar,
the way they gaze.'

He did have a lot to say for someone who always
looked as if he has just had his wheels clamped. Of course,
he wouldn't agree with such sanctions:

'I need to be free. I don't like to be constrained by rules
and conventions . . . To some extent I espouse the idea of
anarchy. What I'm after is an anarchy of thought, a liberation of the mind from all convention.'

'In my home, only my dreams hang from the ceiling.'

In 1993, an interview with Eric appeared in the French
magazine, *Football*. It makes you wonder just who is
more crackers – the reporter asking the questions, or Eric
answering them:

Reporter: 'Have you known happiness?'
Eric: 'Yes.'
Reporter: 'Where?'
Eric: 'At the summit of the world.'
Reporter: 'When?'
Eric: 'At my death.'
Reporter: 'And in your life?'
Eric: 'Never.'
Reporter: 'And do you see why?'
Eric: 'At the summit, the world crushes me.'
Reporter: 'Have you seen down there?'
Eric: 'I have seen the world in suspenders.'
Reporter: 'Naked?'

Eric: 'With a dollar in its arse.'
(Mr Freud – have you a moment?)

Things do improve – well, slightly. Eric told *L'Équipe* he felt 'more open' in Britain: 'It is not that I have changed, I am the same. It is rather as if I am now the son of the person I used to be.'

And to Leeds fans at their Civic Reception: 'Why I love you, I don't know, but I love you.' Surely a sentiment which is a manifestation of a tortured mind!

Commenting on the meeting with French coach, Gerard Houllier, who came to Britain to meet him, Eric said: 'We spoke of my son's drawing, of the child's imaginary world, of life, of Leeds, which is a nice town . . .'

One of Eric's more comprehensible comments, though slightly OTT, was: 'Everything is beautiful. The stadiums are beautiful. The atmosphere is beautiful. The cops on horseback are beautiful. The crowds respect you.' But does Eric respect the crowds, and are not the seagulls beautiful?

Whatever the logic, or the lack thereof, of these *bons mots*, Eurostar has commissioned a series of 'Cantonisms' to persuade the British to use the train to get to Paris. And here we go:
- 'Every man has his hour, it is for him to decide which one.'
- 'It is in his soul that the swallow knows when to leave and in his heart that he chooses a fitting time to return.'
- 'To truly see how the crow flies, one must sit on the train.'
- 'Is it not simpler to leap the stream than to pause on each stepping stone?'
- 'When the body is free, so is the mind.'
- 'For centuries man has pondered the nature of space.'

• 'The expectation of departure should not be hindered by the ignominy of waiting.'

Reported conversation between two Liverpool players:
   'Have you seen some of that s***e Cantona has been writing?'
   'Maybe it is – but you couldn't write 'f*** off' on a mucky car.'

Besides being a sage, not many know that Eric is an embryonic trumpeter who has lessons from John McMurray, the principal trumpeter from the Hallé Orchestra. Apparently Eric is into heavy jazz and – wait for it – is utilizing the 'triple-tonguing technique'.

But Eric is the typical prodigal son who has been forgiven more times than George Best ever was. In December 1991, at the age of 25, he announced his retirement. Earlier in that month he had flung a ball at the ref and incurred a month's suspension.

He continued to slide down the slippery slope when he swore at the disciplinary committee officials and called them 'idiots'. The suspension was increased to two months. Previously, he had called the French manager, Henri Michael, 'a bag of s**t'.

Howard Wilkinson concurred with the aesthetic proclivities of the Frenchman: 'Journalists arrived from all over Europe to meet him . . . He gave interviews on art, philosophy and politics. A natural room-mate for David Batty, I thought immediately.'

But that's not to say Wilkinson admired him: 'Eric likes to do what he likes, when he likes, because he likes it – and then f*** s off. We'd all want a bit of that.'

Few Geordies had any admiration for Eric after the FA Charity Shield when Manchester United beat

Newcastle 4–0:

> Interviewer: 'Were you surprised by the score-line?'
>
> Eric: 'Was I surprised by the score-line? Well, I'll say yes to be polite.'

After Newcastle won 5–0 against the same team a few weeks later at St James's, a member of the Toon Army retaliated in his interview:

'You ask me was I surprised by the score-line. I can honestly say "Oui, Oui, I thought we should have had seven."'

Jordi Cruyff

Jordi, on comparisons between Spain and England:

> Question: 'Is there any difference in the changing rooms?'
>
> Answer: 'Yes, they are so small here. It was the first thing I noticed.'

Kenny Dalglish

Bob Paisley, described by Roy Evans as 'the best talent-spotter I have ever known', once said: 'Kenny Dalglish ran the first five yards in his head'. Kenny, always unassuming, on another occasion caused Bob sardonically to remark: 'Kenny calls all his goals tap-ins until we come to the end of the season and talk of money. Suddenly he changes his mind.'

Former Liverpool Chairman, the late Sir John Smith, said Kenny was: 'the best player this club has signed this century'.

Ali Dea

Graeme Souness couldn't believe his luck when World 'Footballer of the Year', George Weah, telephoned him to recommend his friend, Ali Dea, ex-Senegalese and ex-

Paris St Germain forward. Souness gave him a month's trial, shirt No. 33 and substituted him against Leeds when Matt Le Tissier was injured. Alas, it took minutes to see that Ali was totally out of his depth, and he had to be substituted. The call had been a hoax and not from George Weah at all, and while Ali had been a Senegalese international, he had never played for St Germain's first team, only the reserves.

Dixie Dean

William Ralph Dean, called 'Dixie' – a nickname which alluded to his swarthy complexion and which he detested – scored 60 League goals in 39 games for Everton. A legendary header of the ball, there is the story told of him once meeting the Liverpool goalkeeper, Elisha Scott, at a local railway station. Dean nodded, and Elisha flung himself down and to the right.

Dean was capped 16 times for England, and was a central figure in a 7–1 win against Spain at Highbury in 1931. The Spanish goalkeeper, Ricardo Zamora, was humiliated. An interpreter told Dean afterwards that 'He says he is nothing in Madrid tonight.' Dean replied: 'You can tell him he's not much here in London either.'

Dixie used to tell the tale of when he was playing for Tranmere against Rochdale and their centre-half took exception to the two goals he scored. Dixie recalled: 'A few minutes later, a kick to the genitals laid me out flat. In an attempt to ease the pain, one of my team-mates began to rub them. "Never mind bloody rubbing them – count them!" I yelled. I ended up in hospital that night.' (From Phil Thompson's *Do That Again, Son, And I'll Break Your Legs*.)

Gordon Durie

From time to time Gordon Durie scores goals. But Ladbroke's pre-season odds for the League's top goal-scorer one year included J. Durie. Presumably, this was tennis player, Jo Durie, who they had in mind and also, one supposes, would have been playing for Wimbledon?!

John Fashanu

John Fashanu produced a video for the Central London Training and Enterprise Council which offers 'step-by-step guidance on how to defuse difficult and potentially violent situations'. It doesn't mention anything about creating such situations – but anyway, more power to his elbow! It's a bit like asking Ken Bates to give advice on non-confrontational persuasion.

Steve Bruce of Birmingham tells the story of when he was at Norwich and Fashanu had stated in a newspaper article how he was going to frighten the life out of him. Steve, bravely but perhaps rashly, commented on radio how such threats frightened him not one jot. While having his evening meal on the Friday night, the telephone rang: 'Hello, Brucey, it's Fash – I can't wait to meet you by the far post tomorrow where we will mince heads.' Steve confesses he couldn't finish his meal, and reports how, during the match, both of them went for a fifty-fifty bouncing ball and were flattened. Apparently from then on, Fash's big mate, Vinnie, kept repeating: 'You're going to die – he'll kill you!'

It was of John Fashanu that David Pleat, then Spurs manager, said: 'I could go out and buy Henry Cooper if I wanted a player like that.'

Graham Fenton

One player with mixed emotions in success was Wallsend

Geordie, Graham Fenton of Blackburn, who clinically notched twice to defeat Newcastle in the crucial quest for the title in April 1996. Graham, whose whole family and himself are Toon Army supporters, commented: 'When I go back to Newcastle in the summer, I might have to put a paper bag over my head so that people don't recognize me.' His mam and sister were in the crowd that night, cheering Keegan's army on. 'I hope it hasn't spoiled their day out,' said Graham.

Les Ferdinand

An idea of what Kevin Keegan thought of Les, in the nicest possible way, can be seen from his sentiments after a friendly game against Celtic in 1995: 'Here we've got Les up front, yet at times we were starving him. If you've got a monster up there, you must feed him.' Presumably that was a reference to Les, and not Kevin's advertisement colleague, the 'Honey Monster'.

Duncan Ferguson

'I stepped forward and collided with McStay. Subsequently, he fell to the ground.' (Duncan Ferguson, Everton Striker, giving evidence before being found guilty of assault.)

Having mentioned McStay, that Scottish legend, Jim Baxter, as noted for his lack of effort as he was for his mesmerizing left foot, said of him: 'Stamina? I should give him 12 out of 10, but then I'm not really an expert on the subject.'

When Duncan Ferguson, who once informed team-mate Rangers' John Brown, 'I can drink like a chimney', arrived back at Goodison Park after his release, it is said that he slapped his thighs in delight. Joe Royle, standing next to him, was heard to say: 'Thank God they were your own thighs, Dunc, otherwise you might have been back in Barlinnie.'

Vinny Samways' advice to Duncan after his reserve team comeback in December 1995: 'Now he should get his head down.'

Robbie Fowler

Robbie, that most natural of goalscorers, who can put it in the net with either foot, his head, and from any distance, like all prodigies has his moments of madness. 'God', as he is nicknamed by his team-mates, has bared his buttocks for the Leicester fans and by his own admission came close to death when he perpetrated a prank (*!?*) by ripping up Ruddock's favourite baseball boots: 'If Razor had hit me properly, I don't think I would have been here to talk about it.'

Ray Evans reveals the difficulty managers have of reforming natural footballers: 'You don't want to take away his personality. There's a danger that if we concentrate on developing other facets of his game, Robbie could lose that natural instinct.'

Marco Gabbiadini

After three months and only seven goals at Crystal Palace, it was said that Gabbiadini felt like the biggest intruder at the Palace since Koo Stark.

Paul Gascoigne

The apocryphal story is apparently when Gazza, that 'rebel without a pause', and so unlucky with injuries they reckon his rabbit's foot pulled an Achilles' tendon, turned up for his medical at Rangers in the summer of 1995, the doctor asked him to take his clothes off. 'Shouldn't you take me out to dinner first?' responded Gazza. And when the doctor had a look at the same area that had been gripped by Vinnie Jones and asked: 'How long has it been like that?' Gazza replied: 'It's always been that long!'

The alternative version is that the doctor looked on a stripped Gazza, and said: 'By, you haven't got much down there, have you?' To which Gazza replied: 'I've only signed on here to play football, haven't I?'

Whatever happened at his medicals, Linford Christie was in no doubt about Gazza's physical shape: 'Our shot-putters are in better condition,' he declared.

Before going to Lazio when his knee was the best-known joint in Europe, he said: 'Coping with the language shouldn't be a problem – I can't even speak English yet.'

'I think it's the lightest he's been since he was four.' (Terry Venables on a slimline Gazza.)

Trouble does seem to follow Gazza, and apparently always has done. He told the *Newcastle Evening Chronicle*: 'As an apprentice, John Anderson and John Bailey stuck the nut on me, and Chris Waddle kneed me where it makes your eyes water. And when I nutmegged Billy Whitehurst twice in training, he thumped me.'

In Newcastle, the rumour went round that when the solid bronze football from the statue of local hero Jackie Milburn was missing, it turned up in Glasgow. Gazza, just for a laugh, was about to substitute it for the match ball as McStay was about to take a penalty.

> 'When I look at Gazza sometimes,' said Terry Venables in 1996, 'I see Maradona. I fear for his future.'

George Best tells the story of how he once wrote in a tabloid that he thought the No. 10 on Gazza's shirt was his IQ. A year or so later after saying this, he was watching one of the matches in the World Cup in America with Gazza, and Gazza had asked him: 'Hey, Besty! – What's an IQ?'

But Gazza can't be that daft, can he? Well . . . his mate, Chris Waddle, tells of the time he was with him on tour in New Zealand, and Gazza wanted a full English breakfast. He was informed that, unfortunately, the hotel did not have any bacon. Gazza's reaction: 'What! – 60 million sheep and no bacon!?'

When A. S. Byatt, the novelist, attended her first ever football match, the Germany *v* England semi-final in Euro '96, she wrote: 'I recognized Gascoigne's medieval hair and portly stomach . . .' It was a remark which lent some credence to the observation that when he played against Georgia, the occasion marked 'the biggest export of beef of the year' – or should that be bacon?!

There were several interesting revelations in the documentary on Gazza on 7 October 1996:

- (*On his fitness*) 'I've not had ten pints. I've had 20 halves!'
- (*On his dad*) 'My dad's great! He never asks for anything – apart from a house, a BMW 740, a boat, and a kind of wage. Apart from that, me dad's been all right.'
- (*On the Scotland team*) 'Scotland isn't an international team – it's a mixture of sheep-sh****s.'
- (*On playing a match*) 'I think I want to win so badly. I just hate getting beaten and I just blow up straight away instead of counting to ten or thinking about it.'
- (*On Sean Connery*) 'I shook his hand there. Imagine – that hand's been on so many women's boobs!'

Ryan Giggs

'Giggs was a big problem for us all night, but the biggest problem is that he does not have a German passport.'

(Berti Vogts, German National Team manager – run-up to Euro '96.)

David Ginola

David Ginola, welcomed to Newcastle with the Star headline 'Frog On The Tyne' and who, some would say, turns a minor knock into a scene from Camille, reflects on coming to terms with life on Tyneside: 'It's very difficult when I go out. All the women want to s**g me.'

It has been pointed out that an anagram of David Ginola is *vagina dildo*!

And after his transfer from Paris St Germain: 'When I arrived in England back in July, the Newcastle players would come to my hotel and take me out to the pub for a drink. They were good to me – and still are. But I'm not one for the pub all the time. In Paris everything else is there for you. Not here. I've found the North East very different. Once my family have been to the Metro Centre, then what?'

When Ginola first began playing with Jean-Pierre Papin at Paris St Germain, Papin said: 'I like David, but he is not an attacker' – and as any Newcastle fan will tell you, he's definitely not a defender.

Will the ghost of George Graham ever depart from Arsenal? On the day after Ginola was sent off for lashing out at Arsenal's fullback, one newspaper commented: 'Lee Dixon certainly took a backhander from David Ginola at Highbury last night.'

While another quipped: 'Dixon marked Ginola so tightly that, had Ginola been carried off on a stretcher, Dixon would have gone with him.'

Comment on Ginola's performance at St James's Park after the match against Bolton, which Newcastle won 2–1 on 20 January 1996: 'Ginola sold more dummies than

Mothercare.'

Ginola, after scoring the first goal in their 2–0 defeat of Arsenal, said: 'My father has been here for two weeks and I've scored against Forest and Arsenal in the home games he's seen. I think I'll buy him a flat in Newcastle.'

Valur Gislason

The only foreign signing of the 1996 close season by Arsenal was Valur Gislason of Knattspyrnufelagid Fram Reykjavik – and they wondered why it was taking so long to obtain a work permit!

Ruud Gullit

What is it about foreign players which prompt them to philosophize? Late in the 1995-96 season, Ruud Gullit answered a quite straightforward question by using an old Dutch saying to respond inscrutably:

Question: 'Ruud, do you wish you had come to England eight years ago?'

Answer: 'If your Grandma had a penis, she would have been your Grandpa.'
Well, you can't say fairer than that!

George Hardwick

North-Eastern hero, and English international of 40-odd years ago, George Hardwick, recounts that a player was informed by letter that he was to appear for England. The letter also reminded him to bring his boots, a bar of soap and a towel. The players travelled Third Class by rail, while the selectors enjoyed the comforts of First Class. In later years wasn't there some story about the First Class on 'Cathay Pacific' (Pacific = peaceful). . . ?

Mick Harford

The former Wimbledon Norwegian signing, Oyvind Leonhardsen, who, they say, speaks better English than Joe Kinnear, revealed that the only player's hair Vinnie dared not trim in the 1995 pre-season training was that of Mick Harford. Vinnie, in his turn, reveals that Mick has a saying: 'You've got three seconds to get out of my face.' Vinnie's advice is simple – 'Move.' According to Big Mick himself, he puts his latent ferocity down to 'the glare', which must be something if it can see off vicious Vinnie!

His 'hard' reputation could, of course, have had its origins on the occasion he went to the rescue of his mate Tony Coton in a Hemel Hampstead pub. Says Coton: 'Mick . . . head-butted one of them and decked another three . . .' Pretty impressive – but there's more to come. As they were walking back to the bar, the landlord hit Harford over the head with a big cosh. The thump echoed around the pub and blood began to trickle from his head. Harford put his hand on his head, felt the blood and asked Coton to take him to the hospital. He then turned slowly around to the landlord and told him that, when he got back from hospital, he was going to be in a spot of bother.

And talking about hard men, it was Cloughie who said of Trevor Booking: 'He floats like a butterfly and stings like one too.'

Ron 'Chopper' Harris

Charlie George recounts how he was always hammered by Chelsea's 'Chopper', but gave as good as he got because, he says, he came from Holloway and 'You learn from the pram to nut people who pick on you.' He goes on: 'He whacked me really hard one time, so I jumped up and down on his chest. He was coughing up blood, according to the papers.'

Jimmy Greaves, commenting on 'Chopper', said: 'If he was in a good mood, he'd put iodine on his studs.' On another assassin, Marco Tardelli of Italy, Jimmy had this to say: 'He's put more scar tissue on people than Harefield Hospital.'

(Duncan McKenzie's views on Ron): 'Now "Chopper" was a proper hooligan. He would deliberately decide to give you a vasectomy from 80 yards and afterwards chip you into row "F" of the main stand.'

Apropos of which, Nat Lofthouse, former Bolton and England centre forward, said: 'In my day (post-war years) there were plenty of footballers around who would kick your bollocks off. The difference was that at the end they would shake your hand and help you look for them.'

John Hendrie

When that grand old man of soccer, Tommy Hutchison, was at Coventry, he thought the young John Hendrie, at present with Barnsley, was getting just a bit too cocky. He made him take all his clothes off and stand in the middle of the dressing room singing 'Oh, Susannah'. The same John Hendrie said of his last season with Middlesbrough: 'I was on the bench so much I felt like Judge Dredd. I wasn't in the shop window, I was like a shop dummy.'

Glen Hoddle

Cloughie on Hoddle the player: 'You don't have to bare your false teeth to prove you're a he-man in football. Some people are morally brave – Hoddle is one of them. I've heard him criticized for non-involvement, but I'm not sure what that means. If you can compensate with more skill in one foot than most players have in their whole body, then that is compensation enough.'

Dean Holdsworth

Dean Holdsworth, once Wimbledon's favourite son, after Everton's controversial win against the team at Selhurst Park, in January 1996, continued to assert that the Dons should have had a penalty: 'I was tripped in the box – and no one can accuse me of diving because I can't even swim.'

Pierre Van Hooydonk

Some so-called stars really know how to win over the punters. Van Hooydonk, the Dutch striker, had this to say on turning down the mere pittance of £7,000 a week offered by his old club Celtic: 'It might be enough for the homeless, but not for a top international striker.'

Ray Howard

Scarborough Sunday League footballer, Ray Howard, on scoring his first goal in 28 years: 'I was stunned. Most lads in the team weren't born when I last scored.'

Mark Hughes

Jim White, in his book, *Are you watching, Liverpool?*, described Hughes as 'the centre forward with the on-pitch disposition of something let loose in the streets of Pamplona'.

Such a disposition can prove useful on occasions. The diminutive (5ft 5in) Gianfranco Zola (not to be confused with Radio 5's rendering: 'Score-flash coming in . . . it's Emile Zola again for Chelsea.') appreciates his team-mate. He explains:

'Defenders in England don't give me any presents and sometimes they say things to me and try to be rude. But I don't speak very good English so it doesn't worry me. When I have a problem, I just call "Marco!" and Mark comes and sorts everything out.'

Norman Hunter

Norman Hunter, one of the 'hard men' of the 1970s, and Francis Lee, who made more dives than Commander Crabb, came to blows in a Leeds *v* Derby match and were both sent off for fighting. As the two made the journey to the hot bath and as team-mates protested with the referee, Neil Midgley, battle was resumed with Lee trying to land one on Hunter. Francis, having been provoked beyond measure by Hunter, was fined £250 and banned for four games. Norman was let off scot-free. Years later in retirement, the two met at Maine Road and while chatting, Neil Midgley passed by: 'Have you two finished that fight yet then?' he asked.

This was the same Neil Midgley who shared this snippet of information on his First Division debut: 'My wife, who was in the stand, told me that at one stage the entire row in front of her stood up and gave me the V-sign. I asked her what she did and she said she didn't want them to know who she was so she stood up and joined in.'

. . . and the same Neil who confessed in 1987 before the FA Cup Final: 'Then my eyesight started to go, and I took up refereeing.'

Terry Hurlock
On once winning the 'Man of the Match' award for Southampton against Sheffield Wednesday, Terry Hurlock said: 'We must have some rubbish players if I've won this.'

Vinnie Jones
'You'll hear a new noise in football – it's called the foreign squeal. I own two pot-bellied pigs, yet they don't yelp as much as Ruud Gullit. (Vinnie Jones after being sent off, for the eleventh time, at Chelsea on Boxing Day 1995.)

Comment heard at the Newcastle *v* Wimbledon League match: 'Vinnie Jones has done for football etiquette what myxomatosis did for rabbits.'

At times in the 1996-97 season, Vinnie's tackles had been later than the Christmas post. None the less, Vinnie would frighten a 16-stone Rottweiler, and most certainly a jellyfish. Isn't that right, Gary? Hence the reason he was cast as an underworld debt collector in a thriller.

Daily Mail reporter, Rob Shepherd, claims that most of the time Vinnie can take it as well as dish it out. He cites the occasion of a night out after the PFA dinner, and a little the worse for wear, he gallantly – or foolishly – informed Vinnie that he was a good bloke but couldn't play football. 'Yeah, but I pay my chauffeur more than you earn,' replied the surprisingly docile Vinnie.

When there was some talk of Barry Fry buying Vinnie in the latter half of the 1995-96 season, Vinnie said: 'I need to return to a big club again, and they don't come bigger than Birmingham.'

But they can't come much bigger than Wimbledon, who, late in 1996, on 7 December, lay second in the Premiership behind Arsenal, having gone 18 games without defeat: 'I haven't had a run like this since I went to the curry house,' quipped Vinnie.

When Vinnie spent time in the Genealogical Office in Dublin trying to establish, unsuccessfully, his credentials to play for the Republic of Ireland, Jackie Charlton commented: 'I need him like I need a hole in the head.' Never mind – Bobby Gould was happy enough to have him in the Wales team when Vinnie disclosed his grandfather, Arthur, had been born in Ruthin, Clwyd.

David Ginola: 'Getting kicked is part of the job in France as well as Britain. But the real scandal is that someone like Jones gets to be a star, to make video cassettes and become an example to children.' Vinnie's response: 'Clear off, you French snail!'

And on the subject of Vinnie Jones and Eric Cantona, this is what *The Times* had to say: 'Both sum up all that is resented about their two clubs. Cantona's peacock swagger encapsulates Manchester United: rich, powerful, fed like Strasbourg geese on privilege; a spirit of unalloyed arrogance. Jones's lupine aggression is pure Wimbledon. He's not much of a player, but loves to win, to cock a snook, to put one over the arrogant rich, to hang the aristocrats from the lamppost. With Cantona, Manchester United insist on aristocracy. With Jones, Wimbledon storm the Bastille every week.'

Vinnie certainly doesn't want his tarnished image damaged. When young Michael Roy, from New Kyo, Durham, was training with the 'Olympic 2000' swimming squad at Crystal Palace, who should walk into the hotel where they were staying but the bold Vinnie. Verdict:

'Brilliant!' said Michael, aged 13. 'He even bought us a drink of orange – mind you, he did say: "I don't know why I'm buying this for you – I hate swimmers, Geordies and Newcastle supporters!"'

Vinnie's love and gentleness as a family man and with animals is in sharp contrast to his aggressive and physical postulating on the pitch. When a reporter asked him what Gazza had said when he was grabbed by the particulars, he asked: 'Can you spell "AAARGH!"?'

Juninho

'He's tiny. I half expected him to go out with a school satchel on his back. If he had, I would have trod on his packed lunch.' (Andy Thorn of Wimbledon on Juninho.)

Kevin Keegan

It is interesting to learn from Fred O'Donoghue, in his book, *Scouting for Glory*, that his match report for Liverpool in 1970 on the man who would become the 'King of the Kop', the toast of Hamburg and Southampton, and the deliverer of Newcastle, was: 'Keegan looked like a clanger.' Nine months later, Keegan was signed for £33,000 from Scunthorpe – Fred, who kept his job, informs us he was told: 'Bill Shankley fancies him, Bob Paisley fancies him, Ronnie Moran fancies him and Roy Evans fancies him' . . . and presumably even the tea-lady – and definitely his wife – fancied him.

Mario Kempes

The hero of Argentina from the 1978 World Cup, Mario Kempes, was still playing football (1995-96 season) at the age of 39, for Fernandez Vial of Concepcion in Division II of the Chilean League. His unusual contract required him to appear in home games only.

Ray Kennedy

Shankley's last signing for £200,000 from Arsenal in 1970, and undoubtedly one of his greatest, Ray Kennedy, has said: 'I'm not trying to be bigheaded, but to be honest, playing in that Liverpool team was easy.'

Jurgen Klinsmann

Klinsmann had a profound effect upon the long term development of English football. He demonstrated that a World Cup star could succeed in England, thereby encouraging others to follow and thus ensuring that the game's parochialism would be forever broken. He also showed that Germans can have a sense of humour. He was accused of diving for penalties and attended one press conference in a diving mask.

The not-so-sweet Alan Sugar showed the vindictiveness of a chairman scorned when Klinsmann took his boots elsewhere: 'He gave me this signed Tottenham shirt as a leaving present, but I wouldn't even wash my car with it.' Well, why should he when he can use one of Tez's lawsuits?

Alexei Lalas

The American defender, Alexei Lalas, on the pressure that comes with fame: 'It's not that I can't pick my nose in public any more. It's that, when I do, I have to do it real cool.'

Denis Law

One of the inspirational members of the 1960s Manchester side, Denis Law, was known as 'The King' to the United faithful. His arm raised in triumph will remain an enduring memory and is as much part of the era as The Beatles and kipper ties. Denis was, and still is, a fiercely proud Scotsman. In 1966, he completed a lousy game of golf to be informed that England, with several of his United team-mates figuring prominently, had won the World Cup. Throwing his clubs to the ground, he snapped: 'That makes my day!' He later added: 'I thought it was the end of the world.'

The one occasion when Denis's customary one-fingered scoring salute was not manifested was his eighty-sixth minute winning goal for Manchester City in 1974 which doomed Man. Utd. to the Second Division. Steeped in the Manchester United tradition and a Busby man through and through, he later said: 'It was possibly the most emotional goal I have ever scored . . . But that's football. I was a City player and had a job to do . . .'

He was substituted and for the remaining minutes sat disconsolate on the bench with the countenance of a man who has felt duty bound to take his ailing pet to the vet to end its misery.

For all his balance, breathtaking skills and incisiveness, Denis could look after himself among the 1960s hatchet-men: 'My mother always said that, if they kick you, kick them back, because if you don't, they will kick you for ever. And we did kick them back . . . Fortunately for us, the cameras were not there then.'

Leandros

The practice that Brazilian football stars have of being popularly known by their surnames ran into difficulties in 1995. When the team manager, Zagallo, announced his squad for a friendly, the Brazilian federation put down the nominated player Leandros's club as Internacional. It emerged that in fact Zagallo had chosen another Leandros from Palmeiras. The Leandros from Internacional burst into tears when reporters broke the news to him.

Robert Lee

In 1992, Robert Lee signed for Newcastle for £700,000.
He almost joined his former Charlton boss and mentor,
Lennie Lawrence, 40 miles further south at Middlesbrough. Robert, a home-loving lad, who had been nine
years at 'The Valley', decided to join Kevin Keegan when
he told him Newcastle was nearer to London than
Middlesbrough. 'What I meant,' explained a tongue-in-
cheek Keegan, 'is that there are more flights to London
from Newcastle and more trains ... you'd get there
quicker from St James's.' Nice try, Kevin – but he got the
player he later described as: 'Pound for pound my best-
ever signing.'

Matt Le Tissier

Chris Nicholl, on one occasion comparing the skills of the
hard-working and eager-to-improve Shearer with the
developed and silky talents of Le Tissier, commented: 'He
couldn't trap a bag of cement.' Mind you, Nicholl wasn't
in the job long.

Ally McCoist

David Coleman introduced Rangers' Ally McCoist to a
Question of Sport audience, off-screen of course, with the
words: 'Ally, who has scored 400 times – 200 of them
goals.'

Ally has been a prolific scorer for Rangers none the less
– a fact endorsed by the Celtic defender, John Hughes,
who said in 1995: 'He's like dog shit in the penalty box.
You don't know he's there until the damage is done.'

Paul McGrath

The story at Villa goes that Paul McGrath, who only
plays matches and does not train because his knees have

been ravaged through time and injury, went to the club doctor for his monthly check-up. After he had been examined, he said to the doctor: 'Well, Doc, how do I stand?' 'Buggered if I know, John, buggered if I know!' exclaimed the doctor.

McGrath's colleague at Villa in 1993, Kevin Richardson, voiced what many people thought: 'Just think how good he would be with two good knees.'

Paul, who has a history of suddenly going missing, reveals how once during contract negotiations, Ron Atkinson had joked: 'My problem is whether to include appearance or disappearance money!'

He makes no secret of the resentment he felt towards Alex Ferguson, who got rid of him from Man. Utd., but has since shaken him by the hand – presumably because McGrath's knees prevented him reaching the throat. Paul reckons that Alex's 'kick up the backside' was probably what he needed, and goes on to answer the question:

'Who else has kicked you up the backside?'

Answer: 'Ron Atkinson, Graham Taylor, Jack Charlton, Alex Ferguson, Alex Ferguson and Alex Ferguson.'

Willie Maddren

A former manager and local footballing hero for Middlesbrough, Willie Maddren, who is bravely fighting motor-neurone disease and working on behalf of other sufferers, has given an insight into less prosperous times at the 'Boro while contemplating current signings of Italians and Brazilians. He remembers how in 1985: 'We went to play a friendly at Hibs in a Ford Transit van and I was so ashamed of Middlesbrough not being able to afford anything better that I made the players get out around the corner from their ground and walk the rest of the way.'

Maradona

Did you know that Maradona has his own brand of biscuits on sale in Argentina which are called 'Dieguitas',
that his favourite politician is Fidel Castro, who incidentally is rumoured to be an Arsenal fan, that the going rate
for an interview with him is $50,000 for 30 minutes, his
favourite goal is the one he scored against England, and
that when he was at the Oxford Union, he finished off the
evening by rolling a golf ball from his head to his shoulders, from his shoulder to his forefoot and then to his
ankle, and back to his head again? *Olé!*

Not bad that juggling from Diego, but what about the
Czech player, Jan Skorkovsky, who in 1990 kept the ball
up with his feet during the Prague City marathon without
letting it touch the ground.

Or even the South Korean, Huh Nam Jin, who kept the
ball up for a record-breaking 17 hours 10 minutes 57
seconds in 1991.

Still, old Diego ('the banned of God' – 15 months for
drug-taking) is not welcome everywhere. When it was
rumoured that he was going to sign for American club
Baltimore Blast in 1992, their coach, Ken Cooper, said:
'We are looking for players who are role models, not
parole models.'

Never mind – David Pleat has great admiration for his
free-kick technique . . . well, presumably that is what he's
talking about: 'He gets great elevation on his balls.'

And clearly, someone else, other than the landlord of
the 'Sussex Pad' public house in Shoreham, had a high
regard for his working gear. A football shirt belonging to
Maradona, and valued at £1,000, was stolen. It was kept
disdainfully in the toilet following the 'Hand of God' incident.

Diego would have us believe that he has been

misjudged. On being asked if he would play in a farewell game for his club, Boca Juniors, he revealed: 'I haven't decided yet because I'm very sensitive. I cry a lot.'

Paul Mariner

Paul Mariner, commenting on pre-match superstitions which footballers practised: 'When we went on to the pitch, I always had to come out midway – bit like Ipswich really.'

Stan Mortensen/Stanley Matthews

Despite Mortensen scoring a hat trick in the 1953 Cup Final, it has always been known as 'the Matthews Final', because the maestro eventually obtained the medal the Nation longed for. When, in June 1991, they buried Stan Mortensen, one of the mourners quipped: 'They'll probably call it the Matthews Funeral!'

It is interesting to compare the income of two of the greats over the past 50 years, Stanley Matthews and Ryan Giggs.

Stan earned £50 a week at Stoke, had outside earnings of £1,000 by doing exhibitions in Africa and PR work for the Co-op. Ryan has a weekly wage of £12,000, and his outside earnings are made up of £8 million in a six-year contract with Reebok, £200,000 a year from Fuji Film, £140,000 a year from Quorn Hamburgers and £200,000 from Citroen – an estimated annual income of £1.6 million. Stan's comment: 'It's all relative. When I was earning £8 a week, qualified tradesmen were working for £2.50 and they didn't get to travel the world.'

Jackie Milburn

Much as they would like to, Newcastle fans will never be allowed to forget Hereford's 2–1 win over Newcastle in

their third-round cup-tie replay on 5 February 1972. The
television clip, accompanied by John Motson's: '... Ooh,
what a goal, what a goal! ... Radford the scorer ...
Ronnie Radford!' has led generations to believe that that
was the winner. In fact the honour went to Ricky George,
a one-time Spurs apprentice who had spent his playing
days in the lower echelons. Ricky remembers how he had
resigned himself to sitting out the match on the bench. He
recalls arriving to stay at the Dragon Hotel in Hereford
on the night before the match and being introduced to the
renowned Jackie Milburn, then working as a football
reporter, by John Motson. He recalls: 'Jackie looked at
me and said: "You should be in bed by now, son. It's lads
like you who made me give up management", I said: "It's
all right, I'm only substitute," and he said: "So what? You
might go on and score the winner." And that is exactly
what happened.'

Bobby Moore

The late and great Bobby Moore (better tackle than
Erroll Flynn and a vision more impressive than the
prophet Elijah) grinned at Gordon Banks before the
corner resulting from his amazing save from Pelé in the
1970 World Cup, and said: 'You could have caught that!'

Steve Nicholl

When it comes to being 'intellectually challenged', then it
would seem that players with a Liverpool connection
have the edge. Steve Nicholl can be described most kindly
as being gullible. Tommy Smith, he whose face bears the
imprints of a thousand elbows, once told him in the tunnel as they were waiting to take the field for a Testimonial
on his first outing for Liverpool: 'You can't wear those
boots, son – the soles are too thin. They've got under-soil

heating here and it'll like fry your toes.' Steve was left hopping about, wondering where he could find thicker-soled boots.

Poor old Steve – with his jaw wired up after it had been broken, he sent his wife out for fish and chips. It was only when she brought them back that he realized the problem. Not to be defeated, he put them in the blender and sucked them through a straw.

North Koreans
And some diversions on the 'oldest game'.

It is interesting to note that the North Koreans, who had that magnificent 1–0 victory at Ayresome Park in the 1966 World Cup Finals against the fancied Italians, refrained from sex for two years before the finals. (One wonders how Best ever managed to start, let alone complete, a game.)

Another National side where sex was banned until they were knocked out of the 1990 World Cup was Italy. Bobby Gould, manager of Wimbledon at the time, commented: 'My players have asked for the home numbers of the Italian players.'

It was a comment which prompted this acidic observation from Italy's goalkeeper, Walter Zenga: 'The average English footballer could not tell the difference between an attractive woman and a corner flag.'

Perhaps not Walter, but a report carried by The *Lancet* on 25 October 1996 suggests that, compared to Italian players, they may be better equipped once they have recognized the difference. Apparently tests carried out among young footballers from such clubs as AC Milan and AC Monza reveal that they are in possession of smaller testicles than young men who do not train. It would seem that the rigours of their exercises have an

adverse effect on the flow of sperm. It gives a new dimension to the cry: 'Get rid of the ball.' Many will argue that the report will not apply to British players who don't train as hard, and anyway their libido is already diminished by post-match alcohol.

Roy Hodgson imposed a 'bonking ban' for the Swiss side in the 1994 World Cup – a ban which he partially lifted later. 'Our form has been up and down,' he explained.

Jack Charlton reveals in his autobiography that Don Revie '. . . tried to talk us out of having sex on Fridays. He said it weakened you.'

Meanwhile in Peru in May 1996, soccer players were ordered to have sex no more than twice a week to save their energies for matches – it certainly makes you wonder the frequency during the close season.

Mike Ditka, the Chicago Bears coach, came from a different position, so to speak, when he announced a pre-Super Bowl curfew for his team: 'You can play this game one time. If your wives and girlfriends can't wait, tell them to take a cold shower.'

One is reminded of the true story of a Premiership footballer who, on a close season tour, was caught in *flagrante delicto* on top of the hotel's piano with one of the waitresses. The episode was brought to the attention of the club's supporters by one of the tabloids. At the first away match of the season, the hardcore of travelling fanatical fans gave grudging admiration of his conquest by singing: 'Pia, pia, piano, piano, etc.' every time he got the ball.

There is, of course, the alternative football coach's view which poses a different perception on the theme that sex before a match drains the energy: 'The problem isn't the sex; it's the staying up all night looking for it.'

If that were the case, then perhaps the answer lies in the efforts of these Australian fans:

In September 1996, Sydney Swan's players were banned from having sex on the night prior to the Grand Final of Aussie Rules football against North Melbourne. Swan's officials had not reckoned on Melbourne's 'Top of the Town' brothel which stepped in to offer them 'freebies' to help them keep their routine. 'We are prepared to take it to their door. If the players are used to having sex before the game, they will feel neglected. It might affect their performance,' a spokesman for the brothel smirked.

A sex relationship of a different nature was established when a pub team from York, hitherto known as 'Light Horseman', was sponsored in the 1996-97 season by the lingerie and sex toy firm, 'Anne Summers Foxes'. The type of sponsorship was also appropriate – a strip with the company's name highlighted – and £250. The end result is that the lads have done the business, scored frequently and satisfied home and away.

Perhaps football should take note of the attitude which prevails in other energetic and demanding sports: 'The lads know that nookie is strictly forbidden. You have to be at your physical peak in this game.' (Dick Clegg, manager of the England fishing team.)

He might have added the advice which was given in the *Times Educational Supplement* by a Dr Glass: 'Leave your sex organs with your bedroom slippers, and your day's work will be far more productive and rewarding.' But perhaps not as enjoyable . . .

Alternatively they might listen to the recommendations of the Israeli scientist, Alexander Olshanietzky, who urged his country's athletes to have sex in the Athletes' Village: 'Women compete better after an orgasm, especially high jumpers and runners.' Headers of the ball and hard-working midfield players take note!

Stephen Parks
Stephen, who played for Whitby Town in the Northern League in midfield, was exchanged for one of Stockton FC's turnstiles. 'Turnstiles are very hard to come by, so it seemed like a good idea,' Bob Scaife, the Whitby chairman, explained. 'I just hope it turns faster than Stephen ever did.'

Stuart Pearce
Stuart Pearce, who has that faraway look of mystical revelation in his eyes whenever he scores a goal and would make everyone feel better if he then displayed his 'high' by doing something like nut the goal post, has his name tattooed on his arm (presumably to help officials identify him if he does wander off in one of his post-goal trances).

It was Stuart who uttered the eminently forgettable phrase: 'I can see the carrot at the end of the tunnel.'

After being player-manager at Nottingham Forest for six weeks, Stuart said he has toned down his 'psycho' image. 'I no longer dress up as my mother,' he revealed.

Despite a number of hacks dismissing Stuart Pearce's capacity to communicate effectively on his elevation to managerial status, mainly because he revealed he is an aficionado of the Sex Pistols, whose songs he likes to sing along with in the bath, he has shown himself to be a more than competent commentator. That is not to say that his combative nature does not show through. When, in the final week of January 1997, victory against Newcastle in the Cup was followed by defeat against Coventry, he said:

'I warned the players football can kick you in the teeth. It appears they didn't listen and now they require dental treatment. I don't like people who don't listen when I'm speaking.'

Stuart Pearson

'Bobby Gould thinks I'm trying to stab him in the back. In fact I'm right behind him.'

Pelé

Edson Arantes do Nacimiento (Pelé), who is generally recognized as the greatest player ever, holds the record for the most goals scored in a specified period. From September 1956 to 1 October 1977, he scored 1,279 goals in 1,363 games with his best year being 1959, when he scored an incredible 126.

His natural talent hid a steely resolve and self-preservation which helps to explain his extended career: 'You should never give the first kick, but the adversary has to know that the second will be yours. In my career I got hit a lot, but I also left a lot of people by the wayside.'

Niall Quinn

Niall Quinn, on being asked, no doubt, for some deep theological reason: 'Is there a God?' replied: 'I hope so. Otherwise I've done a lot of wasted praying. Sometimes before a big game I'll look for a bit of divine inspiration.' But even the Lord couldn't work a miracle for Man. City or Sunderland, showing the power of prayer is not all it's cracked up to be.

But one man who will continue to pray is Tommy Burns, now of Newcastle: 'The most important thing in my life is to save my soul. Everything I have achieved in this life is because of God. People don't have to ask me twice about success because I'll no be slow in telling them: it's no come from Tommy Burns, but from Jesus.'

Another who felt the power of the Almighty was Justin Fashanu in 1983, when he was invited to team up again with his old Boss, John Bond, at Manchester City: 'Everything seemed in favour of my rejoining him. But I prayed about it all and afterwards had the unmistakeable feeling that God didn't want me to go.'

Fabrizio Ravanelli

When Fabrizio (*La Penna Blanca* – the white feather) signed for Middlesbrough as their £7 million centre forward, he was asked if he minded being compared with Alan Shearer. He responded, with the merest flicker of a smile: 'It's a great compliment to Shearer.' Pretty sharp, you might think – but then, on arriving at the Riverside, he observed: 'There is something here that reminds me of Parma.' The cheesey smell, perhaps?

When, in December 1996, Fabrizio criticized the 'Boro for not having a gym at their magnificent Riverside

Stadium, rival Geordie fans remarked that it would have been surplus to needs since none of Bryan Robson's foreign signings ever worked out.

Jamie Redknapp

Jamie Redknapp, the target of passes in more ways than one, divulged, 'I got some girl's pants through the post the other day, but I didn't like them . . . well, they didn't fit, to be honest.'

John Robertson

Nottingham Forest winger, John Robertson, played in their Championship and European Cup winning triumphs, and is one of many who are testimony to Cloughie's powers of motivation and inspiration. Reminiscing on those balmy days of success, Clough said of Robertson: 'John was as fat as me now – no, he was fatter – but the way he treated the ball! He treat it better than you would treat a woman.'

Romario

Romario, never the most supportive of colleagues, had this to say about his former PSV team-mates when he went to Barcelona: 'They are workhorses who should keep their mouths shut, save their breath for running, and leave the football and scoring to me. They moan and groan about the things I don't do, like defending and working hard.'

And why does this shrinking violet skimp training? 'I save my energy for matches,' he says.

Never one to underestimate his capabilities, he announced in 1994: 'God created me to delight people with my goals.'

Ronnie Rosenthal

Ronnie Rosenthal was once quizzed by a reporter about the possibility of having to return to Israel if he was called up to do his National Service. Ronnie assured the reporter that he would immediately return if his village was bombed. 'Where exactly is your village?' asked the reporter. 'Birkdale,' answered Ronnie.

Uwe Rösler

'They call me "Splinters". I'm always on the bench!' (Rosler complaining during Alan Ball's stewardship) – and like any good German, he always booked his place with a towel.

Ian Rush

Ian Rush overtook Dennis Law's record of 41 goals in the FA Cup when he scored against Rochdale on 6 January 1996. After the match he made the comment which implied suicidal tendencies on the part of a young team-mate: 'To get the goal at the Kop end was something special. Robbie thought about shooting himself but gave me the ball instead.'

And when Ian Rush was awarded a MBE in the New Year's Honours list, the comment in the Liverpool dressing room was that he expressed the hope that it would have an open-top, and quadraphonic sound.

When Liverpool gave Everton a 5–0 thumping, it was Ian Rush who was the victim of this amazing John Motson statistic: '. . . and Ian Rush has made history here! That's the first ever hat trick in a Merseyside derby! (A pause took place at this point.) Since 1935! – In a league game, anyway!'

Almost as confusing was Ian Rush's explanation for his Juventus debacle: 'Italy was like a foreign country.'

Not a happy time, then, for Ian – Gianni Agnelli, the Juventus president, damned with faint praise: 'We know Ian Rush lets his goals do the talking, but so far he hasn't spoken very much.'

Question: 'What was it like in Italy, then, Ian?'
Answer: 'Bloody awful! For the first week it p****d down!'

Hugo Sanchez

Eric Cantona might philosophize, while others find different ways of expressing themselves. In 1990, Hugo Sanchez of Real Madrid was fined £750 and suspended for two games for grabbing his own genitalia. 'I was making a gesture,' he said, but, perhaps fortunately, did not elaborate.

One year later Michel, also of Real Madrid, was fined £2,750 for groping Carlos Valderrama's testicles during a match with Valladolid. The chairman of the disciplinary committee described it as 'publicly manipulating the gift nature gives only to men'. Nice touch! . . . and all Gazza said after his 'experience' with Vicious Vinnie was: 'The bugger grabbed me balls!'

Steve Coppell was another who was given a none-too-gentle hand by Italian, Claudio Gentile, whom he had been assigned to mark, but paradoxically made a different type of mark on him. 'As I went skidding in (on a greasy pitch), he grasped my testicles. I completely froze, more in shock than pain. Ever since that tackle, I have physically winced every time I've seen Gentile on television.'

And Gentile, on another occasion, after being criticized for continually fouling Maradona (the 'Hand of God' *v* the 'Hand of Claud') explained: 'This is not a dancing academy.'

Len Shackleton
'The Clown Prince of Soccer', Len Shackleton, once beat a fullback by knocking the ball off a corner flag; once ran half the length of the pitch against Chelsea without allowing the ball to touch the ground; frequently took throw-ins off the back of opponents; often would put a two-bob bit on to his instep then into his jacket top-pocket; once played table tennis against Victor Barnes, the British world champion, with the edge of the bat; entitled a chapter in his autobiography, 'What the Average Director Knows About Football', and left one blank page; and five times, under Walter Winterbottom, played for England.

Peter Schmeichel
How Kevin Keegan and the Toon Army must dolefully mourn the day Peter Schmeichel, the finest goalkeeper of his generation and the player who thwarted their ambitions in their quest for the 1996 Championship, was turned down by Newcastle before being snapped up by Man. Utd. from Brondby in 1991. If Cantona's 'steal'

from Howard Wilkinson was like finding a Van Gogh in your granny's attic, then Schmeichel's signing was like getting six numbers up on the Lottery at the first attempt.

Gordon Smith

Remember Gordon's miss for Brighton in the last few seconds of the Cup Final at Wembley against Manchester United in 1983? If you don't, everyone else does, and Gordon isn't allowed to forget it. Put through by Micky Robinson, he only had to beat Gary Bailey to win the cup for his club, and a place in Europe, but instead slid it into the side netting. The miss has been his fame. Passers-by shout at him still; there is a Brighton fanzine, *And Smith Must Score*; and he recalls how, in 1984, playing on tour with Manchester City, a little Malaysian lad asked for his autograph at the post-side: 'Sign, please. You Gordon Smith. How you miss sitter in final?'

He continues: 'When I returned to the club years later for Steve Foster's testimonial dinner, he started his speech by saying: "I don't know whether Brighton supporters will remember Gordon Smith."' He carries the burden well.

Gareth Southgate

The nation's heart went out to Gareth Southgate when he missed the penalty against Germany in Euro '96 – but all credit to the lad for grasping the nettle with both hands while others more experienced washed theirs. That such ordeals are terrifying beyond comprehension is indicated by an observation made by Mick McCarthy, then Millwall manager, after a penalty shoot-out win from 1995: 'I asked the players who wanted to take a penalty, and there was an awful smell coming from a few of them.'

A scenario endorsed by this exchange:

Des Lynam: 'What goes through your mind during a penalty shoot-out, Gary?'

Gary Lineker: 'Your mind? It's the other end you're worried about!'

And while on the subject of unsuccessful penalty shoot-outs, why is it that the Italians have fared so badly in the past? They have been eliminated at the second-round stage on penalties in two of the last three World Cups, and lost to Brazil in the same way in 1994. Giancarlo Galavotti, who writes for the *Gazzetta dello Sport*, has the answer: '. . . Italians are too hot-blooded. We cannot be the best lovers in the world *and* take great penalties, you know.'

As Muhammed Ali revealed: 'When you're as great as I am, it's hard to be humble.'

Poor Gareth's torment can not have been helped when his mam voiced the question the nation had been thinking: 'Why didn't you just belt it, son?'

'We had Watergate and Irangate. Now we've got Southgate.' (Letter to the *Guardian.*)

David Speedie

David Speedie, who on the field did for good behaviour what BSE has done for cattle, expressed the wish to become a referee. When asked what, as a ref, he would say to Speedie the player, he said: 'I would tell him, "Shut your mouth and stop moaning, you whining little sod!"'

Igor Stimac

Jim Smith, Derby's much-travelled manager, enthused about his Croatian import, Stimac: '. . . he's been a revelation. He had one or two setbacks early on. After three days he pranged his club car. Apparently no one told him that over here we drive on the left.'

Gordon Strachan

Gordon Strachan might be small but his tongue can clip a hedge. At Leeds he was known by some as 'King Mouth' and the quality of some of his deliveries make you see why. When he was voted the football writers' 'Footballer of the Year' in 1991, he quipped: 'It's a tremendous honour – I'm going to have a banana to celebrate.' (A reference to his secret of perpetual youth – bananas, seaweed and pills.)

Apropos of which, the down-to-earth Batty commented on Gordon's nutritional inclinations: 'He's got one of these gurus to sort out his diet – me, I just eat out.' David has a reputation for being pretty basic – hence, some have said that that was the root cause of the trouble he had with Le Saux, who reads the *Guardian* and does the crossword. Too cultured by half for David!

But Gordon Strachan, besides being the type of player you would always want in your team, demonstrated by dedication that footballers can remain potent forces well into their thirties. Ron Atkinson, Coventry manager when Gordon celebrated his 39th birthday at the club and was still playing as well as ever, had this to say about him: 'There's nobody fitter at his age – except maybe Raquel Welch.' Gordon revealed in his autobiography of 1992 that, going home after a match he sometimes wondered if he was getting too old. Then, he writes: '. . . I always remember what Kenny Dalglish once told me: never forget that football made you feel knackered when you were 17.'

Mickey Thomas

When Mickey Thomas spent time in prison in 1995, he had this to say about his experience: 'The food is terrible, the tea is like petrol and you get the usual stuff like people asking you to sign your autograph on a piece of toilet paper because they want to wipe their backside on it. And that's just the nice part.'

Bert Trautman

When it was announced, almost immediately after the Second World War, that the German, Bert Trautman, would be playing for Manchester City, there was a great deal of hostile opposition and threats of boycott by the fans. In his first game for the club, he had such a fantastic game that, even though the side was beaten 1–0 when many claimed it would have been 8–0 had it not been for Bert, each and every fan stood and applauded him off the pitch. He turned out to be probably the most popular goalkeeper the club has ever had.

Barry Venison

Barry Venison, Southampton hub and articulate Sky evaluator, has confessed he has a penchant for Versace fashion and powerful cars – '. . . the missus goes mental'. He has been described as 'the best dressed man in his own house'.

Billy Walker

The first player to score a hat trick of penalties was Billy Walker, who played for Aston Villa. It happened in a game against Bradford and the third penalty was awarded when Villa were five goals up. Walker took the penalty against the Bradford goalkeeper, a fiery Scot called Jock Ewart. Walker blazed the ball over the bar on the first two attempts but the referee ruled that on each occasion a Bradford player had moved. It was all too much for Jock, who rolled the ball into the unguarded net and shouted at the ref: 'Satisfied now? He's got his bloody hat trick!'

West Brom Players
In the 1970s Ron Atkinson took his team on a much pub-licized visit to Chairman Mao's China. When asked about his impression of the Great Wall, one player responded: 'Once you've seen one wall, you've seen 'em all, haven't you?' Ron elaborated: 'Some of the lads commented when they saw it that a lot of Irish lads must have been transferred here a long time ago.'

At a reception given by the Chinese, the hosts began to sing Mao's propaganda songs. Not to be outphased, Ron led his 'lads', hands outstretched and clasping handker-chiefs as scarves, in a rendition of 'You'll Never Walk Alone'.

Dennis Wise
Interview with John Motson in the *Sunday Telegraph* Magazine:

> Question: 'Who is the most intellectual footballer you have come across?'
> Answer: 'Eamon Dunphy'
> Question: 'And who is the least intellectual?'
> Answer: 'Dennis Wise.'
> Question: 'What's your idea of a good night out?'
> Answer: 'A drink with Dennis Wise.'

After an incident in the FA Cup Semi-Final between Wise and Manchester United's Keane, Alex Ferguson commented: 'You know Dennis Wise – he could start a row in an empty house.' (Roy Keane has been described as a 'time bomb' – 'You don't know when he's going to go off.')

When Vialli scored his first goal at home for Chelsea against Coventry at the start of the 1996 season, the

Chelsea players slid into a synchronized tableau which one newspaper suggested had found its origins in the 'Creation' of Michelangelo as depicted in the Sistine Chapel. The newspaper presumed that the scenario had been inspired by the Italian imports, Vialli and di Matteo. Club captain, Dennis Wise, was asked: 'Was the goal celebration instigated by Michelangelo's "Creation"?' 'You what?' said Dennis.

Richard Witschge

The Dutch midfield, and ex-Blackburn, player won no friends in England during Euro '96 when he commented: 'In England, football is just like rugby. All the balls go flying through the air or are kicked into the stands. You never think of keeping the ball and trying to play. It may be the culture in England but it has nothing to do with football.' Perhaps his vindictiveness, which went on to criticize the town of Blackburn and Le Saux, who kept him out of the team, was sour grapes at only being called upon to make one league appearance. After that outburst, he wouldn't even get a game with the blue berets of the United Nations, West Ham!

Frank Worthington

Speaking on the skills of modern British footballers: 'Domestic players these days can trap the ball further than I could kick it.'

Ian Wright

Arsenal's outstanding striker, Ian Wright, who opens his mouth more often than a drowning man, and who should have a tee shirt declaring: 'I'll let my football do the talking', managed to upset much more than referees during 1996.

After the FA Cup tie with Sheffield United, Roger Nilssen observed: 'He said to me "You fancy yourself a bit, don't you?" Then he spat in my face.'

Clearly not a circumspect diplomat, Wright pronounced before the Arsenal *v* Borussia Munchengladbach match: 'I just hope we get the credit when we turn over the Krauts.' Alas for Ian, it was the 'Krauts' who did the turning over.

He clearly felt unreasonably persecuted when David Pleat, Sheffield Wednesday manager, complained that Wright had stamped on Stefanovic and yanked Blinker's hair: 'If I have to appear at the FA, I'll have my say about David Pleat. I do so much for football, like charity work, and I always sign autographs. But everywhere I go, the crowd are on my back and other players want me booked. I suppose I'm an easy target.'

Nevertheless he continues to bounce back and can exhibit the odd witty jibe displayed during matches on a revealed white tee shirt, items of clothing which have become the vehicle for his not-so-subtle messages. These have included: 'I love the FA.' (after being cleared of bringing the game into disrepute); 'I don't love the FA any more' (after the FA confirmed his three-match suspension, December 1996).

On the never-ending dispute over Geoff Hurst's World Cup winning goal in 1966, he said quite simply: 'If Roger Hunt had followed the ball in, we wouldn't have had all this bollocks for years.'

In December 1996, Ian had the words: 'Let he without sin cast a stone' tattooed on his right arm because, according to a friend: 'He's sick of all the stick he's taking.' It was revealed that, on a previous occasion, he had a motorbike tattooed on his thigh because George Graham banned him from riding. Self-abuse does seem a bizarre and eccentric form of protest.

Dwight Yorke

When it appeared that Dwight Yorke, on the Aston Villa video, 'The Squaddies' (so called because, for some reason, they appear on the front dressed in combat gear), was confessing to missing 'his mother's cocaine', it seemed reasonable to expect the tabloids to commence sniffing about! It was, of course, his Trinidadian accent which caught everybody off-guard. He was, in fact, talking about her 'cooking'.

Recalling his settling-in period at Aston Villa, Dwight pays tribute to the help given him by such senior players as Platt and McGrath as well as an insight into the mickey-taking: 'One morning I was used as the target in shooting practice because of the bouncers Curtly Ambrose delivered during a West Indies *v* England Test match.'

Sergei Yuran

When Sergei, formerly of Spartak and Benfica, joined Millwall with his friend and countryman, Kulkov, he announced: 'We have played for some of the great clubs of Europe, but this is the pinnacle of our careers.'

It was unkindly suggested that 'the pinnacle' should have been translated as 'the tip', as in rubbish.

The centre forward said: 'It was an open goal – but I put it straight over the crossbar! I could kick myself!' And the manager said: 'I wouldn't bother – you'd probably miss!' (David Frost, TVAM.)

3
Goalkeepers

Introduction

Ruud Gullit's observation during Euro '96: 'A goalkeeper
is a goalkeeper because he can't play football', reveals
more about Ruud's perception of football than it does
about the contribution of the 'last defender'. It is as mean-
ingless a statement as 'a left back is a left back because he
can't score goals'. A goalkeeper is as integral to the game
of football as a defender, midfielder or forward and, like
each one in his own right, requires specific, but none the
less, high quality technical skills. What, perhaps, is more
significant is that a goalkeeper needs a greater mental, and
psychological, toughness since he cannot rely upon team-
mates to extricate him from the mistakes he makes. The
loss of confidence in an outfield player can be critical; in a
goalkeeper it is fatal. The history of goalkeeping is littered
with the memories of once assured and highly acclaimed
keepers whose steely nerves have disintegrated through
irreparable errors. It is no wonder that those who can
withstand the intense pressure are very often eccentrics
and constitute a unique breed of sportsmen who display a

camaraderie exemplified by mutual acknowledgement before and after matches.

Nev Southall's mates at Everton have given their verdict on their elegant goalkeeper. 'He does nothing but moan all the way through the game, moan after the game, moan first thing in the morning . . . Apart from that, the rest of the time he's all right.'

But Nev, one time bin-man, can show wit and humour. While propping up the Premier, Neville was asked what he thought about the chances of relegation: 'I don't think we'll go down,' he said in an unusual burst of loquaciousness. 'But then again, the captain of the *Titanic* said the same thing.'

Bruce Grobbelaar has spoken about his international career with Zimbabwe: 'There I was one day playing in front of thousands of screaming, half-educated savages who know next to nothing about the finer points of the game. Three days later, I was in Harare, playing for Zimbabwe.'

Talking about eccentric goalkeepers, Rene Higuita's scorpion save in the match between England and Colombia, in August 1995, brought this observation from the legendary Gordon Banks: 'What's wrong with a simple catch? If he'd done that playing for England, Jack Charlton would have thumped him and that would have been his last cap.'

Someone suggested Higuita should join Arsenal because they're used to 'kick-backs'.

In Euro '96, the German goalie, Andreas Kopke, made it abundantly clear that he would much rather punch, than catch, the ball. When he turned up for breakfast on the morning after the Italian match, his team-mates welcomed him by punching hard-boiled eggs and bread rolls at him. 'I'm getting fed up of it', moaned Kopke.

Few goalkeepers can have been more unjustly reviled than poor old Gary Sprake, nicknamed 'Cinderella', because he kept missing the ball. Gary – and doesn't the world know it? – had the distinction of throwing the ball into his own net in the Leeds *v* Liverpool match, 9 December 1967. 'I was running towards the halfway line with my back to the goal when I heard this mighty roar,' says Jackie Charlton. 'I looked back and saw the ball in the back of the net – I thought – "f****** hell!".'

Poor Gary had considered throwing the ball to left back, Terry Cooper, changed his mind and tried to pull the ball in to the safety of his shoulder. Inexplicably in the process, he catapulted it into his own net. 'He couldn't do that again if he played for another 50 years,' said manager Don Revie, clearly suffering from yet another aberration. As Sprake held his head in his hands, someone from the terraces shouted: 'Be careful, Gary – for hell's sake don't drop that!'

For years after that Gary had to suffer the ignominy of away fans singing the Des O'Connor hit, 'Careless Hands'.

Another Gary, this time Gary Bailey of Manchester United, had to put up with Scouse humour when playing at Anfield after making the mistake which gave Ireland a goal against England at Wembley in 1985. He was greeted with the chant: 'He's Ireland's No. 1!'

What both Garys could have done with was a bit of the stuff now available to goalkeepers which Sheffield United's international, Alan Kelly, describes in the following way: '. . . gloves made out of latex . . . a shirt with latex on the forearms and chest – you don't have to use your hands any more, you can save the ball by sticking your chest out.'

After Forest's 7–0 defeat by Blackburn on 18 November

1995, it was suggested that Mark Crossley now had achieved the necessary credentials to play for Scotland.

Jess Conrad, the 1960s pop singer who played in goal for the twelfth time for the Showbiz XI Squad in the pre-match build-up to the 1995 Cup Final, said: 'Many goal-keepers would cut off their right hand to play at Wembley – well, one finger anyway.'

John Burridge, the goalkeeper who is always as game as a pheasant, and has had more clubs than Fred Flintstone it seems, will only retire when they have removed his legs. He says: 'When I came into the game as a 15-year-old, one of the trainers said to me: "Son, goal-keepers have got to be crackers and daft. You, son, have got the qualities of an international." I took it as a com-pliment.'

John's wife, Janet, gives this insight into life with a totally-committed goalie: 'Once he is asleep at night, he starts jumping and twitching, and you can feel his arms going. Very often, he'll wake up and say somebody just took a shot at him. I say: "OK – Go back to sleep." I actu-ally heard him give an interview to Gerald Sinstadt in his sleep once.'

John's passion for his chosen trade is manifested still further with his disclosure: 'The sound of the ball hitting the net – the old death rattle, I call it – is the worst sound in the world to me . . .'

Another veteran goalie in the same mould as Burridge is Les Sealey. His former team-mate at Luton, Steve Foster, revealed in 1994: 'One day he announced that he wanted to be known as "The Cat". We'd be playing a match and you'd hear "The Cat's ball!" and Les would come for it. But he didn't always get there, so Mick Hartford christened him "Tiddles".'

Just as zany, and proof that goalkeeping eccentrics are not confined to the British Isles, is the revelation of the Belgian goalkeeper, Michael Preud'Homme: 'When I wake up in the morning and get a burning feeling in my ears, I usually know that I'm going to play well.'

That's not the only feeling goalkeepers from the Benelux countries get, according to Brian Clough, who signed Van Breukelen and Segers from the Netherlands: 'Dutch goalkeepers are protected to a ridiculous extent. The only time they are in danger of physical contact is when they go into a red-light district.'

One goalie who lives for the competition is the Scottish and Rangers keeper, Andy Goram. Before he faced the English team at Wembley in Euro '96 he had this to say: 'See the boy Rudyard Kipling who said it's the taking part, not the winning, that counts? Well, that's a load of s***. It's the winning that counts.'

When Southport played Merthyr in the GM Vauxhall Conference League (19 February 1994), their goalkeeper was called Gamble and Merthyr's, Wager.

Coventry goalkeeper, Ian Gould, in a game against Nottingham Forest Reserves, yelled with irritation at a young lad who had gone to retrieve the ball for him, but in Gould's eyes was not being fast enough about it. The lad turned out to be Roy Keane, visiting his old club.

Gould was lucky to survive injury, particularly when it is learned that, back in his locality in Ireland, Keane, the easily aggrieved midfielder, is known as 'The Man with the Identity Crisis', because he keeps asking people he meets: 'Do you know who I am?'

A little bit reminiscent of the true story of the father of a famous footballer who played for West Ham. He was forever asking people he met in the East End: 'Do you know who I am?' When they didn't, he would enlighten them with great pride. At about 80 years of age, he went to live in a nursing home. He had just arrived and was sitting having a cup of tea next to this old dear. He turned to her and asked the question which had passed his lips regularly for 30 years: 'Do you know who I am?' 'I'm sorry, luv, I don't,' she replied. 'But I'll ask Matron – she'll know.'

The goalkeeper of the Australian national side which lost 17–0 to an FA XI in 1951 was called 'Conquest' – and yes, you've got it in one – his Christian name was 'Norman'.

David Wylie, one-time Scottish under–21 goalie, and Morton 'keeper, was arrested for breach of the peace on his stag night. His barrister told Paisley Court that Wylie earned £125 a week as a footballer, plus bonuses. 'But,' he added, 'he plays for Morton, so there are no bonuses.'

> 'I expect the next rule imposed will force us to play with one hand under our back-sides.' (Barcelona goalkeeper, Julen Lolpetegui, on being informed of the FIFA proposals to widen goals by the diameter of two footballs.)

Jasper Carrott gave David Icke some stick when he claimed he had a mission to rescue humanity: 'David Icke says he's here to save the world, but he saved bugger all when he played for Coventry.'

> 'The goalie was coming out in instalments.' (Joe Royle's comment on Polish goalkeeper failing to stop Shearer's header, 9 October 1996.)

And was it Peter Shilton who said: 'Just when I thought I could make ends meet, someone kept shifting the goal-posts.'

It was Peter who, 16 years ago, was caught with Tina Street, a red-haired mother of three, in his Jaguar, after hitting a lamppost in his attempts to avoid her pursuing husband.

He was found to be positive when breathalysed by the police. In the next match for Nottingham Forest, the South Bank at Arsenal chanted: 'Does your missus know you're here?'

Three years later at White Hart Lane, Spurs fans chanted: 'Tina, Tina, Tina!'

On 21 December 1996, Peter celebrated 1,000 League appearances – home and away.

> Then there's the story about the emerging star footballer sitting with his beloved, having a drink in the pub:
>
> Wife: 'You remind me of the sea.'
>
> Star: 'You mean wild, restless and untamed?'
>
> Wife: 'No – you just make me sick!'

Poor Alan Mullery, as if he wasn't sick enough at receiving a red card against Yugoslavia in June 1968, received a telephone call from his wife, June, saying: 'You're a disgrace to the family.'

> In 1982, Frank Worthington was once asked by a magazine: 'In your career, who has been your most dangerous opponent?' Answer: 'My ex-wife.'

Some football wives are keen supporters. Mike Platt was due to play for Salford City when his wife, Dawn, was about to give birth. A mobile phone was installed in the dug-out to cater for emergencies. At half-time it rang . . . it was Dawn, wanting to find out the half-time score.

> And it's good to see that a player's love for his wife can transcend success. QPR's central defender, Steve Yates, put in a transfer request because people were taking the mickey out of his wife's West Country

accent. 'I can't play well knowing she's upset,' said Steve.

Alex Fynn, in his book, *Dream On – A Year In The Life Of A Premier Club*, recounts the story of the now retired former Spurs and Norway goalkeeper's most embarrassing experience. It was Erik Thorstvedt's first night away with his new team when they were playing a European tie at Munchengladbach and they were staying at a small family-run hotel. He had as his room-mate Andreas Winkholt, and the only bed in the room was a big double one. Erik recalls: 'I was soon fast asleep, and must have thought I was back home. So I wrapped an arm and a leg over the person next to me. . . . Andreas woke with a bolt, and put up one hell of a struggle. We both toppled on to the floor, and eventually he flicked the lights. I didn't know the language, so it was difficult to explain away what I had done.'

It is a story reminiscent of the apocryphal tale of the occasion when an England football squad had gathered before the tour and were being allocated rooms. The newest recruit was allocated to share a room with one of the veterans. He was happy enough until the other players told him, with great glee, that he wouldn't get a wink of sleep because his room-mate had a reputation for snoring all night. The next morning he came down to breakfast and they asked him how he had made out with the snoring.

'There wasn't any snoring,' said the player.

'And how did you manage that?' they all asked.

'Well,' he said, 'I went upstairs, and he was sitting reading the paper, so I went over and gave him a little kiss on the cheek . . . and he stayed awake all night watching me!'

. . . and when he shouted 'My ball!' 'I wrongly assumed he meant the leather one, ref!' (Debilitated centre forward.)

4
Referees

Introduction

Referees must only perform this part-time occupation if they have an insatiable yearning to do so. They cannot do it for the money, so one is left to suppose that it is for the power; or it could be for the uniform? Whatever the reason might be, such individuals are suspect since no one in their right mind would suffer such abuse and persecution willingly. Comments of the type made by Bradford manager, Chris Kamara, after his side's 2–0 defeat at Norwich: 'Even Stevie Wonder would have spotted that one!'; and then Wolves manager, Tommy Docherty, whose side was relegated after the 1985 match against Brighton: '. . . an official asked for two of my players to take a dope test. I offered them the referee!' are mild in comparison with most invective from the terraces.

Michael Parkinson tells the tale of seeing a referee at Barnsley lying on the ground having been felled by a heavy muddy ball. As the trainer raced across to give him assistance, a voice from the crowd shouted: 'Don't revive him – bury the s*d!'

The referee came into the Manchester City dressing room to have a word before the game at the time when the great team of Mercer and Allison was riding high: 'I'm a working man like yourselves. I'm a policeman and today my job is to be referee. You're footballers and you, like me, have got a job to do. So let's get out there this afternoon and play it hard but fair. OK? Any questions?' Mike Summerbee said: 'I have a question, ref – do you think you'll ever catch Lord Lucan?'

Ian Wright failed to demonstrate any subtlety when he observed on the eight yellow cards shown by Graham Barber in the November 1996 clash with Newcastle: 'The referee was booking everyone. I thought he was filling in his Lottery numbers at one point.' A marked lack of diplomacy had been perpetrated by him earlier in the year when, after a confrontation with David Elleray, he referred to referees as 'jumped-up little Hitlers'. Subsequently he was obliged to grovel assiduously.

Ian Wright should have taken note of the finesse of one of Bobby Robson's Ipswich team. Noted for his lack of respect towards officials, the player approached a relatively inexperienced league referee and asked:

'What would you do if I said you were a s***?'
'I'd have to send you off.'
'What would you do if I thought you were a s***?'
'If you only thought it, then I couldn't send you off could I?'
'Right then, I think you are a s***.'

Apropos of Ian Wright calling David Elleray a 'little Hitler', the same referee revealed in *The Times* (16 May 1994) that refereeing was: '. . . a balance between tolerance and neofascism. I tend to lean towards the latter.'

Also a balance between the certain and the uncertain if

his comment from October 1996 is anything to go by: 'In a way referees are almost con men – a lot of the time we're trying to con people into thinking we are very clear in what we have given when we're not very sure.'

If that observation from one of the country's top referees doesn't hasten the move towards the inevitable introduction of Referee-Assisted-Technology (RAT), then what will?

Elleray, an Eton Housemaster, who as a referee has been described as 'fastidious to the point of absurdity', also has an inclination towards the finer things of life and, speaking before the 1994 Cup Final, revealed his public school tastes and assumptions: 'I need lots of liquid to prevent dehydration and I'll be drinking at least 12 cups of tea before kickoff. I hope Wembley have Earl Grey, but I doubt it.'

David Elleray was criticized by Joe Royle in September 1996, when he sent off Duncan Ferguson (who thought Earl Grey was a pub in Glasgow) for swearing. Joe proffered the advice that Elleray should realize that swearing is 'industrial language', and therefore to be tolerated, as presumably it was when Ferguson called Joe a 'b******!' during practice – or even League – matches.

Certainly Kevin Keegan did not mess about when John Beresford countered his touchline instructions with the 'industrial response': 'B******, f*** off, that's c**p!' Keegan, despite the fullback's immediate apology and gestures of repentance, immediately substituted him and Beresford's career came as close to ending at St James's as John Salako's came to starting.

Such expletives are, of course, not new. In a game between Derby and Blackburn (3–2) in 1977, Charlie George, he of the 'lie-down-and-come-and-jump-on-me' Wembley goal, bellowed at manager, Colin Murphy: 'Get the sub on, you big *******!' Colin didn't protest, but the fans did. George apologized and explained: 'There was no offence meant.'

Sometimes it is possible for referees to have their cocoon of self-esteem pierced after a match and not take action. The Swansea referee, Tom Reynolds, had taken the names of five players in the fourth round FA Cup-tie between Chelsea and Birmingham which Birmingham won 1–0. After the match Reynolds found his car blocked in by the City coach so off he went to the dressing room. He put his head round the door and asked: 'Where's your coach driver?' To which a voice replied: 'Come on, ref, you're not going to book him as well, are you?'

Scottish referee, Mr Smith, demonstrated the Scrooge Yuletide spirit of 1995 when he responded to one of Gazza's better antics by taking his name. Gazza had returned the yellow card Mr Smith had dropped by presenting it to him with a typical 'booking' gesture. Presumably Gazza could have argued he couldn't have done that if he hadn't done the other.

Almost as absurd was the referee sending off Partick Thistle's Rod McDonald after two bookable offences in February 1996 – the first yellow card for the heinous crime of making the Sign of the Cross.

It is good to see that not all referees are bereft of humour. The much-respected Dermot Gallagher tells of an occasion when he was approached by a fan at Old Trafford who said: 'I hate you.'

'But you don't even know who I am,' responded Dermot.

'I do know who you are,' replied the red-bobble-hatted fan. 'You're that b******, David Elleray.'

Many might make critical comments about the

propensity of referees at Old Trafford to favour the home team by being generous with 'injury time' and making the type of decisions which would have made Judge Jeffreys resign, but surely things can never deteriorate to the level displayed by one referee in Bogota, Columbia. He was accused by his local FA of 'showing a distinct measure of favouritism towards the home side'. Harsh, perhaps, but he had awarded them seven penalties in one game.

And while Premiership crowds might complain about card-happy referees, they should be thankful they are not in Romania. In the first ten weeks of the 1996 season, officials booked more than 500 players, an average of 5.4 players a game. Recently, one referee booked 12 players in the last ten minutes.

Sometimes the power of the referee can reach beyond the grave. Luigi Coluccio was given a one-match ban nine days *after* being shot dead outside a bar in southern Italy. The ban could not be avoided, said the Italian FA, because the referee's report was submitted before Luigi was shot.

> 'Dartmouth Reserves suffered five bookings –
> including the linesman for smoking on the line.'
> (*Dartmouth Chronicle.*)

Daood Suheil is recognized as the best referee in the Israeli Championship League. Daood, who is a Catholic Arab, says: 'The crowd insults me about my origins. Sometimes they call me Arab or Arafat. But the Jewish referees are insulted just as much as I am. They get called Nazis.'

Some happy combinations of officials at matches. . .
• Cambridge . . . French & Saunders
• Mansfield . . . Smith & Wesson
• Charlton . . . Barber & Hair (other linesman 'Legg')

Others who have officiated together include . . .
- Ryan & Griggs
- Charlton & Law
- Willy & Fury
- Plant & Potts
- Russell & Sprouts
- Day & Dawns

And a few more strange names:
- Duncan Biscuit
- Orson Carte
- Sean A. Legg

Chris Freddi's *Book of Funny Names* contains some unusual monikers:
- Charlie Faultless – a Scottish referee from the 1950s
- Segar Richard Bastard – from the 1880s
- D. Fart – an Iranian referee from the 1940s

The late Jorge Emiliano dos Santos, a Brazilian referee, regularly displayed his homosexuality during matches. When a team scored, he would skip and run his way back to the kickoff, and when he awarded free kicks and penalties, gave little whoops of delight. The crowds loved it, and he was popular with the players. He would say to them: 'I might be a pansy off the pitch, but here I'm a macho man.'

But referees can be given a hard time of it in South America. On Argentine TV soccer coverage when a penalty is awarded, a cartoon ref walks across the screen led by a guide dog.

Also in Argentina in 1992, players in a game got a surprise when a bunch of free fall parachutists made an unscheduled landing on to the pitch. One Estudiantes player picked up the ball believing the match had come to an end, and the referee awarded a penalty.

In Brazil, Serafim Meneghel, President of Uniao Banderante, was highly incensed when the ref awarded a penalty against his team. He ran on to the pitch and asked him: 'Why did you blow your whistle, you s***?!' When he did not receive a satisfactory answer, he pulled out a 0.38 calibre pistol and shot the ball to bits. He asked the question again. This time the referee told him he had had second thoughts, and the offence merely warranted an indirect free kick.

When, in July 1996, Al-Ahly were playing in the Tripoli derby in front of 60,000 fanatical supporters, their owner and chairman, Al-Aadi, the son of Colonel Gadafi, sat in his usual seat, heavily guarded by minders, bristling with armoury. When Al-Ahly scored a goal which was never a goal, the referee, mindful of the win-at-all-costs Rambo-protected chieftain in the stand, and with one eye on his future survival, gave the goal. Result: riot, gun-firing, 50 injured, 20 dead and the Libyan League suspended.

A perceived inadequacy in the referee was seen by West German defender, Uli Stielike, booked in the 1982 World Cup Final which Italy won 3–1 in Spain: 'Of course, he should have sent me off, but that just shows he had no authority. I told him he was whistling for the Italians and he would have done better to have put on a blue shirt from the beginning and swallowed his whistle.'

Matters can get out of hand in Britain too. The Liverpool County FA recorded the case of a father watching his son, who became very angry at a tackle on him, and began to abuse the referee. The referee came over to the line to have a cautionary word, and without more ado was punched to the ground. While he was down, the son, for good measure, kicked him in his side. The 13-year-old was banned *sine die*.

And then there was Ricky Goddard, a North

Warnborough midfielder, who, up to 1992, had been suspended for five out of the nine years of his playing career. He was given an additional six months when he sneaked into the ref's changing room and urinated on his clothes.

And more physically, there is the case of the referee giving evidence to an FA Disciplinary Committee: 'He kicked me, so I bit his ear off.'

> In Spain a referee was banned for four games, for wrongly sending off a player in a match between Atletico Madrid and Oviedo.

When the writer was standing watching a school football match in Hartlepool in 1981, youngsters on the line kept referring to the referee as 'Leghead'. On enquiring whether that was the ref's actual name, it was explained that some years earlier, he had had an accident to his scalp, which had required a skin graft from his thigh – hence the nickname.

Referees can give as good as they get. When Real Madrid defeated Barcelona by a penalty on 1 February 1993, Johann Cruyff said the ref, Manuel Diaz Vega, should stick to children's matches. Manuel responded by saying: 'He's losing his nerve. Every time he plays Real Madrid, he p****s his pants.'

> Altercation in Derwentside League:
> Player: 'Ref – are you blind?'
> Referee: 'Bonny lad, I can see the sun OK – and that's 93 million miles away!'

Then there was the referee from the Liverpool Association who was known as 'Isaiah' – not because his parents had a commitment to the Old Testament, but because, when he was viewed from the front, one eye appeared to be higher on his face than the other.

Nowadays, referees get more flak thrown at them than

a Second World War Lancaster Bomber. 'Not like the 1960s,' says John McGrath, previously manager of Halifax. 'Then referees were OK, as long as tackles were kept below the throat.'

John remembers the advice given to him by Manager, Joe Harvey, when he played centre half for Newcastle during the 1960s: 'Retaliate first. If you can't get the man, you'll have to go for the ball.'

If it's tough for referees, it can be even tougher sometimes for the linesman. In 1972, an Argentine team was jailed for kicking a linesman to death.

But you have to feel for Martin Perry from Dorset, who was refereeing the match in the Dr Marten's Cup (the Southern League's knock-out competition) between Witney Town and Clevedon Town. Witney Town left the pitch believing they had won their two-legged first round tie on away goals and proceeded to get bathed and changed. As they were about to go for the after-match pint, who should appear but an embarrassed Martin, confessing that he had made a mistake in thinking that away goals scored in extra time counted double. A penalty shoot-out was necessary, so the players had to divest themselves of their clean clothes and re-clothe with dirty kit. It was 10.30 p.m. by this time, and spectators had left, thereby missing the climax of the whole evening. Perhaps it was just as well for the referee when Witney Town won the shoot-out 4–2.

Question: 'What was it that Wendy Toms kept sticking up when she became the first woman to spend one-and-a-half hours participating in an activity which involved a group of 30 men, on 29 January 1997?'

Answer: 'A flag. She was the first woman to act as assistant referee in a Coca Cola Cup match.' (Southampton *v*

Stockport County.)

The FA were obliged to discipline referee Mrs Janet Fewings, 41, who showered naked with players after matches in the Exeter and District Sunday League. The reason she gave was that there was a lack of changing facilities for women officials. She was charged with bringing the game into disrepute. She is reported to have made a clean breast of it and disappointed players are looking for the FA nark who reported the cock-up. They want him black-balled!

. . . and finally in this section, what every crowd thinks about every referee:

'The only thing worse than being a bachelor is being a bachelor's son.'

5
Clubs and Fans

Introduction

Eric Cantona could not praise British fans enough – that is, of course, apart from the odd Crystal Palace supporter. He compared them to their French counterparts who, he said, do not have the same lifelong attachment to a local team and will only follow success. It is something which does appear to be unique in Britain, where there is a plethora of football teams, and rabid devotees can build up an obsessional commitment to less prestigious ones such as Cowdenbeath and Marine. How could the French, or for that matter the rest of this country, appreciate the chant of pure pride and emotion encapsulated in the singing of the Darlington fans, who, at the match in 1990 which marked their return to the Football League, bayed rapturously: 'Are you watching, Hartlepool?'

Kevin Keegan, when he took over at Newcastle, commented how the fans had followed the club through thick and thin, but in his last weeks at St James's, it seems it was a case of 'thin and thin'. A greater source of amazement than the lifelong dedication to a club is often the level of passion which transcends class barriers, overshadows marriage and family obligations, as well as financial good sense. It is sometimes a phenomenon as inexplicable as examples of road rage, where perfectly normal individuals suddenly lose all sense of sanity and flip. How else can you explain two Australian Manchester United fans who spent £8,000 travelling to Britain in the hope of getting a ticket for the 1996 Championship decider against Middlesbrough. Meanwhile, back home, their wives learned that their homes had been re-mortgaged and their husbands were not away on a kangaroo hunting trip. Clearly, pockets of fanaticism do exist abroad, as can be witnessed by Bjorge Lillelien's hysterical words of triumph when his country, Norway, beat England in 1983 at what was probably their finest hour: 'Yurggggh! Der Stod Ingelland. Lord Nelson, Lord Beaverbrook, Winston Churchill, Henry Cooper, Clement Attlee, Anthony Eden, Lady Diana! Der Stod dem all. Der Stod dem all. Maggie Thatcher, can you hear me? Can you hear me, Maggie? Your boys took one hell of a beating tonight!'

Arsenal

In October 1995, Arsenal's Youth Development Officer, Terry Murphy, received a phone call from a parent, singing the praises of his son's ball control and passing skills – it transpired that the child was two years old.

David Seaman, *numero uno* goalkeeper, has taken to wearing a specially made lightweight padded jockey jacket to protect his ribs after a serious injury. 'Only did it,' said a Spurs supporter, ''cos the guy who plays in front of him has a donkey jacket.'

A few seasons ago, when Arsenal went six weeks without a home fixture, it was suggested that the local cinemas should be showing 'The Gunners of Never 'ome'!

Aston Villa

When Aston Villa had Tony Daley playing for them and
then signed Dalian Atkinson, one fan could not work out
how it was that Aston Villa only won 1–0 when he was
convinced the commentator had said: 'Daley and
Atkinson' had scored.

A similar story concerns a cricket fan who listened to
the heroic deeds of an Australian cricketer called 'Lilian
Thomson' – it completely evaded him that the references
were to Dennis Lillee and Jeff Thomson.

Apropos of Eric's slip-up – with two feet at Crystal
Palace – 78-year-old Aston Villa fan, Charles Taylor,
recalls seeing Pongo Waring in the 1930s wading into the
crowd during a game, soundly thrashing a barracker and
returning to the field of play. No action was taken.

More recently, in 1984, David Ward, of Fisher in the
Beazer Homes Southern Division, pushed himself
through a crowd during the match and punched a fan
who had been giving him 'grief'. He was given a two-week
ban.

Aston Villa has banned the ever increasing popular
request for the scattering of the ashes of deceased supporters upon the pitch. A spokesperson for the club said:
'Players have expressed reservations about the practice
and it is their working environment after all.' It seems it
can be off-putting to end up face down on the penalty
spot and have to live with the possibility of having inhaled
perhaps a part of the remains of Willie Ogden, the pie-
man of the East End. Besides that, the groundsman was
complaining that the practice was ruining the grass in the
goalmouths and the centre spot.

Clubs might follow the example of Ajax if their pitches
ever become surplus to needs. When the Dutch club
moved to their new stadium, they donated the turf to the

city's crematorium. This meant that the last wish of some supporters to have their ashes scattered over the hallowed ground could now be granted. However, there is still a measure of disappointment, in that a number of the deceased had hoped to achieve in death what they could not attain in life, which was to make an appearance in front of thousands. Had that happened, one supposes there would have been the possibility of someone ending up on his favourite player's thigh after a last-ditch sliding tackle, and then sharing the bath with the whole team.

Banners

In Britain, there does exist a deep-seated and bitter rivalry between fans from the north and the south which is reflected in such a universal chant as: 'You're just a soft Southern b******,' a chant, which is, incidentally, even directed at Leeds players by Middlesbrough supporters. In Italy, the land of football placards, where there is disdain for teams and supporters south of Rome, there exists bitterness which is akin to hatred. Wherever Naples travel, they face banners which proclaim:

WELCOME TO ITALY

and

STOP THE NUCLEAR TESTS AT MUROROA
DO THEM IN NAPLES

The Neapolitans have retaliated by displaying banners with the message:

MILAN, TURIN, VERONA – IS THIS ITALY?
IF SO, IT'S BETTER TO BE AFRICAN

And a banner about Andy Gray at the 1977 League Cup Final between Aston Villa and Everton proclaimed:

HE'S HERE,
HE'S THERE,
HE'S EVERY
F****** WHERE

To which the Everton faithful responded:

HE'S FAT
HE'S S***
HE'S NEVER
F****** FIT

It is the same Andy Gray who was described by the Bayern Munich coach, Udo Lattek, in 1985, as having a 'style suited to rugby union' and whose views on Sky in 1996 brought this jibe from a sportswriter: 'If he wore soundproof trousers, we wouldn't hear a word he said!' Unfair when Andy is here, there and every. . .

This banner appeared at Anfield when Wales beat Scotland in 1977 in the World Cup qualifier:

JOE JORDAN
STRIKES FASTER
THAN
BRITISH LEYLAND

And during Liverpool's record-equalling 29-game unbeaten start to the 1987-88 season, these banners were seen:

I HAVE SEEN LIVERPOOL BEATEN

and

I HAVE SEEN A GOAL SCORED AGAINST
LIVERPOOL

More recently and with smug, if understandable, satisfaction, Manchester United fans unfurled the following provocative banner at Leeds:

MERCI POUR CANTONA, SCUM

A banner at St James's Park where the French were playing during Euro '96:

HOWAY THE FROGS

Advice for Kevin Keegan when Manchester United clinched the 1995-96 Premiership title:

STICK TO SELLING SUGAR PUFFS, KEV!

Banner at Scotland *v* Soviet Union game, 1982:

ALCOHOLISM *v* COMMUNISM

Billingham Town

Shouted abuse at a Billingham Town *v* Ashington match when the visitors' well-groomed star took what appeared to be a 'Ginola' tumble and required the services of the trainer: 'The only attention you need, yi big lass, is from a hairdresser!'

When the officials from Lancaster Gate visited
Billingham Town's ground, one of the best amateur stadiums in England, to inspect the pitch after hasty repairs,
they were met by the committee, resplendent in smart
suits and ties, who fussed over them to obtain their seal of
approval. Everything was going well until a scruffy local
appeared with a ferret, and assured the notables that he
could rid the pitch of its perennial problem of rabbits.
Fortunately, the officials were unable to understand the
Teesside accent, and Billingham Town men explained
that the gentleman had arrived to deal with the guttering.

Birmingham City
Ricky Otto, one of Barry Fry's many signings, was
quoted in the *Birmingham Sports Argus* in January 1995:
'Once I'm settled in, I will get better and the fans will see
me fly.'

Blyth Spartans
When Blyth Spartans beat Ashton United in the FA
Trophy 2–0 on Saturday, 20 January 1996, the scorers
were Proctor and Gamble.

Bolton
Despite their calamitous 1995-96 season, Bolton fans,
who had to put up with such cracks as: 'Bolton have been
very unlucky because other teams have been turning up',
could still demonstrate a fine sense of humour when they
beat Middlesbrough at the February meeting at the
Riverside stadium by singing: 'Can we play you every
week?'

It must have been a similar type of black catastrophic

humour which prompted Frank Bruno's fans to chant to Mike Tyson before their fight in Las Vegas: 'You're going down with the Bolton.' Another football chant, which must have bemused the Americans, was directed at the fuzzy-headed Don King: 'Get your hair cut for the lads!'

Boscombe Celtic
A local club from the Bournemouth area, Boscombe Celtic, is a team for ex-drug and alcohol addicts who are recovering. When the club's supporters wrote to League clubs requesting spare kit, the only one which responded was Millwall. Unfortunately, they were sponsored by 'Captain Morgan'.

Bristol City
When Bristol City played Shrewsbury in the Auto-Windscreens Shield tie in 1995, there was only one fan in the visitors' enclosure who was welcomed by the announcer, and cheered by the home supporters, who could honestly chant: 'You must have come in a taxi.'

Cardiff City
When Trevor Senior scored a hat trick against Cardiff City in 1985, they were prepared to let him have the match ball – if he would pay them £40.

Celtic
Celtic fans' chant about Duncan Ferguson, 1995:
> 'He's tall, he's skinny, he's going to Barlinnie.' (Her Majesty's Prison.)

In a city where football and religion are inextricably entangled, one definition of an atheist is: 'A bloke who goes to a Rangers-Celtic match to watch the football.'

Maurice Johnston, who emulated Paul of Tarsus by crossing a sectarian divide, and plied his trade in both the Rangers and the Celtic camps, was realistic about his binding impact: 'For a while I did unite the Rangers and the Celtic fans. There were people in both camps who hated me.'

Chelsea

Question from the Terraces: 'What is the difference between Chelsea and Psycho?'

Answer: 'At Chelsea the shower is trying to put the knife in Bates.'

Chelsea fans could read in their programme that match sponsorship in the 1995-96 season included the following benefits: '. . . Car-park facilities, directors' box seats, exclusive use of Sponsors' Lounge, three-course lunch including win.'

When Ray Wilkins, Chelsea's 1970s square-ball passer, and darling of southern media personalities, put a ball ten yards behind the player he was aiming for, Jimmy Hill praised him.

'He might not have got the ball to his own player,' said Hill, 'but just look at the effect his pass had. A defender went to intercept the ball and pulled a hamstring.'

North of Leeds they used to say he was eulogized for having his shirt on the right way round.

Coventry

Sticker on Coventry fan's car: 'God give me patience – but hurry.'

Cowdenbeath

Keen Cowdenbeath fan, the Rev. Ronald Ferguson, was

called upon to make the presentation to the player of the year at a dinner in 'Wee Jimmy's Bar' before Christmas 1996. The recipient of the award had only played a few games but had been chosen by the fans, it was explained by the clergyman: 'Because he had played so seldom, he won by inflicting least damage on the team.'

Darlington

Avid Darlington fan, Neil Raper, was mascot for the day in the local derby match against Hartlepool. It was a surprise treat organized by his family. Nice gesture it might seem, but it was a wind-up plotted by wife, Angela, for his 40th birthday and witnessed by a guffawing crowd who hooted as he led the team out with a big '40' on the back of his shirt.

But wait – it has come to light that Swindon have had

mascots aged 50 and 82, mere youngsters compared to Harold Farnell, who turned out as mascot for Bradford in the match against Bolton on his 96th birthday. Harold did not cause the same bother as Newcastle's five-year-old mascot against Aston Villa, Jonathan Levey. Both teams were lined up, waiting for the whistle, when he was spotted dribbling his way through the Newcastle team with the match ball. Much to the delight and encouragement of the crowd, he popped the ball past Pavel Srnicek before being carried off in triumph.

The ill-feeling between the Darlington Board and the fanzine, *Mission Impossible*, continued into the 1996-97 season, and took a new twist. The Board banned the sale of *Mission Impossible* anywhere on club property. And this at the club nicknamed 'The Quakers', and which likes to be known as 'the friendly club'.

One visitor to see Darlington play was mightily impressed. Zakaria Yusuf Mwamzandi from Nigeria changed the name of the team he manages back home – Msambweni – to Darlington FC (The Quakers). The reward for such esteem and veneration was a full set of first-team shirts.

Neville Chapman, who played for Middlesbrough, then moved on to Darlington, tells the tale of when he paid a visit to Feethams some time after leaving the Club. He met the groundsman-cum-general-administrator who had always, during Neville's playing days, been accompanied by a huge labrador called Blackie, – but this time Blackie was nowhere to be seen.

'Where's Blackie?' asked Neville.

'Oh, the Board decided to get rid of him,' was the reply. 'You know he was only kept to guard the safe, but it was costing £3.50 a week to feed him, and there was never any more than £2.50 in it!'

Just how important football is to youngsters can be gauged from the comment of one lad, a Middlesbrough supporter, 24 hours before he was due to set off for Wembley to give support to another north-eastern team, Darlington, in their 1996 Play-Off Final against Plymouth. He came bouncing downstairs, declaring to his mum: 'I'll never forget today for as long as I live! It's the day before I go to Wembley.'

Derby

Question aimed at referee during Derby match, 1991: 'Are you Maxwell in disguise?'

Sometimes the daftest part of a visit to a match can be the 'attractions' which more and more clubs are providing in the quest for added hype and entertainment. At Derby they have Rammie the Ram (alias Dean Mottram), their lucky mascot, whom Paula Cocozza of *Goal* magazine interviewed in the 1995-96 season. He said: 'People think you're a bit nutty, but once I walk through them gates, I've changed. I've become somebody else. I'm still Dean, but it's like I leave Dean in the changing room, then I dress up as Rammie, if you know what I mean. I can play Dean, but doing what Dean wouldn't normally do and get away with it. To a degree, I've got a split personality.' You don't say!

Dynamo Moscow

A football fan at a European tie with Dynamo Moscow in that city returned to his hotel and asked one of the more amiable guides: 'Where is the nearest night club I can go to for a good meal?' She smiled and replied: 'Helsinki.'

El Salvador/Honduras

A three-match series to decide whether Honduras or El Salvador would qualify for the World Cup in Mexico ended in a war in which, after four days of fighting, 3,000 people were killed and 100,000 made homeless. On Saturday, 7 June, El Salvador played their away leg in Honduras and were beaten by a Honduran goal in the last minute. Back home in El Salvador, 18-year-old Amelia Bolanios took her father's pistol and shot herself dead. *El Nacional* said: 'The young girl could not bear to see her fatherland brought to its knees.' The sad thing was that, in the deciding game, El Salvador won 3–2 – and also, incidentally, the war.

Everton

After suffering five consecutive defeats, including the 3–1 Cup-tie humiliation by Bradford, Joe Royle travelled to St James's Park on 29 January 1997. He was booed off the bus to shouts of: 'The taxi's waiting, Joe!' – a none-too-subtle reference to the way former Everton boss, Harry Catterick, was sacked in the back of a cab, and a tale which has become entrenched in Evertonian folklore.

Falkirk

Before joining Bradford in the 1996-97 season, Chris Waddle had a short spell with Falkirk.

> Reporter: 'Chris – How do you feel playing at Brockville Park after Marseille?'
> Answer: 'Anything's got to be better than the sausage factory.'

Fanzines

> Comment on a particularly hard-working female fan in a Midlands' fanzine: '. . . does a lot of work for

charity – like handling the football team's balls'.

The hostility between the Darlington fanzine, *Mission Impossible*, and the powers-that-be at Feethams who hold the League record for the highest turnover of managers since the war at 29, with eight in the last five years, did not decrease, despite the club's success under Jimmy Platt. When asked by the national supporters' magazine, *When Saturday Comes*: 'If you could do one thing for Darlington, what would it be?' without the slightest hesitation, the heartfelt response was: 'Explode a small but powerful incendiary in the board room.'

Also noted in one issue of the fanzine.

'LORD LUCAN SPOTTED IN HARTLEPOOL TROPHY ROOM'

Often the funniest part of a fanzine is the title itself and some show a sense of humour in the best traditions of the game. Here are a few of the best:

Dial M for Merthyr – Merthyr Tydfil
More Dead Wood than the Mary Rose – Portsmouth
One Man and His Dog – Scottish junior football fanzine title
Loadsamoney – Blackburn Rovers
Only one 'F' in Fulham – Fulham
Mass Hibsteria – Hibernian

The Manchester City fanzine, *Electric Blue*, has changed its name after a threat of legal proceedings by the porn magazine, *Electric Blue*. The name was changed to *Bert Trautman's Helmet*.

One Heart of Midlothian fanzine is called *Always the Bridesmaid* because they have been runners-up so many times in domestic competitions.

Fulham

The apocryphal tale was that Ian Branwell, in the 1995-96 season, was seen by one of his players standing in Trafalgar Square, looking up at the pigeons, wiping his eye and saying: 'Go on, do it again. Everybody else does.'

> Car sticker spotted in Fulham: 'There's a place for you at Craven Cottage . . . mine.'

Terry Angus was voted the fans' man of the match after Fulham's 1–1 draw with Chesterfield in 1995. He spent the entire game on the bench, but polled 20 more votes than any other player.

Ernie Clay, Fulham FC chairman in 1980, had a clear vision for the future: 'We've got a long-term plan at this club and, except for the results, it's going well.'

Fifty Fulham supporters boarded a coach to travel to the match with Colchester. Half-way up the M11 they realized they were going the wrong way. When they pointed this out to the Alf Garnett-like driver, he told them: 'My instructions were to go to Cambridge and that's where I'm going.' They never did see the match, and now travel by train.

Glasgow Rangers

Graffito in Glasgow in Rangers' territory: 'No Pope here.' Underneath someone had written: 'Lucky old Pope.'

Glentoran

Broadcaster, Vincent Hanna, recalls how once he watched a seagull sleep throughout the second half on the Glentoran crossbar.

Hartlepool United

Can you believe it? When the new stand was being built at the Victoria ground, Hartlepool, the construction team continued to work while the team played Torquay.

When Hartlepool had their record-breaking run without a goal in 1993, the local *Hartlepool Mail* had this to say: '(Since Hartlepool scored last) . . . you could have watched all three *Godfather* movies, waded through every Technicolor moment of *Gone With The Wind* and still had time to settle down to a two-hour episode of *Inspector Morse*.'

The last thing players see as they leave the tunnel at Anfield is: 'This is Anfield' – designed to strike terror into the hearts of opponents. At Hartlepool, the sign has depicted the lower half of a lady bedecked in frilly black knickers, stockings and suspenders, and the message: 'Good luck, lads!' Rationale? Uncertain, but perhaps an attempt to encourage the home team to score.

The fastest British League goals (six seconds) came in matches between Hartlepool *v* Aldershot (Albert E. Mundy, 1958), Notts. County *v* Torquay United (Barrie Jones, 1962), and Crystal Palace *v* Derby County (Keith Smith, 1964). The record for the fastest own goal (six seconds) is held by Pat Kruse in the match between Torquay United and Cambridge (1977).

Hereford

At the FA Cup replay at Spurs in February, 1996, Hereford wanted to parade their mascot, the Hereford Prize Bull, on the pitch before the match. The request was denied, presumably because, as one fan put it: 'There is enough bullshit at White Hart Lane as it is.'

Ireland

It is amazing the adrenalin which can flow even when fans

find themselves in the most extreme adverse situations.
When Irishman Brian Keenan was being held hostage in
Lebanon and watched Ireland play England in the World
Cup, 1990, grim humour prompted this comment: "It was
a bit hard to jump up and down with chains on.'

Juventus

It is interesting to learn that until 1903, when Juventus
acquired the now famous black and white stripes, they
played in pink. Had they turned out in that colour for the
match against Manchester United on 11 September 1996,
in the Champions League (Juventus 1 – Man. Utd. 0), it
might have given the Lancashire Lads a bit more confidence – especially if the home fans were shouting: 'Come
on, you Pinks!'

Kenya Ales

Six players have been dismissed by Kenya Ales soccer team
for using witchcraft. Kenneth Matiba, chairman of the
Kenya Football Federation, had already warned clubs this
year about witchcraft, 'which has become an epidemic in
football'. The six, all internationals, 'paid more attention
to ju-ju than their own coach'. Strange how in Britain
players belonging to a team of that name are more likely to
pay more attention to 'brew-brew' than their own coach.

Leeds United

Millions of gallons of water were 'lorried' into the
drought-ridden Yorkshire Water Board area from
Kielder Reservoir in the week leading up to Leeds playing
Newcastle at St James's Park. When Leeds had the
temerity to score, the home crowd chanted: 'P**s in your
water, we're gonna p**s in your water.'

 You might have thought they could have shown the

type of decorum Eton boys demonstrated when they played Harrow:

'If you hate Harrow, clap your hands!'

But back to the subject of relief. Maureen Walton, who wrote *The ABC Guide to Football Grounds*, has this to say on the provision of toilets: 'In the Premier League, women are well catered for. But in the Lower Divisions, they were often like air raid shelters with just two cubicles, which meant queues a mile long.'

and . . .

In the Paramount Bar, Aberdeen, three TV screens have been built into the Bar's stainless steel urinals, and have been covered with perspex. Customers on their way to the toilets can request a particular video footage or individual upon which they can relieve their pent-up venomous fluid. Paul Gascoigne, Gary Lineker and Bryan Robson come in for a lot of splatter – as do Will Carling,

Margaret Thatcher and Paul Daniels – 'the wee magician'. One female customer commented: 'The men really seem to have a good time in there. You can hear them cheering each other and giving directions.'

> John Borg was refused entry to a Leeds home game on the grounds he was carrying a Cornish pasty.

An anagram of 'George' + 'Leeds' = 'Le Greed Goes'.

Lincoln City
Crystal clear clarity from a Lincoln City programme: 'It is also a dangerous feeling to consider that where we are in the League is of acceptable standard because standard is relevant to the standards we have set which thereby may well indicate that we have not aspired to the standard which we set ourselves.'

Liverpool
The wit of the Liverpool fans is legendary – a humour often heightened by its spontaneity. The story of a five-year-old, bedecked in red, running on to the pitch to retrieve a ball before the start of an Anfield match in the early 1980s, prompted the chant of: 'Sammy Lee, Sammy Lee, Sammy Lee.'

Scouse wit was further evident when their goalkeeper, James, appeared in one of his many *avant-garde* hair-styles. The voice from the Kop loudly pronounced: 'James, that's not a f****** haircut – it's a cry for help!'

And here is an interesting query for Liverpool fans. Which Liverpool player played 224 games for the club between 1925 and 1933, studied Classical Greek at University, became a marine engineer and packed in the game to become a Presbyterian minister? Answer: James Jackson.

But what of the stranger who, standing for the first time

half-way up the Kop, enquired of the man behind where the toilets were, and was advised to p*** in the pocket of the bloke in front. 'I can't do that', ventured the stranger. 'Why not?' replied the Kopite, 'I've just p***ed in yours!'

The 'Anfield' story is told of an opposing fullback who was having a nightmare. The longer the game went on, the worse he became. The Kop was very kind to him until, towards the end, he had to retrieve the ball from behind the goal at that end. As he did so, a voice hollered from the midst of the masses: 'Mate, I've seen better backs covered with dandruff!'

And to an unhappy winger: 'You useless b******! You couldn't put a cross on a f****** pools coupon!'

Liverpool can themselves taste humour of a high order. The chant which went up from the Crystal Palace supporters after their 9–0 defeat at Liverpool:

'Oh lucky, lucky,
Lucky, lucky, lucky,
Lucky, lucky Liverpool!'

But try beating this for pure fanaticism: 'I am a young housewife who used to follow Liverpool but now, with my little boy to look after, leave it to my husband. I would like to nominate him as Fan of the Year. Here are the facts:

Our house is called "The Kop".

Our sitting-room is "The Anfield Den".

He has a lounge full of football pennants.

If Liverpool win, we receive six Sunday and six Monday papers and all the cuttings are stuck in the scrapbook. He has a fantastic collection which no one dares touch because he says one day they will be "priceless".

If Liverpool lose, there are no papers in the house, and no lunch.

If they are playing an away match that he cannot get to, he wears the red socks, red hat, scarf, tie and cardigan in the house as he waits for the result on the telly.

We have called our son "Robbie Steve ____".

He interrupted our honeymoon to get back for the vital Championship games in 1988. After the victory we returned to our honeymoon hotel.

When Everton lose, he dances.

He calls the team "The Red Gods", the ground is "The Anfield Temple", the opposition are "sacrificial offerings", and Roy Evans is "The Lord Almighty".

Signed: Wendy Dee'

Manchester City

When Alan Ball announced at City's AGM in December 1995, that the mother of homesick Georgiou Kinkladze had been given permission to join her son in Manchester, a voice shouted out: 'Great! Where does she play?'

Question: If they love him so much, how the hell can they call him 'Kinky'?

Strange but true: Charlie Phillips, a member of Manchester City's ground staff, was introduced to the Maine Road crowd as one of the few surviving war heroes holding the George Cross. Imagine his surprise when, at the next home game of the new season, he was greeted with scores of German flags. Rösler and Gaudino had arrived!

Already disillusioned by Ball's coaching flair in their relegation season in 1995, the City fans could still show a glimpse of humour with the chant: 'Alan Ball's a football genius', as their team climbed temporarily from the bottom of the Premiership.

On the last day of the 1995-96 season, Alan Ball received inaccurate information from the radio-listening fans in the crowd that a point would be enough to keep them in the Premiership. Drawing at the time, he relayed the message to the players to relax and play for time. When he realized his mistake, Ball had to shout instructions to cancel his previous orders and ordered them to bust their guts to score.

> Chants of the early part of the 1996-97 season during the interregnum when Alan Ball had been sacked and Asa Hartford was looking after the first team: 'Nobody's Blue and White Army.'

And on 28 September, when Sheffield United were 2–0 up against City, United fans struck up with their usual: 'We hate Wednesday! We hate Wednesday!' City fans, once more showing resilience by being able to laugh at themselves, responded: 'We hate Saturday! We hate Saturday!'

Stephan Boler, who has a £7 million stake in Manchester City, making him the largest shareholder, has as his first concern the preservation of the black rhino, which in 30 years has diminished from 40,000 to 4,000. He has left the preservation of that other endangered species, the Manchester supporter, entirely in the hands of chairman, Francis Lee.

Manchester United

Football fan, Alan Fraser, browsing at a news-stand while on holiday in Menorca, overheard this conversation:

'Oh, good – the English papers.'

'What's happened to Fergie's tits?'

'A bit better. They beat Nottingham Forest 2–0.'

No hablo español! Ten Manchester United fans were imprisoned for ten weeks in Spain after violence following the Barcelona *v* Manchester United Cup-tie. The trouble began when the fans asked for 25 beers at a bar in the city. The barman said '*frío*' (cold); they, believing him to have said 'free', said 'thanks', picked them up and walked away!

A magistrate had no mercy on a fan caught shoplifting from a Chester store in spite of the plea from his solicitor: 'Being an ardent Liverpudlian, my client is already deeply embarrassed enough about being in possession of a Manchester United shirt.' He was fined £100.

Fans can be very insensitive. When Dani Behr was going out with Ryan Giggs, she recalls that, when she visited Old Trafford, some fans said to her: 'You leave Giggsy alone. He's been playing crap since he met you.'

Mansfield
An incident involving a trouserless fan appeared in the *Staffordshire Evening Sentinel*: 'In the Mansfield incident, the Court heard, Robson ran on to the pitch and took down his trousers. He then removed his underpants, bent forward and showed his backside to the crowd. Judge Garrard commented: "It might be possible for a football club to get photographs of people like this and refuse them admittance to the ground."'

Meadowbank Thistle
It's not only players who sometimes go over the top. Chairman Bill Hunter had extreme opposition from a dedicated bunch of fans when he successfully, and for very sound and generally popular reasons, moved the Edinburgh club, Meadowbank Thistle, to the nearby West Lothian town of Livingston. Pat Lynch, a mere boy of 16, was banned by Mr Hunter for shouting: 'This is a dictatorship, Blobby.' For similar sentiments, approxi-

mately 50 fans have been denied access. If Mr Chase had been as sensitive at Norwich, the team would have been playing in front of the substitutes, and 'Blobby' must have money if he can afford to cast aside what must be a good crowd on a bitter afternoon.

Middlesbrough

Song at Middlesbrough during their period of 13 league games without success in the 1995-96 season: 'We'll win again, don't know where, don't know when. . .'

After Middlesbrough had played in the Zenith Data Systems Cup Final against Chelsea and were beaten 1–0 by a Tony Dorigo goal, one of their coaches was pelted with stones by triumphant Chelsea supporters as they made for the A1. The coach stopped and one of the 'pelters' was 'captured' by the 'Boro fans who dragged him on to the coach and kept him there until they arrived at the A19 turn-off, some 230 miles further north.

In October 1996, 'Boro fans wanted to release a recording of their favourite chant to the tune of 'Hey Macarena' in praise of Fabrizio Ravanelli's sensational goal-scoring start and subsequent practice of pulling his shirt over his head. Alas, because the Club, which has the contract on his name, did not wish to have unauthorized exploitation, the world will never enjoy the refrain: 'He scores great goals and you will see his belly – Hey, Ravanelli!'

However, two local radio men were given the go-ahead to record a version of Simon and Garfunkel's 'Cecilia' for the charity, Task Brasil, which provides shelter for that country's street children – and a sample: 'Juninho, we're down on our knees, begging you please, score a goal.'

And while on the subject of apocryphal tales from the town – early January 1997:

Science teacher: 'What is the respiratory system?'

Boy: 'That's all to do with the lungs and how we breathe.'

Teacher: 'Good! Now tell me about the circulatory system.'

Boy: 'It's how blood gets round the body – the heart, the arteries and the veins.'

Teacher: 'Well done! And the nervous system?'

Boy: 'Easy, Miss. That's Fleming, Cox, Whyte and Vickers – it's the 'Boro's back four!'

When the 'Boro's revised history, *From Doom To Boom*, appeared in the wake of Ravanelli's criticism of the club, Branco's sacking and vitriolic attack upon Robson, Emerson's absence-without-leave and a dozen games without a win before Christmas 1996, cynics suggested the words: '. . . And Back Again' should be added to the title.

Heard from the Riverside's terraces when 'Boro's defence was as slack as Nora Batty's tights: 'Robson, your f****** team couldn't defend our front door against Jehovah's Witnesses.'

One senior supporter, septogenarian Tom, was known by all around him as a hater of linesmen and referees. It got to the point of annoyance with some of the fans when, as the ref ran on to the pitch, Tom always, and without hesitation, greeted the official with the words: 'You're bent, ref!' The time came when one of the men in black was standing on the line right in front of the North stand, and he decided that a 'Boro player was offside. 'Linesman, you need glasses!' yelled the irate pensioner. The crowd in front of him took great delight in turning round, and informing him that it was not the linesman standing ten yards from him – it was the ref!

It made no difference – Tom is still plaguing them at

the Riverside.

Professional footballers quickly learn that it is point-less trying to justify a bad performance. Middlesbrough's 1970s centre forward, Billy Ashcroft, excused himself for failing to score from several clear-cut chances by claiming that he had suffered from double vision. It only made one fan more furious. 'That means he could see *two* balls,' he moaned, 'and he couldn't get a boot to either of them!'

The crack going around Teesside when Emerson was ensconced in Brazil:

> Question: 'What's the difference between Ronnie Biggs and Brazilian footballer, Emerson?'
> Answer: 'It's easier to get Biggs to return to Britain from Brazil!'

Chant at the Riverside during the Coca Cola tie by Huddersfield fans after their team scored a goal when 'Boro were 5–0 up: 'You're not singing anymore . . . !'

> Headline in local paper when 'Boro postponed their Premiership match with Blackburn because 23 players were unfit:
> ''BORO'S CRY-OFF CAUSES ILL-FEELING'

Bill McNeil is the half-time commentator for the schools' penalty competition at 'Boro's Cellnet Riverside Stadium. Several years ago, he was made captain of a Middlesbrough Sunday League team of teachers and received a visit from the ref before the first match of the season. 'Lads,' Bill warned his team-mates sternly. 'The ref has told me that he wants no back-chat. He's the man in charge, and he will make the decisions. Just keep your mouths shut!' In the first minute, Bill thought he had stopped the ball from going for a corner. The ref thought otherwise, and Bill had to walk through an avenue of players all wagging their fingers as he advanced towards the glaring official to explain his cry of: 'You must be blind, ref!'

When Uwe Fuchs signed for Middlesbrough, a lot of fans found difficulty in pronouncing his first name. They were calling him 'Hughie'.

And when Uwe was sent off in Middlesbrough's 1995 First Division match against Sheffield United, there was the inevitable Ceefax headline: 'Fuchs off at Ayresome'!

A group of away supporters making their first visit to Middlesbrough's new Cellnet Riverside Stadium complimented the town on the excellent signposting leading to the ground. 'Don't think it's to help you,' said one 'Boro supporter. 'The signs are there for Emerson!' Newcastle supporters suggested that the signs had been put up for 'Boro supporters.

Talking about the Geordies, it is a source of amusement in the North-East that the majority of inhabitants living south of Scotch Corner think that Geordieland begins just north of Darlington. In consequence, supporters of the 'Boro and Sunderland are always perplexed when away fans start chanting: 'We hate the Geordies! We hate the Geordies!' and they then tend to join in with: 'So do we! So do we!'

Before the match with non-League Hednesford Town at the Riverside on 25 January 1997 in the fourth round of the FA Cup, Rodney Marsh commented on Hednesford's chances: 'It's very romantic to think they might win, but like all romances Hednesford are going to get dumped.' He was right, but only just – 'Boro won 3–2.

Rodney was not so accurate in his prediction of the Everton *v* Bradford tie: 'There is an old North American Indian saying: "Beware the wounded bear!"' Rodney's reference was to the fact that Everton had been beaten in their previous five games and would be up to demolish

First Division Bradford. Bradford won 3–1 and Chris
Waddle scored a wonder goal.

Any player unfortunate enough to have the name
Kinnell should also have the good sense to have it
changed by deed poll before he does anything stupid.
When Middlesbrough were playing at Derby County on
Boxing Day, 1968, George Kinnell cost the 'Boro a win
when he inexplicably handled in the penalty area.
Imagine the cry which erupted from 'Boro fans – and con-
tinued all the way back up the A1!

Shoot! magazine did a feature on 'Brough's ex-star
Juninho, and it explained how well he had settled on
'Wearside'. Everybody, of course, except the writer of
that article, and perhaps Roger Whittaker, knows that
Middlesbrough is *Teesside* and Sunderland is *Wearside*.
Roger had a hit in 1969 with 'Durham Town', which he
describes as 'on the banks of the River Tyne'.

Millwall
Message on the scoreboard at Millwall: 'Ex-wives dis-
posed of without a trace.' It was an advert for a tattoo
parlour.

Newcastle United
It was another packed-out ground at St James's, Newcastle, the first match after Christmas. The seat in the
Jackie Milburn Stand was occupied for the first time in
the season. 'Have you been working away?' asked his
neighbour who, like all the rest in that part of the ground,
had been wondering why such a valuable acquisition had
never been used. 'No', replied the centre of attention.
'The wife bought the season ticket and gave it to me for
Christmas.'

Newcastle fans working in the post office have been

reprimanded by their manager, Tony Fawcett, for writing contemptuous comments on postage destined for Sunderland FC. He informed them that anyone caught inscribing such remarks as 'Toon Army', 'Failures', 'Rubbish', and the like, on packages and envelopes would be summarily dismissed. He made it clear that he wanted it all 'stamped' out.

Graffito at Newcastle docks:

'David Ginola rules – *au quai*'

Illustrations of football fanaticism are widespread. Who could not feel for the hapless Newcastle supporter who had a portrait of his hero, Andy Cole, tattooed on his thigh only to learn, later on the same day, that he had been transferred to Manchester United?

While on the subject of thighs, Jordan Williamson from Gosforth, near Newcastle, is only five, but can recognize, and give the name of, any Premier League player by looking at his legs.

Animal lovers will feel more deeply for the now deceased budgie belonging to another Geordie fanatic, Dominic Hurd. He kicked out in frustration at Stan Colleymore's late winner for Liverpool at Anfield on 3 April 1996, in the crucial top-of-the-table fixture. Unfortunately, his kick knocked the budgie's cage off its stand and his budgie died of shock. Dominic was offered money to replace his beloved Peter. 'But,' said a grieving Dominic, 'if I did have another budgie and Newcastle kept losing, I could become known as a serial budgie killer.'

There is the story of the Newcastle fan who, after the away Spurs match, joined a coachload of Geordie supporters in a pub and matched them pint for pint. By the time they were ready to go home, the lad had passed out. They loaded him on to the bus and took him back north. When they arrived in the early hours

of the morning, they searched his pockets and found
an envelope with a Byker address on it. They took
him to the house named, and began to ring the door-
bell continuously until an upstairs window eventually opened. A middle-aged lady demanded to know
what they wanted.

'Does Billy Smith live here?' she was asked.

'Yes he does, but he's just got married and is down in
London on his honeymoon.'

Mam and Dad Park, fanatical Newcastle supporters,
have given their son and daughter 'St James' as a middle
name, refuse to eat bacon (red and white) because of their
dislike of Sunderland, but still cannot get tickets to see
their team.

'I take them to the training ground all the time,' says
Dad.

At a Newcastle Garden Centre, gnomes which were not
selling are now being snapped up as soon as they reach
the shelves. They have been painted black and white and
buyers, for a little extra, can have the number and name
of their favourite player painted on the back.

At another Garden Centre in Newcastle, Graeme
Darling, the owner, offers to fans three white and three
black pansies. Visiting Sunderland supporters have suggested that 'pansies' is an appropriate word to describe
the Newcastle side.

One story from Newcastle is that when Mike Walker
was manager of Everton, he telephoned Kevin
Keegan: 'Kevin, I want to do a straight swap –
Cottee for Cole.' Kevin thought for a minute, then
said: 'OK – how many bags do you want?'

The Rev. Lyn Jamieson, a football-mad vicar in
Gateshead, has had a 1950s-style Newcastle shirt fitted
with a dog-collar. 'I thought I'd combine my twin

passions,' she said.

And Sister Josepha, Headteacher at St Vincent's Primary School in Walker, Newcastle, where a whole corridor is dedicated to Kevin Keegan memorabilia, and where pupils are allowed to sing Newcastle slogans to hymn tunes, jokes that she only became a nun so that she could wear black and white.

Sister Josepha, like other 'Toon Army' fans, was devastated on Wednesday 8 January, when Keegan resigned. As the news spread during the morning, hundreds made their way to St James's to seek solace in their bereavement. The atmosphere was reminiscent of the sadness of a burial and the song the fans had concocted for their messiah and idol – 'Walking in a Keegan Wonderland' – reverberated around the rafters of the Exhibition stand.

Others were more dramatic in the loss of 'King Kev'. Keith Clegg commemorated the manager's sudden departure by having a tombstone tattoo emblazoned on his arm with the words: 'RIP Kevin Keegan, 1992–1997 NUFC.'

Victoria Rickaby was another distraught fan: 'How can Kevin Keegan leave us? He is God around here. He is even bigger than God. He is the life of Newcastle. People name their children after him – there are even dogs named after him.' Deification indeed!! In fact, many Geordies considered Keegan's description as Messiah was entirely apt since, as Jesus breathed life into His friend, Lazarus, so King Kev raised NUFC from the dead.

King Kev was dead, but within a week and with the changing of only the final consonant (less work for the graffiti-ists), King Ken's reign began.

Sister Josepha, perhaps the most devout of Newcastle's fans – though Cardinal Basil Hume would have to be in the frame – had, by the night of Kenny Dalglish's appointment, penned an 'Ode to Kenny', which began:

> 'Welcome Kenny to St James's, you can hear the Toon Army sing,
> It's goodbye Kevin, hello Kenny,
> Tyneside's brand new King. . . .'

The graffito which, in the centre of Newcastle, had once declared:

> KING KEV RAINS – OK

now reads:

> KING KEV HAS STOPPED RAINING – KO
> KING KEN RAINS NOW – OK

During the 1995-96 and 1996-97 seasons, publicans and others in Newcastle exploited a loophole in the law, whereby they screened a live Saturday afternoon match picked up from a Norwegian satellite station. Peter Robinson, who runs a shop where the satellite dishes are sold, said: 'We had a recent game on in the shop window, and about 100 people watched from the pavement.'

When John Paul II was elected Pope, Cardinal Basil Hume, already identified as an ardent Newcastle fan, was a member of the conclave which was to elect him. Before the result was known, the following headline appeared in the local *Newcastle Evening Chronicle*:

> UNITED SUPPORTER TO BE NEXT POPE

Shout from the terraces at St James's, December 1996: 'Ginola – You couldn't tackle a Christmas Dinner!'

When, as manager of Nottingham Forest, Frank Clark was asked whether he felt sorry for Kevin Keegan when Newcastle had just drawn 1–1 with

Frank's team in a crucial title-chasing match. Despite being a firm 'Toon Army' fan, Frank had no sympathy: 'Me feel sorry for Kevin Keegan? – when he's got Asprilla, Barton and Clark on the bench!'

Geordie fans nickname Sir John Hall 'Turtle', because he was forever saying, in his semi-refined Geordie accent: 'I'm "turtley" behind Kevin Keegan!' He said of Keegan's appointment in 1992: 'It was a business decision and I am a hard businessman.' There is no doubt Kenny Dalglish was chosen for the same reason and that Sir John will be 'turtley' behind him as well.

Norwich
Banner at Norwich, 1995, read:
> GOD MIGHT LOVE YOU, CHASE –BUT
> EVERYONE ELSE THINKS YOU'RE
> A F****** B******!

After Norwich were beaten 3–1 by Reading on the Saturday before New Year, 1995, a group of aggressive fans waited for the unpopular chairman, Robert Chase, and began chanting abuse about allowing talented players to depart. 'Have you sold your wife and kids?' they sang.

Nottingham Forest
You'll not remember the name Sean O'Hara, but you will remember the incident. It was the Nottingham Forest *v* QPR, Littlewood's Cup Semi-Final of 1989 at the City ground, and Forest had just won 5–2. As hundreds of fans invaded the pitch, two of them were confronted by a demented Clough who gave Sean a good clout round the ears. In a blaze of publicity two days after the bout, Sean

and his mate, Jimmy McGowan, went to the City ground to clear up the fuss and save Cloughie from a charge of assault which had been caught on video. In an act of contrition, Cloughie leaned over to Sean and said: 'Give us a kiss!' – and he did. Sean's life was never to be the same again. He still gets called: 'Cloughie's bum boy!' Sean says: 'One minute you're cast as a down-and-out 'cos you ain't got a job. The next, you're the boy who got kissed by Cloughie. I was thinking: "What am I doing here?" and I thought of telling him to p**s off in that second. But at the time, I just kissed him.'

In 1980 Cloughie had taken a different and irreverential view of football disorder – 'Football hooligans? Well, there are 92 club chairmen for a start!' and 'There are more hooligans in the House of Commons than at a football match.'

In the same year, and on the same subject, Alan Clarke, manager of Leeds, had this to say: 'The most violent offenders should be flogged in front of the stand before home games. I feel so strongly on this matter, I'd volunteer to do the whipping myself.'

Did he feel the same way when, under Don Revie, Jack's 'Little Black Book' came to light?

Bobby Roberts, Colchester manager in 1980, felt more strongly: 'It sounds drastic, but the only way to stop the hooligans is to shoot them.'

Oldham

Oldham's poor start to the 1996 season brought with it strong protests from the fans. When asked to comment on the criticism and gripes, Graham Sharpe commented: 'I can tell you what – if Jesus came here, he'd have a hell of a hard job.'

Piacenza

Peter Brackley, commentating on Channel 4's Sunday afternoon Series A game in September 1995: 'We all know how critical Italian fans can be, even about their own players, but do they really crucify them?'

. . . and later in the same match: 'Taibi (the Piacenza goalkeeper) was struggling on the cross.'

Port Vale

From a programme, February 1994: 'Kathleen K. Sorry to hear about all your nither. We hear that you've had a hysterectomy and had a fireplace put in, all in one day. Get well soon. Love, Sandra, Mick and Janice.'

Very entertaining, the Vale programme. Here is what George Andrews, a Radio Stoke DJ, wrote in September 1996: 'England's game against Moldova was a non-event. The pitch was as flat as Pamela Anderson's sweater on a cold day . . . If England's instructions in the second half were to do bugger all, then the boys did us proud. It's no wonder the grass was growing so thick and fast because of the huge amount of crap on it.'

QPR

Most frightening fan chant of the 1995-96 season comes from Loftus Road: 'Ray, Ray, show us your hairy chest.' What is worse is that Raymond did!

St Mirren

Even home fans can be vicious – cite the case of Paul Kinnaird when he was playing for St Mirren in 1992. He says: 'I knew my days were numbered when I was warming up behind the goal at Parkhead one day, and one of the fans shouted: "Kinnaird, we like the Poll Tax more than we like you!"'

Sampdoria

Sampdoria players were very upset when, after the match against Middlesbrough to mark the opening of 'Boro's new Riverside stadium in November 1995, there were no plug adaptors for their hair dryers. Apparently the groundsman told them they would 'have to hang their heads out of the bus window'.

Scotland

But what of the Scottish fan who had travelled from his workplace in Africa and was picked up by the Italian cameras at a Scotland *v* Italy World Cup qualifying match in Naples in 1965? Here was a kilt-clad Scotsman in full regalia, on his feet and cheering wildly along with a demented stadium when Italy scored their third goal. He was even captured by an Italian commentator after the match and, not understanding the question, just shouted: 'Viva Italia, Viva Italia, you are the most sporting nation in the world.' It was only some hours later he learned that Italy, and not Scotland, had been wearing the blue shirts.

When Estonia failed to turn up for the world qualifying match, and Scotland played and should have been awarded the points and weren't, what would have happened if Scotland had lost the toss?

Scottish supporters' chant after Estonia failed to turn up for the World Cup match: 'There's only one team in Tallinn.'

Scunthorpe

Fans at Scunthorpe have suggested that one of the stands in the eight-year-old Glanford Park be demolished to enlarge what is a small pitch where visiting teams can pack defences and repel attackers with ease. Apparently the pitch was originally measured out to a large full-size area, but no one realized until the stands went up that no allowance had been made for the perimeter track.

Sheffield United

Sean Bean, the actor, who is better known for his role as Major Sharpe than as a zealous Wednesday, emblem-tattooed fan, has been bemoaning the disappearance of his team's traditional stripes: 'Blades' strip looks as if it was designed by Julian Clary when he had a migraine', he comments.

Shrewsbury

When Shrewsbury were due to meet Liverpool in the next round of the FA Cup, 1996, their coach, Kevin Summerfield, went to watch them play Leeds, whom they destroyed 5–0. Afterwards he commented: 'The gaffer sent me to see if I could spot a weakness and I found one. The half-time tea's too milky.'

Southampton

Question from the terraces: What is the difference between Nigel Mansell and Matthew Le Tissier?

Answer: It's only Le Tissier's face that doesn't fit.

Chant from Stockport fans during their 2–1 victory over Southampton in the Cup-tie at The Dell on 29 January 1997, taunting Le Tissier: 'You'll never play for England!'

... and the home fans' chant: 'He'll never play for Stockport!'

Sunderland

The seven toddlers playing the dwarfs in St Joseph's Primary School pantomime in Washington, County

Durham, were told to wear their Newcastle United shirts for the part. It was just too much for one of them, who defiantly arrived in his Sunderland top – and, no, he wasn't playing Dopey.

Jubilant Sunderland fans, celebrating their team's elevation to the Premiership in May 1996, caused Newcastle fans to see red (and white). They clad the famous statue of Jackie Milburn, located in the centre of the town, in a red and white Roker shirt.

To celebrate Peter Reid's achievements in the 1995-96 season, Sunderland fans released their own version of the Monkees' hit, 'Daydream Believer', and called it: 'Cheer Up, Peter Reid!' In the first week, it sold over 10,000 copies. And the lyrics:

> Oh I could fly without wings
> On the back of Reidy's Kings
> At three o'clock I'm as
> Happy as can be
> 'Cos the good times they are here
> And the Premiership is near
> So watch out world as all of
> Roker sings
>
> (Chorus)
> Cheer up, Peter Reid
> Oh what can it mean
> To be a Sunderland supporter
> To be top of the league
>
> We once thought of you
> As a scouser dressed in blue
> Now you're red and white
> Through and through
> We had all dreamt of the day

When a Saviour would come our way
And now we know our
Dreams are coming true
(Chorus)

Newcastle fans could not, of course, resist producing a bastardized version which went something like:
F*** off Peter Reid
Oh what can it mean
To be a sad Mackem b******
In charge of a s*** football team.
So much for North-Eastern camaraderie.

It seemed magnanimous at first sight, in September 1996, when the Geordies proclaimed that Sunderland would last for three seasons in the Premiership – autumn, winter and spring. Of course, they were right!

In February 1996, a Sunderland AFC spokesman urged all Sunderland supporters to boycott 'Sugar Puffs' because Kevin Keegan appeared on television in the advert: 'We are calling on all true Sunderland fans to stop eating "Sugar Puffs" now. If action isn't taken, this cereal killer could affect the lives of thousands of children across Wearside.'

The ban worked – sales came to a halt and 'Sugar Puffs' orders were cancelled. A 'Sugar Puffs' representative went on local radio and appealed for a truce. Sales never recovered.

Sunderland invited people to suggest names for their new ground on the site of the old Wearside Colliery. Newcastle supporters suggested: 'The Pits'.

The construction of a spanking new stadium and Premiership status is a far cry from those days in 1985 when Ian Aitken, a former Sunderland captain who moved to Everton, jibed: 'If you think champagne, you drink champagne. At Sunderland they think water.' . . . A touch of the bitterness of sour grapes?

The stadium gave Sunderland fans a unique, and lasting, method of exacting retribution. In December 1996 the club was selling at £25, bricks for the new construction which could be inscribed with the names of friends and workmates who were Newcastle supporters. One victim, Franky Clarke (Jnr) from Lanchester, complained: 'For somebody who won't eat mint rock because it's red and white, this has been a serious embarrassment. It's worse than driving a three-wheeled Reliant – I might sue 'cos I never gave permission for my name to be used to build such a gruesome place – I'm appealing for the brick to be removed and I hope it's in the foundations.'

Tannoy announcements

The target of the tannoy announcement made at the Brentford *v* Brighton Boxing Day match: 'Your wife says can you turn off your mobile phone; all she can hear is the game', got off pretty lightly by not being named. Have sympathy for the fan who, five minutes into the game at the sell-out Newcastle *v* Liverpool match, was requested over the tannoy to go immediately to his car because his wife was ready to go home. Easily identified as the only one making his way from mid-row, he had to suffer the jeers and hooting of fellow fans as he made a vain attempt to sneak out.

Tannoy announcements can, from time to time, bring greater enjoyment than the play itself. Witness this announcement from the Wrexham tannoy announcer at the sell-out FA Cup replay against West Ham in 1992: 'Visiting supporters will be kept behind for ten minutes after the final whistle to allow the ground to clear . . . and the Wrexham fans will be kept in until Saturday's match with Blackpool.'

And at Highbury: '. . . , your partner has just given birth, and here you are at the Arsenal *v* Spurs match. Just to make matters worse, she's calling it "Chelsea".'

While on that subject, the American producers of the tee shirt: 'Leave Chelsea Alone', could not understand why so many Londoners were inundating them with orders for something to do with President Clinton's daughter.

While at Grimsby in December 1993, when the request: 'Would the owner of car, registration number 777 Romeo, Romeo, . . .' came over the tannoy, the crowd responded: 'Wherefore art thou, Romeo, Romeo?'

Tottenham
It is a matter of record that, at White Hart Lane in 1930, the Spurs winger centred the old type of leather ball with such velocity on a wet Saturday afternoon, it struck the centre forward, bounced off him and hit another player, resulting in both of them being carried off with concussion.

Verona
Verona authorities were forced to cancel plans to name a stadium after Italy's World Cup-winning goalkeeper, Aldo Olivieri, when they discovered he was still alive. Everything was ready for the inauguration until the Verona authorities discovered that Aldo, of 'unforgettable memory', was not dead but a sprightly 86-year-old living in western Italy. 'Thanks for the initiative,' said the old hero, 'but I hope to live a while longer, touch wood.'

Watford
At Vicarage Road, the chant is often intoned of: 'Old Git,

old git, give us a wave.' Whereupon Peter Lawson, a 65-year-old retired plumber and Watford steward, obliges.

The refrain comes from the younger element, who have a grudging respect for him despite his continuous attempts to get them to sit down.

'I take it in the spirit I hope is intended,' says Peter. 'There has to be some give and take. Sometimes they come up and ask for my autograph – I sign: "The Old Git".'

Wimbledon

From the Wimbledon Boxing Day programme, 1993: 'Coaching generally starts at the age of five. We want to start at the age of one for outfield players, and six months for goalkeepers, so they can work on their groundwork prior to being able to walk. The Scottish FA have revised this plan to include goalkeeping sessions with pre-natal classes as extra work is needed.'

Question from the terraces: 'What is the difference between the Wimbledon midfield and clocks?'

Answer: 'Clocks go forward at least once a year.'

Wimbledon's lofty Premier position stopped Joe Kinnear's mockers in their tracks after they had pooh-poohed Joe's early season prophecy that he would take his side into Europe. The only way Wimbledon would get into Europe, they jibed, would be through Club 18–30.

Wolverhampton Wanderers

A suggestion as to why Wolves are called 'Wanderers' is that it describes the propensity of the team's defenders.

6
Euro '96

Football supporter, Steve Weatherill, celebrated the English wins against Scotland and Holland in Euro '96 by painting the St George Cross all over his garage and vowed to paint his whole house if England won the final. Steve and his wife, Julie, from Huddersfield, were expecting their first child. Steve wanted to call it 'Shearer', but Julie, clearly the voice of sanity in the household, said: 'No'.

The programme for the England *v* Bulgaria match in March 1996 contained features on six players who were either not playing or were not in the starting line-up, and – food for thought – at the height of the meat crisis, a full-page advert asked: 'Guess who's beefing up the England Squad? Burger King, the official fast food of the England Team.' So that explains the madness on Cathay Pacific, and the Hong Kong night club.

As was expected, the mega-sports firms were out at Euro '96 to get the fans to buy their products:

Coca Cola, which spent £14 million and themed its Euro '96 'For the fans', produced a poster which proclaimed:

'WALKING IN FRONT OF THE TV IS A BOOKABLE OFFENCE'

One of Reebok's offerings was a picture of Peter Schmeichel making a spectacular save and underneath a caption which read:

'The last time he dropped a ball his voice broke.'

NIKE scored a brace of own goals by featuring Eric Cantona and David Ginola who did not even make the French squad. Still, up Eric popped giving a threatening stare and the message: 'I have worked hard to improve English football. Now it must be destroyed.'

Another NIKE advert portrayed Italy's defender, Paulo Maldini with confident and supercilious countenance proclaiming: 'Italy's goalkeeper: easiest job in Europe.'

Wonderbra even bounced in and exposed their Euro '96 pointed revelation – a well-cleavaged model pouting athletically and the words: 'Cup Fever'. Must be nice to have such wonderful support!

Shariff Abubakar Omar, a witch doctor from East Africa, was very serious when he wrote to Terry Venables, offering his services to him to win Euro '96: '. . . if you consult me . . . I could use my magic charm to make things work in England's favour.' His letter ended, threateningly and inaccurately: 'Your predecessors, Don Revie and Bryan Robson, paid the price by ignoring my advice.'

Until the games with Scotland and Holland, when the English players became good guys in Euro '96, Terry might have reconsidered Shariff's offer because there was plenty of media vitriol aimed at them, especially after the Cathay Pacific and Hong Kong nightclub shenanigans.

> (After the Switzerland match): 'The best draw England had of the Euro '96 Tournament was with Cathay Pacific.' (Joe McGinnis – *Sunday Times.*)

'And what about that phrase "collective responsibility"?
Who do Venables' squad think they are? The Cabinet? A
cocktail cabinet maybe.' (Patrick Barclay – *Sunday
Telegraph*.)

> And whose bright idea was it to have the band of the
> Royal Air Force with fixed bayonets playing 'The
> Dambusters' March' for the Germans? It was the
> Wembley disc jockey who played 'Tequila' at half-
> time in the England *v* Scotland game, in memory of
> a good Hong Kong night out.

Scarborough Council won the battle against Darlington
to be hosts to the Bulgarian team for Euro '96 when they
played the preliminary rounds at Leeds and Newcastle. It
was at some cost – £20,000 for hotel bills and £5,000
spending money for the players. The Labour Council
sanctioned this spending, perhaps in the belief that hordes
of Bulgarians would descend upon the Yorkshire resort
and bring wealth and prosperity for its inhabitants. They
failed to realize that few in Bulgaria could afford the trip
and there would be a veritable glut of empty hotel beds. If
they couldn't get that right, it is no surprise that when the
Bulgarian team arrived to inspect Scarborough in
January, they were presented with a flag of the country's
hated and rejected previous regime.
    Still, Scarborough, for all its efforts, did not deserve the
criticism meted out by their star, Hristo Stoichkov,
explaining why the squad was going to new headquarters:
'Scarborough is boring!' – especially when they were
moving up the road to Stockton-on-Tees, which is not
exactly the Las Vegas of the north.
    But, 'one man's meat is another's. . .' How else can you
explain the unbridled enthusiasm of Lev Zarakhovich,

the Russian Press Officer, who announced: 'Training has been cancelled. They have the day off and are planning a shopping spree in Wigan.'

But you have to feel for the Portuguese supporters who, on their arrival in Sheffield, asked: 'Where's the beach?'

> 'The French squad is full of foreigners who don't know the words of the Marseillaise.' (French National Front leader, Jean-Marie Le Pen.)

The German based International Federation of Football History and Statistics informed UEFA before Euro '96 that the system of sudden death, the so-called 'Golden Goal', was instituted by the Nazis in 1935 and used in more than 460 games up to 1944.

After England's defeat by Germany in the semi-finals, one disbelieving fan spluttered: 'I just don't understand it. How the hell did we manage to beat them in two world wars?'

The *Daily Mirror* got it wrong again – its 'cut out 'n' keep' front page for England's semi-final with Germany read: 'Achtung! Surrender – For you, Fritz, ze Euro '96 Championship is over.'

Things in Euro '96 were certainly looking up for England after the victory over the Dutch: 'To be totally realistic, we were out-played in every aspect of the game. We were vulnerable in every position.' (Holland Coach, Guus Hiddinck.)

'Shocking, bewildering, disgraceful and scandalous.' (Dutch newspaper *De Telegraaf*'s verdict on Holland's Euro '96 defeat at Wembley.) How much nicer it is when the boot is on the other foot!

Dennis Bergkamp had complimentary words for

England after the tournament: 'Europe can now see that you can play football in England. Before the tournament, everyone was laughing at the way football is played here. Now they are envious, England proved everyone wrong.' With such praise, he might even win over the Arsenal fans!

And it must have been comforting for Dennis to have heard that Tony Adams, his Arsenal colleague, was relishing the confrontation with him in the game against Holland: 'Dennis is such a nice man, such a tremendous gentleman with such a lovely wife – it's going to be very hard for me to kick him.'

The Spanish were bemused and bewildered by the xenophobic insulting rubbish shovelled out by sections of the British press. It did for Anglo-Spanish relations what the Iberian sun does to unprotected skin. Fortunately, the more responsible Spanish press would not lower themselves to such a level, dismissing the jibes as the rantings of 'some sensationalist British papers' (*algunos diarios sensacionalistas ingleses*) – pretty mild really – and riposting with a far more eye-catching and humorous headline for the game:

　　'Toros Bravos contra Vacas Locas'
　　('Brave Bulls versus Mad Cows')

El Mundo Deportivo (The Sporting World) chipped in: 'Not only the cows are mad in England. The English press is also infected.'

After losing out against England in the championships on Saturday, 22 June, the Spanish, already goaded by certain tabloids (for example, 'The day we sent the paella-eaters packing'), firmly believed that they had lost to an inferior team in a match decided by penalties. A reader from Murcia voiced the feelings of the country in the *Marca* sports paper: 'Spain fought the mad cows and placed a pair of banderillas around their ears.'

One report of the match on 22 June in the Spanish *AS* concluded: 'The cruelty of football verges on the masochistic; yesterday, the Marquis de Sade had a stand ticket at Wembley.'

It was not only the excesses of certain sections of the British press which perplexed the Spanish – one spokesman at their FA headquarters in Leeds remarked: 'Leeds United's idea of welcoming fans has been to play endless Julio Iglesias records over the PA.' He should have thanked God it wasn't the Brighouse and Rastrick Band.

When the net was cast wider, anti-Hispanic sentiments, which plumbed the depths as it were, came from a more expected source. Terry Bunker, a West Country trawler skipper, warlike by name and warlike by nature, commented: 'I don't particularly like football, but I shall be following the match just to see the Spaniards kicked to death.'

. . . and you can't say he would have been gutted by the result.

Arrigo Sacchi, the Italian coach, joked his way to failure and eventual dismissal: 'Come the end of the tournament, they'll want to kiss my bald head or throw tomatoes at it.'

Shades of despair clearly consumed Scottish captain, Gary McAllister, after missing a penalty against England. 'I know there are far more important things in life than football, but if you cut me open and had a look inside right now, it would not be a pretty sight. I don't know if I can sink any lower.'

Peter Gibbons of Harrow caught the Euro '96 Final football when it was kicked into the crowd after the match, and you would have thought he would be happy – but no! 'I am very nervous about having it. I have lost sleep and I am off my food.' His anxiety was reflected in the way he deposited the ball with the jewellers, Garrards.

Hoddle did, however, inherit a team with status and repute, unlike the team Venables acquired from Graham Taylor which had plummeted downwards to a world ranking of 24th, faster than a Guy Fawkes' spent-rocket.

Sign on Leeds Sports Shop window during Euro '96:
CUSTOMERS GIVING ORDERS
WILL BE
SWIFTLY EXECUTED

7
Spoken And Written Gaffes

Introduction

We must thank God for mistakes, cock-ups, and misprints, for they brighten up the listening and the reading of sports fans. You have to laugh when Des Lynam says: 'More football later, but first let's see the goals from the Scottish Cup Final.' Or when John Motson, in a face-to-face interview with David Pleat, asks: 'What do you think, Trevor?'

The pleasure can be equally, if not more, satisfying, when a statement or a headline in the newspapers gives a different type of message than was intended. This headline from the *Nottingham Evening Post*, following an outburst of football hooliganism, is an example:

FOOTBALL VIOLENCE
JUDGE HITS OUT

It's a relief to see that the cock-ups are not solely confined to football. Murray Walker, the David Coleman of motor racing, regularly comes out with some pearlers, to wit: 'Unless I am very much mistaken ... Yes, I am very much mistaken.' And from Ted Lowe of the 'green baize' ... 'Fred Davis, the doyen of snooker, now 67 years of age and too old to get his leg over, prefers to use his left hand.'

From time to time, however, it may be a different sport but a familiar football pundit. The story is told of how Jimmy Hill was, on one occasion, acting as anchorman and had to hand over to the newly appointed rugby commentator, Nigel Starmer-Smith. Jimmy was a little concerned at getting a difficult name correct and so he practised it time and time again – 'Nigel Starmer-Smith, Nigel Starmer-Smith, Nigel. . . .' When the great moment arrived, Jimmy announced: 'And now I'll hand you over to our rugby commentator, Nigel Starmer-Smith, who has had seven craps as scrum-half for England.'

And wasn't it David Coleman who handed over '. . . to our Boxing Carpenter, Harry Commentator'?

While it is appreciated that the pressure of live broadcasting and, for reporters, the burden of having to write to meet deadlines, will inevitably lead to blunders, they are, none the less, very entertaining. Wouldn't each of us feel a right prat if we said, as John Helm did on ITV: 'Viv Anderson has pissed a fatness test.'

For those who do commentate, it is advisable that they be really well prepared because, as Bob Hope once said: 'It's amazing how many people hear you. . . After I did my first broadcast, five million sets were sold the next day. Those people who couldn't sell theirs threw them away. . .'

And so, accepting Ted Lowe's observation and excuse that 'Commentating isn't as simple as it sounds' – and groaning with sympathy – let's have a laugh . . . !

Football Commentators
Anonymous
'For those who know the Selhurst Park ground, West

Ham are playing from right to left.'

'And now, as the evening wears on, the shadows cast by the floodlights get longer.'

'The score is Liverpool 0, Norwich 0 and it's only the absence of a goal we're waiting for.'

Ron Atkinson
'Someone in the England team will have to grab the ball by the horns.'

'I'm going to make a prediction – it could go either way.'

(On Manchester United's Norman Whiteside): 'He's not only a good player, but he's spiteful in the nicest sense of the word.'

Alan Ball
'I'm not a believer in luck, although I do believe you need it.'

Dave (Harry) Bassett
'Obviously for Scunthorpe, it would be a nice scalp to put Wimbledon on our bottoms.'

Alan Brazil
'He held his head in his hands as it flashed past the post.'

Trevor Brooking
'Being naturally right-footed, he doesn't often chance his arm with his left foot.'

'He went down like a sack of potatoes and made a meal of it.'

'Merseyside derbies usually last 90 minutes and I'm sure today's won't be any different.'

Alistair Burnett (News at Ten)
'And in the Cup Winners' Cup, Spurs will play either Eintracht or Frankfurt.'

Bryon Butler
'Fifty-two thousand people here at Maine Road tonight, but my goodness, it seems like fifty thousand.'

'And Wilkins sends an inch-perfect pass to no one in particular.'

David Coleman
'He's 31 this year; last year he was 30.'

'Kevin Reeves, who's just turned 22, proving that an ill wind blows nobody no good.'

'Manchester United are buzzing around the goalmouth like a lot of red bluebottles.'

'Both of the Aston Villa scorers – Withe and Mortimer – were born in Liverpool, as was the Villa manager Ron Saunders, who was born in Birkenhead.'

'The pace of the match is really accelerating, by which I mean it is getting faster all the time.'

Barry Davies
'Poland nil, England nil, though England are now looking better value for their nil.'

'Andy Cole – only his second goal of the season.' (Failed to mention he had been slightly hampered by two broken legs, and pneumonia, and had not, until this point, started a first-team game.)

Fred Dinenage
'The rest of the football team are very large . . . they dwarf above you.'

FA Spokesman
'The referee didn't change his mind. He merely amended his view.'

Judy Finnigan (TV Interviewer)
'So you went to the hospital with your alcoholism problem? That must have taken a lot of bottle.'

Gerry Francis
'Jurgen Klinsmann has taken to English football like a duck out of water.'

  'What I said to them at half-time would be unprintable on the radio.'

Paul Gascoigne
'I never predict anything, and I never will do.'

Alan Green
'It was the game that put the Everton ship back on the

road.'

Brian Greenhoff
'All the Leeds team are 100 per cent behind the manager, but I can't speak for the rest of the squad.'

Ron Greenwood
'Glen Hoddle hasn't been the Hoddle we know. Neither has Bryan Robson.'
   'Playing with wingers is more effective against European sides like Brazil than English sides like Wales.'

John Greig
'Celtic Manager, David Hay, still has a fresh pair of legs up his sleeve.'
   'The game is finely balanced with Celtic well on top.'

Tony Gubba
(After Matthew Le Tissier scored an eye-catching goal to equalize against Newcastle on 18 January 1997:) 'The goal of the century.'

(Trevor Brooking on *Match of the Day*, taking the mickey out of Gubba's extravagance, said of QPR's Trevor Sinclair's spectacular goal:) 'The goal of the millennium.'

. . . and

(Alan Hansen, going one stage further, said of Chris Waddle's goal for Bradford against Everton in the FA Cup-tie:) 'The best goal of all time.'

Reg Gutteridge
'The referee's done very well. He's let the fight flow as they say in football.'

Peter Jones
'Arsenal have plenty of time to dictate these last few seconds.'

Vinnie Jones
'Winning doesn't really matter as long as you win.'

Kevin Keegan
'I don't think there is anyone bigger or smaller than Maradona.'

Joe Kinnear
'We rode our luck, but that's what the goalposts are there for!' (29 January 1997 match *v* Manchester United.)

Lennie Lawrence
'Sunderland are suffering from *déja vu* – a case of "what will be, will be".'

Gordon Lee
'Even when you're dead, you must never allow yourself just to lie down and be buried.'

Alex MacDonald
'We ended up playing football and that's not our style.' (1991, after defeat by Aberdeen.)

Lawrie McMenemy
'The last player to score a hat trick in an FA Cup Final was Stan Mortensen. He even had a final named after him – "The Matthews Final".'

Ian McNail
'We actually got the winner with three minutes to go, but then they equalized.'

Archie Macpherson
'That's the kind he normally knocks in in his sleep – with his eyes closed.'

Brian Moore
'History is all about todays and not about yesterdays.'

'When you speak to Barry Fry, it's like a 1000-piece crossword.'

'Remember, postcards only, please. The winner will be the first one opened.'

'Rosenborg have won 66 games, and they've scored in all of them.'

'Mark Hughes, Sparky by name and sparky by nature, and the same can be said of Steve McMahon.'

'The European Cup is 17lbs of silver, and is worth its weight in gold.'

'And now the familiar sight of Liverpool lifting the

League Cup for the first time.'

Cliff Morgan
'Sadly, the immortal Jackie Milburn died today.'

Mike Morris
'Some of the fans come on to the pitch and shake the players on the back of the chest.'

John Motson
A further selection of Motty own goals . . .

'The World Cup – truly an international event.'

'Peter Reid is hobbling, and I've got a feeling that will slow him down.'

'For those of you watching in black and white, Spurs are in the all-yellow strip.'

'All the Brazilian supporters are wearing yellow shirts. It's a fabulous kaleidoscope of colour.'

'We're back to 1–1.'

Motty doesn't make many blunders, and his thoroughness is legendary. Who else would count the steps leading up to the Royal Box at Wembley so he could announce when Martin Buchan went to lift the FA Cup for Manchester United: 'How appropriate it is that a man called Buchan should be climbing 39 steps to pick up the Cup.'

'There are 11 men sitting on yellow cards, and that's a very uncomfortable position to be in.'

Phil Neal
'It's a case of putting all our eggs into the next 90 minutes.'

Alan Parry
'The ball was glued to his foot – all the way into the back

of the net.'

'With the last kick of the game, Bobby MacDonald scored a header.'

'2–0 is a cricket score in Italian football.'

Stuart Pearce
'His return gives England another key to its bow.'

David Pleat
'He's got two feet, has Zola.'

Bruce Rioch
'Long-term we are looking at a rebuilding situation.' (Famous last words – August, 1996. Bruce Rioch was sacked from Arsenal the next day!)

Andy Roxburgh
'Hagi is a brilliant player, but we're not getting psychedelic about him.'

Joe Royle
'Kanchelskis has not been right in the mind for us this season and it's time he moved on.'

John Sillett
'Venison and Butcher – they're as brave as two peas in a pod.'

Terry Venables
'If you can't stand the heat in the dressing room, get out of the kitchen.'

'If history is going to repeat itself, I should think we can expect the same thing again.'

'I felt a lump in my throat as the ball went in.'

Jimmy Hill: 'Don't sit on the fence, Terry. What chance do you think Germany has got of getting through?'
Terry Venables: 'I think it's 50–50.'

'It may have been going wide, but nevertheless it was a great shot on target.'

Chris Waddle
'My legs sort of disappeared from nowhere.'

David Webb
'He showed everyone the right attitude and was as game as a pebble.'

Elton Wellesby
'And now for the goals from Carrow Road, where the game ended 0–0.'

'Football today would certainly not be the same if it had not existed.'

Howard Wilkinson
'Once Tony Daley opens his legs, you've got a problem.'

Non-Footballing Commentators
Rex Alston (Cricket)
'Hundreds of small boys are playing with their balls.'

Anonymous (Golf)
'Arnold Palmer, usually a great putter, seems to be having trouble with his long putts. However, he has no trouble dropping his shorts.'

Anonymous (Wildlife)
'In winter, bullfinches are best fed on bacon rinds and great tits like coconuts.'

Anonymous (Yachting)
'Aristotle Onassis, the Greek shitting typoon . . .'

John Arlott (Cricket)
'Bill Frindall has done a bit of mental arithmetic with a calculator.'

Alec Bedser (Cricket)
'He's about a stone and a half overweight and has been told to get it off.' (Referring to England captain, Ian Botham.)

Winston Bennett (Rugby)
'I've never had major knee surgery on any other part of my body.'

Henry Blofeld (Cricket)
'Brian Toss won the close.'
  'And the score is half past four.'

Frank Bruno
'I was 18 about six years ago – I'm 28 now.'
  'My mum said I used to fight my way out of the cot. I can't remember. That was before my time.'

Harry Carpenter (Boxing)
'He looks up at him through his blood smeared lips.'
      Harry: 'Well Frank, after that defeat by Mike Tyson, have you got a message for your British fans?'
      Frank: 'Well, you know what I mean Harry – I gave it my best shot, but that's cricket, in'it?'
  (Boat Race 1977) . . .
  'Ah! Isn't that nice, the wife of the Cambridge president is kissing the cox of the Oxford crew.'

David Coleman (Athletics)

'Moses Kiptanui – the 19-year-old Kenyan who turned 20 a few weeks ago.'

'It's a great advantage to be able to hurdle with both legs.'

'They came through absolutely together. . . . with Allan Wells in first place.'

'He won the bronze medal in the 1976 Olympics, so he is used to being out in front.'

'There's going to be a real ding-dong when the bell goes.'

'There is Brendan Foster, by himself, with 20,000 people.'

'The pacemaker shook everyone by staying in front and finishing third.'

Tony Cozier (Cricket)

'The Queen's Park Oval, exactly as its name suggests – absolutely round.'

Frank Crawford (Boxing)

'The dumbest question I was ever asked by a sportswriter was whether I hit harder with red or white gloves. As a matter of fact, I hit harder with red.'

Jay 'Dizzy' Dean (Baseball)

'There is a commotion in the stands – I think it has something to do with a fat lady . . . I've just been informed that the fat lady is the Queen of Holland.'

Mickey Duff (Boxing)

'I only hope people will come along in peace and enjoy a good fight.'

Farokh Engineer (Cricket)
'There must be something on Gooch's mind, and he wants to get it off his chest.'

Chris Eubank (Boxing)
  Question: 'Are you going to write your autobiography?'
  Chris Eubank: 'On what?'

Major Ronald Ferguson (Polo)
'Swearing at the Polo club? It's a load of bollocks.'

John Francombe (Racing)
'He must have discovered euthanasia. He never seems to get any older.'

Ray French (Rugby)
'It's Great Britain in the all-white strip with the red and blue V, the dark shorts and the dark stockings.'
  'Shaun Edwards has happy memories of Wembley. On his last appearance here he received a fractured cheek.'
  'And there's Kevin Ward raising his crutch to the fans.'

Tony Greig (Cricket)
'Well, the day began this morning . . .'

Bryan Johnston (Cricket)
'There's Neil Harvey at leg slip with his legs wide apart, waiting for a tickle.'
  'Henry Horton's got a funny sort of stance. It looks as if he's shitting on a sooting stick.'
  'Play has ended here at Southampton, but they play until seven at Edgbaston, so over there now for some more balls from Rex Alston.'

'. . . the batsman's Holding, the bowler's Willey.'

Ted Lowe (Snooker)
'And that's the third time this session he's missed his waistcoat pocket with the chalk.'

Bill McClaren (Rugby)
'You can almost hear the crowd's audible sigh of relief.'

Christopher Martin-Jenkins (Cricket)
'It is extremely cold here. The England fielders are keeping their hands in their pockets between balls.'

Dan Maskell (Tennis)
'The British boys are adopting the attacking position – Cox up at the net.'

Alan Minter (Boxing)
'Sure there have been injuries and deaths in boxing, but none of them serious.'

Julia Morley (Miss World Organizer)
'Miss World is still popular even though it has its fair share of knockers.'

Alex Murphy (Rugby League)
'The conditions were very hot. I asked one of the lads after the match how he felt. I won't repeat what he said but it begins with "N".'

Greg Norman (Golf)
'I owe a lot to my parents, especially my mum and dad.'

Oxford Union President
'Cox are Cox no matter what sex they are.'

Alan Parry (Athletics)
'Zola Budd, so small, so waif-like, you literally cannot see her – but there she is.'

Ron Pickering (Athletics)
'The French are not normally a Nordic skiing nation.'

Chris Rea (Rugby)
'Ferguson is a Fijian, a native of Fiji . . . he's from Tonga, actually.'

Brough Scott (Racing)
'And there's the unmistakeable figure of Joe Mercer . . . or is it Lester Piggott?'

Jo Sheldon (Cricket)
'A brain scan has revealed Andrew Caddick is not suffering from a stress fracture of the shin.'

Marlon Starling (Boxing)
'I'll fight Lloyd Honeyghan for nothing if the price is right.'

Fred Truman (Cricket)
'One day Yorkshire cricket will arise like a Spartacus from the Ashes.'

   'We didn't have any metaphors in my day. We didn't beat about the bush.'

Murray Walker (Motor racing)
'And now the boot is on the other Schumacher.'

'The lead car is absolutely unique, except for the one behind it, which is identical.'

'Either the car is stationary or it's on the move.'

'Two laps to go then the action will begin, unless this is the action, which it is.'

'Just under ten seconds for Nigel Mansell, call it nine point five in round figures.'

'You can't see a digital clock because there isn't one.'

'Here's Giacomelli driving like the veteran that he isn't.'

'Do my eyes deceive me, or is Senna's car sounding a bit rough?'

Julian Wilson (Horse racing)
'There's been an effing copedemic.'

Written Gaffes
'There's an unmentionable four-letter word in Northern Ireland's World Cup vocabulary at the moment ... defeat.' (*Daily Mirror.*)

'COLMAN-BALLS – The engagement is announced between TIMOTHY, son of Mr and Mrs B. P. Colman, of 40 Fakenham Road, Drayton, and MARIE, daughter of Mr and Mrs R. E. Balls, of 122, West End, Old Costessey – Love from both families.' (*Eastern Evening News.*)

'Bury 2, West Ham United 2
When the First Division leaders meet a Fourth Division team, even quite a good one, they are expected to win. West Ham duly did so last night.' (*The Times.*)

'Impressive display by Germans
by Cyril Chapman
Aston Villa 0, Southampton 1'
(*Grauniad.*)

'Town boss, John Maggs, had big defender, Tommy Warrilow, back in the heart of defence following a groin injury, but was missing striker, Frank Ovard, out with a badly bruised rectum.' (*Crawley News.*)

'During his time there, he grabbed FA Cup and UEFA Cup Glory. Another possible candidate for the job is Midlands man, Don Howe, the former Arse-' (*Sun.*)

'Sutton United Supporters' FC, who play in the Morden and District League, require players for all positions to strengthen the tea this season.' (*Sutton and Cheam Herald.*)

'Three players on the moon', on Teletext, should have read: 'Three players on the move.'

The game between Chadderton of the NW Counties League and Glossop had to be abandoned when it was eventually discovered someone had nicked the nine halogen lamps from the floodlights. What made it more embarrassing was that it was a Floodlit Trophy Tie!

Teams and players have their own way of celebrating a goal, ranging from the waddling of the Aylesbury (ducks) team to the abuse of a corner flag by Lee Sharpe. In Serie A, when Botafogo of Tulio scored the first of his two goals against Fluminense in their 2 – 1 win, he ran to a public telephone behind the goal and pretended to make a call.

A television listing pointed out by the Stockport fanzine,

The Tea Party:

> '4.45 Bad Influence!
> Ryan Giggs' Soccer Skills.'

'Seventeen football supporters, ten English and seven German, were arrested and a policeman was injured in Dusseldorf last night before West Germany beat England 3–1. Mr Colin Moynihan, Minister for Sport, said he was delighted with the way it had gone.' (*The Times.*)

'A minute's silence for the deceased Honorary President of FIFA, Sir Stanley Rous. Shot against the post by Maradona (57 mins).' (*FIFA News* match report.)

'The match was unfinished owing to measles. Graghurst was compelled to scratch.' (*The Harrovian.*)

'"Get on with it!" shouted the crowd, as halfback James paused with his foot on the ball. He did, and it produced a goat.' (Sports news in a Sunday paper.)

'The kickoff is at 3.15, and the teams will be found elsewhere.' *(Cambridge Daily News.*)

'Bonner looked over his shoulder to see the ball skimming through his legs.'

'Bonner, winning his 72nd cap, equalling Liam Brady's record, was unemployed at the other end.'

'Wales and their manager, Mike Smith, were considering their futures on the 27,000-mile retreat from Tbilisi last night.'

'Swindon's manager, John Gorman, yesterday called off his quest for the unsettled West Ham winer Joey Beauchamp.'

'Sent off: Wayne Biggins (Stoke) 54 min. Descent.'

'They are 11 pints off the lead, but if Arsenal can
start putting results like this together . . .'

'Gascoigne received an early booking for dissent, only
three days after his off-pitch alteration.'

'Celtic supporters woke up today believing they are
about to witness the end of an error.'

'Le Tissier revealed how, as schoolboys in the Channel
Isles, he had many a dual with Graeme Le Saux.'

'According to Scottish sources, Rangers have
brought some sophistication to their play this
season. Players just used to boot the ball straight up
to Hateley. Now they pass it to Laudrup who boots
it up to Hateley.'

'A 60-year-old grandmother has been banned from
attending any more soccer matches at her town ground.
Mrs Alice V—, of Stourbridge, Worcs., has been accused
of "ungentlemanly conduct" by the committee of the
Southern League club after an incident at the end of their
home game with Weymouth. The club has been ordered
to appear before an FA disciplinary commission to
answer a charge of crowd misconduct. During a scuffle,
Graham Williams, formerly West Bromwich Albion and
Wales, now player-manager of Weymouth, was punched
in the mouth and a linesman was struck with a rattle. Mrs
V—, whose son has also been barred from the ground,
claimed yesterday that the ban was unfair. She said she
had shouted at Williams during the game when he
charged the Stourbridge goalkeeper. "He waved two fingers at me." ' (*Daily Telegraph.*)

'England soccer captain Bryan Robson was banned

from driving for three years after admitting a drink-driving offence. "He was standing by his car which had run out of petrol and Mr Robson smelled strongly of petrol. It seemed he had been drinking."' (*Yorkshire Post.*)

'Brentford Reserves were involved in a nine-goal thriller when they beat Orient 4–3 on Wednesday.' (*Ealing Gazette.*)

'High as the goal bar this effort came skimming along, with every eye of the vast throng watching its progress on tiptoe.' (*Glasgow News.*)

'Time and again the Scots found space down the left. Hughes was not a great deal more reassuring, his lack of a left foot again being apparent.' (*Sunday Times.*)

'Palace are hoping Milligan will be fat enough to play.' (*Croydon Advertiser.*)

'Three fine goals from Frank Watts was indeed a tonic in this rain-lashed match, and his rat-trick had manager Jimmy Garson beaming at the finish.' (*Sunday Express.*)

'In an Everton attack, Royle was injured and lay writing in the centre of the field.' (Middlesex newspaper.)

(Joe, incidentally, was nicknamed 'Cadbury' by his manager at Everton, Harry Catterick: 'after my favourite soft-centred chocolate'.)

'A fixture that has brought nothing but defeat since 1949 was won at last by the shooting of two Football League forwards.' (*Daily Mail.*)

'John Harkes going to Sheffield, Wednesday.' (*New York Post.*)

'When Bingham announces his team at noon today

he will almost certainly name either John McClelland or Sammy McIlroy as captain . . . There is less doubt that Pat Jennings will appear in gaol yet again.' (*Grauniad.*)

'God, who was transferred from Manchester City to Rotherham on the same day that Doyle moved, was also dismissed in his second match in new colours.' (*Scottish Daily Record.*)

'After the Hungarian uprising of 1956, Kocsis moved Switzerland and layed for Young Fellows. Subsequently, he signed for Barcelona.' (*Daily Telegraph.*)

'Dead-eye, Stewart Fraser, who got three against the League of Ireland recently, attempted a shit from 20 yards, but was so wide of the target that he actually found Carlyle with his attempt. The outside right was so surprised at the "pass" that he made a mess of his shot at goal.' (*People.*)

'Shearer picked his spot.' (*Sunday Sun.*)

(Sofia, Bulgaria, Tuesday) 'It remains to be seen whether Chelsea can make as much impact here with their football as they have done with their fashion. They have already brightened the grey countenance of this Balkan city with a tapestry of colourful ties and skirts.' (*Yorkshire Evening Post.*)

'Borussia Munchengladbach 5, Borussia Dortmund 1. That's Munchengladbach won the Borussia derby then!' (Gary Newton, Taek Radio – the two teams are located 80 miles apart.)

'The high point of the afternoon came when Les Ferdinand scored with an absolutely beautiful goat.' (*Newcastle Evening Chronicle.*)

'Keane, who has 12 months left on his current deal, will have talks straight after today's Final on a mega-improved contract. It's expected that he will be offered £15,000 a year in wages to make him the club's highest-paid player ahead of Cantona and Ryan Giggs.' (*Mirror.*)

'And that's a priceless goal worth millions of pounds.' (Alan Parry describing the winning goal in the European Cup Final.)

From the programme of a Premier League side: 'Correction – In our continued efforts to ensure safety and good order, Miss — has been appointed as General Supervisor of AREA SIX and not (as was stated in last week's programme) of AREA SEX.'

At a Lancashire football ground undergoing structural changes: 'We would like to apologize for the improvements we are making.'

When Ossie Ardiles came to Britain, he was required by the DHSS to complete the necessary forms. It is reported that answer to the question: 'Length of residence in the United Kingdom?' He wrote: 'Approximately 26 feet.'

On the subject of bureaucracy, the annual FA Information Reply form asks: 'Total number of staff (Broken down by Sex)': To which Arsenal might have replied: 'Drink and drugs appear to be a bigger problem!'

From a changing-room at a club in the Wirral: 'These hooks are for players only.' Underneath someone had added: 'They may also be used for coats and trousers.'

From St Mary's Old Boys' football section of the school magazine: 'Old St Mary's players are requested to complete the form and return it as soon as possible. News of old players who have died will be particularly welcomed.'

Placard held by two teenage lads hitch-hiking on the A1 near Scotch Corner on a Saturday morning: 'Anywhere but Wimbledon.'

Sign next to the Sports Injury department at a London Hospital:

CAUTION !
GUARD DOGS OPERATING

Sign on a stall in a London street market:
Coloured football shirts.
Guaranteed not to run.

Notice in the staff canteen at a Coventry factory:
The football club meets for instruction and practice in the games room every Tuesday at 7.00 p.m. New

blood always welcome.'

Notice outside Glasgow Video theatre:
> Grand Double Horror Bill Tonight:
> JAWS 2 and England *v* Switzerland, Soccer

Notice in football club snack bar:
> **ASSISTANT REQUIRED**
> (No Objection to Sex)

Notice in football club bar:
> THE LOWENBRAU LABELLED BOTTLES IN THIS BAR HAVE ALL BEEN TASTED AND PASSED BY A PANEL OF GERMAN BEER EXPERTS

Sign at garage/petrol station near Roker Park, Sunderland:
> **TOILETS**
> Quadruple stamps on four gallons or over

In Barnsley supporters' club:
> HAPPY HOUR, 6.30 p.m. UNTIL 7.00 p.m.

At the Victoria ground:
> TRY OUR HOME-MADE PIES.
> YOU'LL NEVER GET BETTER.

At another supporters' club:
> GOOD CLEAN ENTERTAINMENT,
> EVERY NIGHT EXCEPT THURSDAY.

A lawyer tells of a form he once received from a professional footballer which included the question: 'Are you a natural born British subject?' His client had replied: 'No – by Caesarean section.'

'Samuel Bagshaw, aged 73, of The Dimple, Matlock, a sportsman, was buried yesterday with a double six domino clasped in his hand. Bagshaw once played football against a circus elephant and won a silver cup.' (*Daily Dispatch.*)

Did you know that football fanatic, Rod Stewart, has his own private football pitch on which he holds matches which often include professionals such as Dean Holdsworth of Wimbledon? He is always captain and is never substituted!

Malcolm Allison, former manager of Manchester City and itinerant manager to many others, was sacked in February 1996 from the southern section of Century Radio as match pundit. The commentary programme has the local reputation of being lively but biased in favour of Middlesbrough, and makes no apologies for it. Commentator and anchorman, Alistair Brown, invites phone calls, then bombs out anyone offering any baseless criticism of the 'Boro team. Big Mal exclaimed: 'F***ing hell!' when goal-keeper Gary Walsh let in a weak shot from Les Ferdinand and was given his marching orders. But how's this for a bit of enterprise? A couple of days later he was on Century Radio again, but this time advertising bathroom fitments. He began the advert with: 'I may have been sent for an early bath but . . .' Malcolm was forgiven and once again installed as the resident expert at the start of the 1996-97 season, only to blot his copybook again on 28 December. 'Boro were beaten 3–0 at Highfield Road by Coventry and after the second goal Malcolm once more used the 'F' word in frustration at the team's performance – an early bath and red card. (*Sine die*?) A manager on Radio Cleveland also made a 'cock-up' in one sports programme:

'Yes, we've had a lot of injuries this week. But some of the players are going to have to turn out. Stevie's had a groin injury, but he's going to play and we'll see if it stands up.'

BBC Radio announcement for travelling fans:
'There will be widespread fist and mog.'
And . . .
'More about that delay on British Rail Southern Region. We have our reporter on the line . . .'

In the bitterly cold weather of 10 February 1996, Macclesfield took off Power and put on Coates!

And then there are the groups which might sponsor the most suitable team:

Arsenal: The Temptations/The Mindbenders/Exploited/Addicts
Birmingham City (under Barry Fry): Pickettywitch
Blackburn: Flash and the Pan/The Walker Brothers
Blackpool: The Beach Boys
Chelsea: Stylistics
Chester: Four Pennies
The Columbian Team: Scorpions
Coventry: Wing and a Prayer
Leeds: Consortium
Manchester United: Status Quo/The Supremes
Middlesbrough: New Seekers
Newcastle: Enigma/The Heartbreakers/The Pretenders
Plymouth: Johnny Kidd and the Pirates
QPR: Cockney Rejects

Southampton: The Drifters
The Spanish Team: Los Bravos
Spurs: Gerry and the Pacemakers
West Ham: Motorhead/The Aliens/Foreign Choice
Wimbledon: The Animals/Iron Maiden/Wombles/
Break Machine

The same can be done by suggesting which product would
be best suited to the team:

Chelsea: Liquorice All-Sorts
West Ham: 'Heinz 57' Varieties
Manchester United: Top Man
Newcastle: Platignum Gold/7-UP
Nottingham Forest: Nestlé 'Cheerios'
Southampton: Turkish Delight
Wimbledon: Quaker 'Oat Crunchies'
Middlesbrough: Brazilian Airways

And some suggested Christmas presents for a selection of
footballing personalities:

A Robin Reliant for **David Ginola** because he can't get
past anyone/Swimming hat for his diving

A boxing manual for **George Graham** to avoid back-
handers

Two £5 notes for Blackburn because they are also useless in Europe

Some gunpowder for **The Gunners' directors** – to maintain their firing power

A copy of *How To Make Friends And Influence People*
for **Ken Bates** at Chelsea

The following headline and story appeared in the
Middlesbrough Evening Gazette in 1996:

ROBBO PUT OUT TO PASTURE

'Robbo has been forced to quit, it was dramatically revealed today. Trainers say that, although Robbo is still physically fit, he is no longer able to complete a full day's work.'

It turned out, in fact, that the story concerned a 19-year-old Cleveland Police horse.

And which popular songs might suit some teams and personalities? . . .

Alan Ball: Adios Amigo (Jim Reeves)

George Best: Bermuda Triangle (Barry Manilow)

John Burridge: Happy Wanderer (Oberkirchen Choir)

Eric Cantona: 'The Seagull's Name was Nelson' (P. E. Bennett); 'Feet Up' (Guy Mitchell); 'I've Been a Bad, Bad Boy' (Paul Jones); 'One More Chance' (Diana Ross)

'Razor' Ruddick: 'Sixteen Tons' (Frankie Laine)

England Players (in Hong Kong): 'One Drink Too Many' (Sailor)

Alex Ferguson: 'Paranoid' (Black Sabbath)

Duncan Ferguson: 'Hit and Run' (Girlschool)

Barry Fry: 'Ain't Got a Clue' (Lurkers)

Gazza: 'Life on Mars' (David Bowie); 'Baby Stop Crying' (Bob Dylan); 'Big Girls Don't Cry' (Four Seasons); 'The Crying Game' (Dave Berry)

Gazza/Vinnie Jones: 'Great Balls of Fire' (Jerry Lee Lewis); 'Handy Man' (Jimmy Jones)

David Ginola: 'All Fall Down' (Lindisfarne)

George Graham: 'Questions I Can't Answer' (Heinz)

Sir John Hall: 'Big Spender' (Shirley Bassey)

Oyvind Leonardsen: 'Goodbye, Sam' (Cliff Richard)

John Holmes (Agent): 'Gonna Make You a Star' (David Essex)

Kevin Keegan: 'As Long as the Price is Right' (Dr Feelgood); 'Attack' (Exploited)

Gary Lineker: 'Goody Two Shoes' (Adam and the Ants)

Gary Lineker, Vinnie Jones, and **Peter Beardsley:** 'The Good, The Bad and The Ugly' (Hugo Montenegro)

Son of Manchester City Supporter: 'Don't Jump Off the Roof, Dad' (Tommy Cooper)

T. Maxwell (Billingham Town Chairman): 'If I Were a Rich Man' (Topol)

Newcastle's Defence: 'Get Back' (Beatles)

A. Shearer (at Blackburn): 'Tired of Being Alone' (Al Green); 'Bend It' (Dave Dee, Dozy, Beaky, Mick and Tich); 'Going Back to my Roots' (Odyssey)

Neville Southall: 'My Old Man's a Dustman' (Lonnie Donegan)

Gareth Southgate: 'Hit and Miss' (John Barry)

Garry Sprake: 'Butter Fingers' (Tommy Steele); 'Careless Hands' (Des O'Connor)

Mickey Thomas: 'They're Coming to Take Me Away, Ha Ha!' (Napoleon XIV)

Jack Walker: 'The House That Jack Built' (Tracie)

Wimbledon: 'Bad Boys' (Wham); 'Beer Drinkers and Hell Raisers' (Motorhead); 'The Crunch' (Rah Band)

X, Y and Z on Cathay Pacific: 'Smash It Up' (Damned)

In August 1992, *World Soccer Magazine*'s monthly quiz received for the very first time an entry with *all* 20 questions incorrect. The decision was made to send a winner's prize of a tee shirt and a free annual subscription to the loser in his home in Ireland.

An annual five-a-side competition at Leicester, on 15 January 1994, involved 240 players, every one of them called 'Patel'. It makes you wonder how 'quite remarkable' David Coleman would have managed to commentate on that one.

An Irish football club secretary entrusted his wife with the job of getting a presentation tankard engraved. The inscription read: 'To Mr M. P. Clark in appreciation for the Whitsun 1974 tour', and this duly appeared on the tankard's side. Unfortunately, as the words had been written out on a shopping list, the engraving went on: 'One bottle of shoe cleaner and a pair of white laces.' (*World Medicine.*)

Headline in the *Middlesbrough Evening Gazette* in May 1996, when there was intense speculation that Ian Rush would sign for the 'Boro . . .
'RUSH FOR THE RIVERSIDE'
It was, in fact, a story saying that, because the Brazilian, Emerson, had been signed, there was a great demand for tickets for the 1996-97 season. Ian Rush, of course, ended up at Leeds.

But It Also Happens in Other Sports . . .

'Thoroughbred filly, two years old, for sale, by Shit in the Corner out of Lady Dromara, approximately 15.2 years old.' (*Dumfries & Galloway Standard.*)

'Another heavily-backed horse was Church Parade, owned by the Queen. But housewives who rushed to back the horse with the royal wedding in mind to see Church Parade finish were disappointed. The Queen was at the course well back in fifth place.' (*Daily Mail.*)

'I'm looking for a kind home for my 15.1 heavyweight

Cob Gelding, he's quiet in every way, but gay, £700 ono.
– Exeter.' (*Western Morning News.*)

    'Queen Elizabeth walked one block to King's
Saddlery, where she spent over 45 minutes, bought a
belt, a pair of gloves and some raiding equipment.'
(*Trinidad Guardian.*)

'M. James, Cheltenham: "I'm surprised the stewards did
not reprimand Christy Roche and Pat Eddery for excessive use of the ship during the Derby. It made me feel sick
for the poor horses."' (*Daily Mirror.*)

    'Kit Patterson, Carlisle's clerk of the course, says:
"The prospects for racing are very remote. There is
snot and frost on the course and we will hold an
inspection at noon tomorrow."' (*Herald Express.*)

'Bill does it again
on Miss Tweedie'
(*Racing*): Denis Foley

'Lady Roborough
fancies pigeons'
(*Western Morning News.*)

MINISTER SEES THE CESAREWITCH – PUTS
NOTHING ON
(South London newspaper.)

'Amazing luck in the Irish Sweep fell to a Kentish man
who drew two tickets and a Sussex woman.' (*Yorkshire
Post.*)

    'A motor horsebox carrying a live horse can travel at 30
mph. If the horse dies in transit the vehicle immediately
becomes a carrier of horseflesh and by law must reduce
speed to 20mph.' (*Daily Mail.*)

'Explore France on a horse!
Village Gits
Self Catering or Full Board'
(*Horse & Pony.*)

'Willie Carson, riding his 180th winner of the season, spent the last two furlongs looking over one shoulder, then another, even between his legs, but there was nothing there to worry him.' (*Sporting Life.*)

'Good horse, complete with saddle and bridle, 6 volt battery, pistons, connecting rods, etc.' (Advert in the *Nigerian Times.*)

His Lordship: I suppose the word 'horse' in the rule does not include an aeroplane?
Counsel: No, I think not.
His Lordship: It ought to – it is much the same thing.
Counsel: I think that it was put in for the relief of the archdeacon. (*The Times* – Law Report.)

'Glider Crash – ASPATRIA: Hang glider, Gordon Rigg, ended up in hospital this week with an arm injury after crashing during a flight from Great Cockup Fell, Skiddaw.' (*Cumberland News.*)

'LIES! LIES! LIES! – Pages 4 and 5' (*Sun.*)

'Our women lick male sportsmen' (*Sportsweek.*)
(Advert): 'Your own LOG SAUNA for as little as £220 plus erection.'
'Golf, tennis, bowls, riding, sailing, fishing, indoor amusements and night porter completes the ideal holiday.' (Advert in St Ives guide book.)
'It is possible to dry angleworms until they are only

46 per cent water, and still revive them, but they die if they become only one-fifth of 1 per cent drier than 46 per cent.' (*Binghampton (NY) Press.*)

'Sir, When I was a judo instructor I always used to ask trainees to stand on their heads at the first interview. Those who swayed towards the left ear were nearly always women, and those who swayed towards the right ear, nearly always men. The test was 99 per cent infallible. Yours etc.' (Letter in *Observer.*)

'Personal: Nabil, come home, your mother forgives you, and your brother is going to be president of the Badminton Club – Your fiancée, Tu-Tu.' (Advert in *Outlook* (American University of Beirut).)

'Chelsea College of Physical Education in Eastbourne is recovering with eight broken ribs in a clinic at Sierre in the Rhone Valley.' (*Evening Standard.*)

'If you bought our course: '*How to fly solo in six easy lessons*', we apologize for any inconvenience caused by our failure to include the last chapter, titled: 'How to land your plane safely'. Send us your name and address, and we will send it to you post-haste.' (Advert in *World Magazine.*)

Headline: 'MAN SHOT BY DOG' (Hunting dog trod on gun, shooting his Japanese owner in the stomach.)

'MAN SAVAGED BY HERD OF COWS'
(Bob Floyd, walking with his dog through a field of cows near Banbury, was attacked by the cows, and had his ear bitten off. He had to have it replaced by micro-surgery.)

'Mlle Veronica, holder of the world's high kick record of 5,121 kicks in 2 hours 22 minutes, hopes to beat this figure this afternoon on the roof of a North End department store . . . Veronica will be accompanied by Giovanni, the world celebrated pickpocket.' (*Croydon Advertiser.*)

'New York ban on boxing after death.' (*The Times.*)

'It was a sort of David and Goliath battle, in which the stronger and bigger man always appeared to hold the mastery.' (Scottish newspaper.)

'But Foster showed he has a magnificent left jab as well, and several times all 79 inches of his lean left arm slammed into Finnegan's face.' (*Sun.*)

'John Wright hit 55 off 44 balls, but New Zealand failed by 5 runs to overhaul Pakistan's total of 157 for 5 in 20 years.' (*Grauniad.*)

'India was without Kapil Dev, because of a bruised finger, a legacy of the first Test, and England omitted Chris Cowdrey and fielded three spacemen.' (*Brighton Evening Argus.*)

'This does not detract from the achievements of the charging Northants' bowler, whose balls came off the pitches so fast batsmen were hustled into errors.'

'The last wicket fell just before lunchtime. After the interval a very pleasing improvement in the dimensions of the spectators was to be seen.' (*East Anglian Daily Times.*)

'How England must wish that Statham were just a little younger! Even at three, however, his consistent accuracy is without equal, and he sets a magnificent example to the younger men under his command.' (*Grauniad.*)

'Carr was given out leg before, as he appeared likely to make a good score.' (Report of village cricket match.)

'Here's Miller running in to bowl. He's got two short legs and one behind.' (BBC Commentator.)

'Greg Norman, hot favourite for the Card Classic at Royal Porthcawl, missed a five-inch putt on the 11th green yesterday. The blind Australian tried to tap in the tiddler one-handed but hit the ground with his putter and only just moved the ball.' (*Sporting Life.*)

'Not even my colleague, Captain Heath, with Professor Einstein and Dr Gallup to assist him, could work out the odds against that astonishing coincidence on the Worthing golf course on Sunday morning when two brothers killed two seagulls with two balls during the same round.' (*News Chronicle.*)

From a West Country golf club bulletin: 'As in previous years the evening concluded with a toast to the new president in champagne provided by the retiring president, drunk as usual at midnight.'

'CYCLING HOLIDAYS: Shakespeare country/ Cotswolds. Great accom., everything supplied. Penny Farting, 4 E— Rd., Warwick. Telephone—' (*Observer.*)

'MILK RACE: It's a strong strategic base for next week's operation, but unfortunately Bayton, who would have been Edward's natural deputy, is still suffering from his fall. He finished at New Brighton with the bunch, but his back still pains, and he felt every bum in the road.' (*Observer.*)

'FALL OFFER – BICYCLE SALE
SYKKEL o O Huset
Lokkev. 33 – tif. 53 38 68'
(*Saga Weekly* – Norway's News in English.)

'Pretty And Fit Cyclist – Seeking male Jewish partner, 35–45, to travel highways of life making titstops for marriage and kids. Will take all cultural, intellectual and recreational detours. 9702' (New York magazine.)

'Gent's three-speed bicycle, also two ladies for sale, in good running order.' (Lancashire newspaper.)

'As the four finalists hit the last bend, he produced an electrifying bust which swept him past his opponents into the home straight to breast the tape.' (*Carmarthen Journal.*)

'As an old age pensioner, I wish to draw the attention of elderly readers to the dangers of the tricycle. The other day I stepped off my doorstep, and two racing tricyclists came hurtling upon me. But for my startled cry of horror I am sure I would have been knocked to the ground. Recently I have seen children riding tricycles crawl behind old ladies, and deliberately batter their calves. The hurt cries of the victims have caused fiendish chuckles from the children.' (Letter in the *Manchester Evening News.*)

'During the past few days three bicycles have been stolen from Exeter streets. The police consider that a bicycle thief is at work.' (*Western Morning News.*)

'STAND-IN: Former England Rugby skipper, Steve Smith, replaces the injured Nigel Melville as scum half.' (*Daily Mirror.*)

'Michael M—, who toured with the All Blacks, at the match on Saturday last, kicked three gals in succession.' (New Zealand newspaper.)

'There were no failures in the Scots line-up. The forwards fought for every ball and rampaged in the loo.' (*Evening Citizen*, Glasgow.)

'The Transvaal team for the match against the Western Province today will not, it is stated, be chosen until tomorrow morning.' (*Rand Daily Mail.*)

INJURY FORCES
MISS TRUMAN
TO SCRATCH

'Deryk stood watching her, his hands in his pockets, a splendid specimen of English manhood in his white flannels, his tennis racket in his strong brown hands.' (Story in Church newspaper.)

> 'In the women's singles semi-finals of the Victorian lawn tennis championships, Miss Turner, playing her usual baseball game, confused Miss Casals.' (Birmingham *Evening Mail and Despatch.*)

Tennis commentator: 'Well there it is then, Steffi Graf has won yet again in straight sex.'

'Mary's two boobs sink Britain'

'Mary Rand, the golden girl of the Tokyo Olympics, yesterday dropped the biggest clanger in British Athletics – a relay baton that knocked Britain out of the new European Cup competition in Fontainbleau . . .' (*Sun.*)

> 'The flame will burn for 16 days and nights until the closing ceremony on 8 December. It is fed by cylinders of profane gas.' (*Bristol Evening News.*)

'Tynedale Council, which was organizing the event, advised that the river was "unsuitable" for bathing due to bacteria including food poisoning orgasms, in the water.' (*Newcastle Journal.*)

> Irish Sportswriter, Peter Byrne, reporting once on his country's achievement in one day in swimming, wrote: 'Ireland triumphed in the Olympic pool yesterday. Nobody drowned.'

'She used an ordinary casting rod and light tickle.' (*Freeport (Illinois) News.*)

'FOR SALE, motorbike, suit 34 bust' (Advert in local paper.)

'Lots of orange juice and lots of sex – it's important to have plenty of calcium and relaxation.' (Jim Courier's explanation for his return to form.)

> 'I would have loved it sometimes if an umpire or linesman had just said: "Look, p*** off, you little s***."' (John McEnroe.)

'Jonah Lomu? Joanna Lumley more like.' (Damien Hopley, when asked if he was England's Mr Lomu.)

> 'I'm not interested in him because he's got nothing I want, except a Harley-Davidson motorbike.' (Benn scorns Chris Eubank.)

A successful move is reported from Pennsylvania to get motorists to slow down on a stretch of road there. Three words on a newly-erected sign have done the trick: 'Caution – Nudists Crossing'.

'Even the stubble on his chin hurts you.' (Glen McCrory on Mike Tyson.)

8
You've Got To Laugh

A Geordie was down at the front of the ground at Newcastle when the bottles and cans began to fly. He couldn't concentrate on the match and kept looking over his shoulder. Somebody near him said: 'Look mate, don't worry. It's like the war – if there's one with your name on it . . .' 'That's the trouble', he said, 'I'm called McEwan!'

McDermott, a Rangers supporter, knew he was in a Celtic pub, but when he had drink in him he became very aggressive. 'Down with the Pope!' he yelled for his third toast. Mick O'Neill stepped up and drilled him into the floor. When he came round, his mates said to him: 'You silly man – you must have known O'Neill was a Catholic.' 'I did,' said McDermott. 'But why didn't you tell me the Pope was?'

Talking about the religious and football rivalry which pervades Glasgow, there is the tale of the Orange branch of the Masons having a football match against the exclusive and private Catholic club of the Catenians. Apparently they had to abandon the game at half-time because neither would tell the other the score.

It took a long time, but the manager eventually did develop an attachment for the chairman – it fitted over his mouth.

'I have always tried to pay the transfer fees to the other clubs with a smile,' said the chairman, 'but invariably they want money.'

Then there was the footballer who was a very competent golfer and went to the professional for some lessons. 'What's your handicap?' asked the pro. 'Seven,' he replied. 'Right,' said the pro. 'Will you go over there and drive a few balls?' The man did so. 'What did you say you played off?' asked the pro. 'Seven,' said the man. 'Well,' said the pro. 'You must be a f****** good putter.'

'The only hole in one he's ever had has been in his socks!'

Question: 'What has four legs and flies?'
Answer: 'A dead horse!'

'I can't understand it,' said the footballer. 'The wife asks for £100 every Monday, and then she says she needs another £100 on Tuesday – and exactly the same on Wednesday. Every week's the same.' 'What, in Heaven's name, does she do with all that money?' asked his mate. 'I don't know, do I? – I never give her any!'

It was explained to Billy at the ground that seats were £20, £15 and £10 and that programmes were £2. 'OK' said Billy. 'I'll sit on a programme.'

On the bus going to the Aston Villa-Coventry derby, a Villa fan decked out in maroon and blue was sitting with a large duck under his arm. Straight opposite him was a Coventry fan resplendent in blue. 'They won't let you

take a donkey into the ground you know,' he said loudly.
'It's not a donkey, it's a duck you divi,' said the Villa fan.
'I wasn't talking to you,' said the other, 'I was talking to
the duck.'

> The gateman went up to the ticket distributor at a
> big match and said: 'There's a bloke outside who
> says he's the ref's father and has lost the ticket he
> gave him. What should I do?' 'Tell him to p*** off –
> I know this ref, and he doesn't have a father.'

There was the bald prima donna superstar who was asked
whether he had ever considered a transplant and replied:
'Don't be silly, I'd look ridiculous running round the
pitch with a kidney on top of my head!'

> A man took his collie into the pub on Saturday after-
> noon and was having a quiet drink until the scores
> came on the telly. When it was announced that his
> team was beaten, the dog went berserk, knocking
> over tables and snapping at customers. 'What's the
> matter with your dog?' demanded the landlord. 'Oh,
> he's always like that when our team get beat,'
> explained the owner. 'Bloody hell, what does he do
> when they win?' 'Don't know,' replied the owner.
> 'I've only been supporting Middlesbrough six
> months.'

A bloke went into a pub with his dog to watch the match
on Sky. Every time his team got a goal, the dog used to get
up on its hind legs and clap its paws together. 'That's
great,' said the landlord, 'but what does he do if the
others score a goal?' 'Somersaults,' replied the owner.
'How many?' asked the landlord. 'It depends how hard I
kick him up his a***.'

It is said that Norman Hunter was always hard, even

as a young lad. His mother recalls him coming home
from a school match one day with a broken leg. She
made him take it back straight away.

A Manchester United fan had gone to the Holy Land on
a pilgrimage. His mate asked him if he had managed to
visit the Wailing Wall in Jerusalem. His mate replied:
'Couldn't get near it for City supporters.'

A spectator, who is a regular at Maiden Castle,
Newcastle's training ground, tells the story of when
David Ginola had his first session. Keegan holds up
the ball in front of the assembled players, points to it
and says: 'Ball, ball, ball.' Then he points to his head
and says: 'Head, head, head.' Finally he points to the
goal and says: 'Goal, goal, goal.' 'Head, ball, goal.'
At this stage Peacock says: 'Howay, Gaffer, Dave's
English isn't that bad.' Whereupon Keegan says:
'I'm not talking to Ginola, I'm talking to David
Batty.'

At a Rotherham match, ten minutes before half-time, a
recently converted fan went to the toilet and, while abluting, heard a mighty roar. On his return he asked his mate:
'Have they scored?' 'No,' replied his mate. 'The pies have
just arrived.'

A Hartlepool fan was on the edge of the roof at St
James's Park. He was about to jump off when someone asked: 'Why don't you go to the Victoria
ground, your own ground, and jump off there?' He
replied: 'Have you seen the queue?'

After Wimbledon's victory over Arsenal, Joe Kinnear
spent time signing his autograph on any bit of paper put
in front of him. One fan, somewhat the worse for drink,
asked him to sign his bum. 'No way,' said Joe. 'Ask Harry

Redknapp – he's the one who signs all the bums.'

The groundsman at Huddersfield telephoned the chairman to tell him there had been a fire at the ground. 'Are the cups OK?' he asked. 'No problem!' was the reply. 'But the saucers are well knackered.'

Try saying this out loud: 'Weir, Young and Speedie, Ure, Auld, Bald, Gray and Duff.'

A man was walking his dog along Scarborough beach and came across a brass lamp. He rubbed the sand off it and a genie appeared. 'Thank you,' said the genie. 'You have released me from the cold North Sea and for that I shall grant you a wish.' 'What I wish is that my dog here becomes Supreme Champion at Crufts.' The genie looked at the decrepit mongrel standing shaking on the sand – no teeth, bits of hair missing and a permanent limp. 'Sorry,' said the genie. 'No way – that's an impossibility. Give me another wish.' 'I wish that Scarborough win the League and get promotion this year.' The genie looked at him and said: 'Here, let's have another look at this dog of yours.'

Question (1996): 'What have Coventry City and John Major's underpants got in common?' Answer: 'They've both been on the bottom of the Premier.'

A psychiatrist was doing good business, especially in the football season. He used an idea-association test on one of his patients one day and asked him what came into his mind when he thought of something brown and firm, with smooth curves. 'A football,' replied the patient at once. 'Good! And what do you think of when two arms slide around your waist?'

'An illegal tackle,' was the immediate reply. 'Now, picture a pair of firm thighs . . .' 'A fullback.' 'Great!' said the psychiatrist. 'Your reactions are quite normal. You wouldn't believe some of the stupid answers I get.'

A young Merchant Seaman from South Shields was shipwrecked on a beautiful tropical island. On the first evening, he watched the sun set over the palm-covered beach as he leaned on a rock. Suddenly the most beautiful native girls appeared, carrying a silver tray upon which was an ice-cold bottle of Newcastle Brown Ale. He drank it greedily as she disappeared. The next night, at the same time and in the same place, she appeared again. This time she had upon the tray a huge plate of fish, chips, mushy peas, bread and butter and a pot of tea.

Again he greedily scoffed her offering. The following night the scene was the same. This time she appeared without a tray and came beside him as he leaned on the rock. She squeezed up to him and asked him in a very attractive and seductive accent: 'Would you like to come down to the beach with me where we can play a little game?' Young Geordie looked at her, eyes popping, and replied: 'Don't tell me you've got a football an' all!'

The Club chairman visited the team manager who was sick in hospital. 'Gordon,' he said, 'the Board decided to send you a "Get Well" card and I'm sure you'll be pleased to hear that it was a majority decision.'

A bloke was walking home one Saturday evening, when he was confronted by a drunken Arsenal fan with a gun in one hand and a bottle in the other. He pointed the gun at his victim, pushed the bottle towards him and said: 'Take a drink of this.' The poor man took a swig then spat it out. 'That,' he said, 'is terrible!' 'I know,' said the drunk. 'Now you hold the gun on me while I have a swig.'

> Question: 'What is the difference between the urinal at a football ground and an anniversary?'
> Answer: 'None. Men usually miss them both.'

The latest signing, Robert Cox, had not turned up for training and the trainer was told by one of the players he had gone to get his hair cut. 'Go and find him now!' ordered the trainer. The player dashed off to the nearest hairdresser's, opened the door and asked: 'Bob Cox in here?' 'Sorry mate,' said the barber, 'but we only do shaves and haircuts.'

> Alan Sugar, who had started his business career by selling TV aerials out of the boot of his car, met an ex-Tottenham player, down on his luck, as he parked his rolls in front of the Ritz. 'Hello Alan, remember me?' 'Jimmy, of course I do. Haven't seen you in years. How's business?' 'Alan,' says Jimmy, 'I've hit a really bad patch. In fact, I was wondering if you could let me have a tenner for a bed.' 'No problem, Jimmy – bring it around in the morning, and I'll have a look at it.'

Billy, a fanatical Rangers supporter, took his crocodile into a pub and said: 'Do you serve Catholics?' The bar man assured him that he did. 'In that case,' said Billy, 'I'll have a pint and two Catholics for the crocodile.'

> Jackie, an ex-footballer, now in his seventies with legs in a terrible state, went into hospital. When he came around after the operation, he looked up at the surgeon and said: 'Doc – I can't feel my legs.' 'Not

surprised Jackie, my old mate,' he replied. 'We had to take your arms off.'

Another footballer came around after his operation to find the doctor by the side of his bed. 'I have good news and bad news for you,' said the doctor. 'I'll have the bad news first, Doc,' said the old pro. 'Well – we've had to take your legs off.' 'And what's the good news?' moaned the old man. 'The fellow in the next bed says he'll buy your slippers.'

Another footballer, after a major operation to his dodgy knees, was told by the doctor that he had good news and bad news. 'The bad news is that your playing days are over,' said the doctor. 'And what's the good news?' asked the miserable lad. 'Well, you see that good-looking nurse over there? I'm going out with her tonight!' replied the doctor.

The team was playing away and because there was no-one to look after his labrador, one of the players asked the gaffer if he could take the dog with him. He refused until the player told him that it would be useful because, on the coach to the match, the dog played cards and could make up a school. Keen to see what would happen, the boss let him take the dog and was amazed when it did play. 'I've got to say,' he enthused, 'I know labradors are intelligent, but this one's fantastic.' 'Ah, he's not that good,' said the player. 'Every time he gets a good hand he wags his tail.'

Then there was the intellectually challenged foot-baller who thought:
- Intercourse was a ticket for the races.
- Bigamist was an Italian fog.
- Joan of Arc was Noah's wife.
- A penal colony was an all-male nudist camp.
- Hypocrisy was a Greek philosopher.

- Judicious meant washing up after dinner.
- Monotony meant being married to one woman all your life.
- The four seasons were pepper, salt, vinegar and mustard.
- Red, pink, orange and flamingo were colours of the rectum.
- Mozart was a child orgy.

The Captain of the Premier League football side went to the doctor and explained to him his problem. 'It's like this, Doc. I am greatly troubled by wind in the most awkward of situations – during team talks, at the toss-up and such occasions as presentations. I just can't help it. Fortunately, there is one good thing about it – they never smell or make a noise. In fact, Doc, while I've been explaining this to you, it's happened twice. Is there anything you can do for me?' The doctor reached for his prescription pad, scribbled something down and handed it to him. 'Nasal drops,' he read. 'I don't need these.' 'Listen, bonny lad,' replied the doctor. 'When we've got your nose sorted out, we'll have a look at your ears.'

After getting a nasty bang on the head, the centre forward was carried off and came round in the dressing-room. 'Are you comfortable?' asked the physio. 'Well, I've just moved into a new 5-bedroom detached and I drive a BMW with a personalised numberplate. Does that answer your question?'

A Celtic supporter went into a butcher's shop which was painted and tiled out in green and white and asked for a meat pie. 'We don't sell pies to Celtic supporters,' said the butcher. 'But you're a Celtic supporter yourself. This is disgraceful.' 'Have you tasted our pies?' asked the butcher.

The footballer arrived half an hour late for training. 'You should have been here 30 minutes ago,' said the trainer. 'Why?' responded the player. 'What happened?'

Sign in football dressing room:

IF YOU HAVE TROUBLE WITH ALCOHOL,
PHONE 01435-967425

One of the players did – and found that it was the local off-licence.

There was the referee whose wife informed the press that he had been a premature baby – he was born before his parents were married.

A motorist stopped a pedestrian in Newcastle and asked him the quickest way to get to the Royal Victoria Infirmary. The pedestrian pointed to the pub across the way, 'The Barking Dog', and said: 'Nip into the bar over there and shout out "Dalglish's a B******".'

This footballer had a weakness for Vindaloo curry, which he wanted every night, but restricted himself to a Saturday night after the match when he'd had a few pints. Then he would return home and eat the curry his wife had collected from the take-away. On this particular night, he returned home, but when his wife went into the kitchen to serve it, she found that the cat had eaten it. The footballer went loco, pulled the cat inside out, opened the back door and stuffed the cat into the water butt. Five minutes later there was a knock on the door and when he answered it, there was the cat. 'You couldn't give me another drink of water could you?' it asked.

A Rabbi died in Glasgow and his brother flew over from Israel for the funeral. It was the night before the ceremony and he asked to have a last look at his brother. When the lid was taken off the coffin, there lay his brother, resplendent in a Glasgow Rangers football strip. 'What's this?' asked the brother. 'It was his very last wish,' replied his wife. 'But why?' asked the brother. 'You know and I know he was never interested in football. What exactly did he say?' 'His very last words,' his wife said, 'were "I want to be buried in the Gaza Strip".'

A Turkish town hall was twinned with a German town, and at one of the early arranged cultural visits, the Turkish Planning Officer went off to meet his German counterpart. The German gave the Turk a tour of his splendidly efficient, well-designed and clean town, and then took him to his house for a meal. The Turkish councillor was very impressed by the size of the German's house, grounds and swimming pool, as well as the Mercedes which cluttered the drive.

'Councillors must be very well paid in Germany,' remarked the Turk with a great deal of envy. The German grinned, and asked his new acquaintance to follow him as he moved up the stairs. On the sunroof, which commanded wonderful views of the surrounding countryside, he said: 'Look over there – can you see our new football stadium?' The Turk nodded, and the German winked as he tapped his breast pocket. 'Twenty per cent,' he said.

The following year, the German visited the Turkish town, and was in turn shown around the somewhat shabby and dilapidated town by his Turkish colleague, and then invited to share a meal at his home.

The German was astounded. The Turk's home was massive with two pools, a golf course and two

Rolls-Royces standing outside the house at the top of the mile long drive. Beautiful, scantily-clad girls draped themselves around the pool and food of all descriptions hung heavy on laden tables. 'I see you learned the lesson well,' said the German. 'Aha!' grinned the Turk as he beckoned the German to follow him. On the top floor he threw open a door leading on to a verandah and said: 'Do you see that new football stadium over there?' The German looked and looked and then looked again before finally saying: 'I'm sorry, I cannot.' The smiling Turkish councillor tapped his breast pocket: 'One hundred per cent!'

As the goalkeeper trudged off after letting nine past him in a Sunday League match, a little man approached him. 'I'm interested in you,' he said. 'I'd like to sign you on.' 'Are you a scout?' asked the goalkeeper. 'No son, I'm an optician . . .'

'Have you anything to say about this disgraceful hooliganism?' asked the Judge of the thuggish looking fan.
'Stuff all!' replied the fan.
'What did he say?' the judge asked the Clerk of the Court.
'He said: "Stuff all!", Your Worship.'
'Funny,' said the judge. 'I could have sworn I saw his lips move.'

They reckon that Matt Le Tissier is so laid back he would be more active if ever he took valium.

The footballer returned home to find his wife in bed with a stranger. He asked his wife: 'What are you doing with him in bed?' His wife turned to her partner and said: 'There you are – I told you he was thick.'

When the England job was up for grabs and it was given to Graham Taylor, Notts County fans supported Cloughie for England Coach. They reckoned his teeth should have been taken out and seats put in.

A little lad became lost at the football match and was crying his eyes out. When the policeman approached him, he told him: 'I've lost my dad.' 'What's your dad like?' asked the copper. 'Beer, women and the odd bet!' said the little lad.

The lads were talking in the changing-room about what had been on telly the night before. One of them said that he'd seen a good film which was called Moby Dick. 'I don't like sex films,' said one of the less bright team-members. 'It's not about sex,' he was informed. 'It's about whales.' 'I don't like the Welsh either!' he said.

You can tell a Manchester United fan – but you can't tell him much.

A Scotsman won a million and a half on the Lottery. 'What will we do about the begging letters?' asked his wife. 'Keep sending them, keep sending them!' he replied.

A keen looking young lad dressed in Spurs gear asked a London Bobby: 'How do I get to White Hart Lane?' The bobby replied: 'Practise, practise, practise!'

At the Gateshead Football and International Athletics Stadium an officious looking official approached an athlete. 'Are you a pole vaulter?' 'Indeed I am,' he replied. 'I'm from Warsaw. But tell me – how did you know that my name was Valter?'

The reporter was pressing the old footballer on his 100th birthday as to why he had lived so long. 'There are two reasons,' said the old man. 'The first is my life-long practice of having ten Woodbines a day.' 'And the second?' 'Cancelling my voyage on the *Titanic*,' he replied.

At the football match they were selling Oxo at £1.50 a mug. The line of mugs stretched right around the corner.

The lads were getting changed for football. 'What's that mark on your shoulder?' asked the local Trigger. 'A birthmark.' 'Had it long?'

The footballer was having his regular check-up. 'When did you last have sex?' asked the doctor. 'Nineteen fifty-eight,' said the footballer. 'Good God! That was some time ago,' said the doc. The footballer looked at his watch. 'Well, it's only twenty-two fifteen now!' he said.

The centre forward was asked: 'Can you telephone from a submarine?' 'Of course,' he replied. 'Anybody can tell a phone from a submarine.'

As the Fourth Division footballer said, when his contract was not renewed at the end of the season: 'One door closes, another slams in your face.'

The football supporter was sitting in the club, staring at what seemed to him to be the hardest barman he had ever seen. He wore a filthy vest with muscles popping out of his arms, his face was unshaven and his hair in tatts. The barman caught sight of him staring and asked him: 'What the hell do you think you're staring at?' 'It's the remarkable likeness . . . you're a dead-ringer for my wife – if it wasn't for the moustache . . .' 'I don't have a moustache,' said the barman. 'No, but my wife has!'

A Rangers supporter stared at the barman. 'Are you
all right?' asked the barman. 'Not really,' he said. 'I
think I've got the Yaws.' 'What's Yaws?' asked the
barman. 'Thanks very much. I'll have a triple
whisky.'

The footballer went into Boots and asked the supervisor:
'Where can I get some talcum powder?' 'Walk this way,
sir,' she said. 'Madam,' said the footballer, 'if I could
walk that way, I wouldn't need the talcum powder.'

The ex-footballer was desperate to find employment
and went to a prominent theatrical agent to try and
get work as a bird impersonator. 'There's no call for
that – they're as common as pop singers,' said the
agent. 'Just leave me your name and number.' He
gave his name as Dickie Bird, took a numbered ring
off his leg, and put it on the desk, laid an egg,
crapped on the window and then flew away.

A footballer went into the pub during pre-season training
and told the barman he was a little stiff from shuttles. 'I
couldn't give a damn where you come from mate,' said
the barman, 'as long as you have the money for your
pint.'

The same footballer arrived back from the pub and
his wife was ironing one of her bras. 'I don't know
why you bother', he said. 'You haven't anything to
put in it.' 'You know what?' said the wife. 'I always
think the same thing when I iron your underpants.'

He was an unlucky player who not only suffered many
injuries, but one day when he was driving into training,
his car horn accidentally jammed while he was driving
behind a group of Hell's Angels.

A dyslexic footballer was taking a break skiing and
went up to a man and said: 'Excuse me, but could

you tell me whether I should be zig-zagging or zag-zigging down this slope?' 'It's no good asking me, mate,' said the other fellow. 'I'm a tobogganist.' 'Well, in that case,' said the footballer, 'can I have 20 Embassy Silk Cut?'

At the World Cup some international footballers were having a chat. One asked another: 'Where's the best place to go to get stoned with just one drink?' The other replied: 'Iran.'

Then there was the footballer who was told that his wife was having an affair with his best friend – so he went out and shot his dog!

What do you say to a Liverpool supporter in a suit? 'Will the defendant please rise.'

'Tell me, why is your team-mate known as Martini?' – 'Any time, any place, anywhere . . . !'

Ten Chelsea supporters went into a pub and the leader ordered 11 pints. 'Why do you want 11 pints? There're only 10 of you,' asked the barman. The leader grabbed the barman, nutted him, and slapped him around. 'If I ask for 11 pints, just give me 11. Understand?' said the chief fan. 'No offence meant,' said the barman. The fans' leader took the extra pint to a little old man who was sitting in the corner of the pub. 'Well, that's a very nice gesture,' said the old man. 'No problem,' said the leader. 'I don't mind helping a cripple out.' 'But I'm not a cripple,' said the old man. 'You will be if you don't get the next round in!' said the leader.

Why won't a rattlesnake bite a football agent? Professional courtesy.

What's the difference between John Barnes playing well for England and Martians? There are at least a few people who have claimed to have seen Martians.

What is the difference between Jack Walker and Mussolini? Both wasted millions but Mussolini got further in Europe.

What's black and white and hard? A Newcastle supporter with a flick knife.

(Heard in St James's bar post-match *v* Wimbledon): 'Come in, Vinnie – make yourself at home – hit somebody!'

The dashing Third Division player sauntered into Top Man and asked the assistant: 'Can you show me the cheapest suit in the shop?' 'Yes, Sir,' said the assistant. 'You're wearing it.'

One footballer confided to one of his team-mates: 'I don't want you to tell anybody, but I'm having an affair.' 'Is that right?' asked his friend. 'Who's doing the catering then?'

The footballer asked his wife what she wanted for her birthday and when she said: 'Something with diamonds in it.' He bought her a pack of cards.

Two football apprentices were going through a graveyard and came across a headstone with the inscription: 'Here lies a Football Manager and an Honest Man.' One of them said: 'I wonder how they got the two of them in the one grave.'

Have you heard about the Middlesbrough supporter who thought Manual Labour was Bryan Robson's latest foreign signing?

The Premier League footballer's contract was up and not renewed. Eventually he found a place with a Third Division team and the income was severely reduced. 'We'll have to cut down on some of the luxuries,' he told his wife. 'If you could learn to cook, we could fire the chef.' 'In that case,' replied his wife, 'if you could learn to make love, we could fire the gardener.'

A football steward decided that, for defensive reasons, he would take karate lessons. Nothing ever happened at the match, but one night on his way back from the pub, he was mugged. But by the time he managed to get his shoes and socks off . . .

The ex-footballer was sitting in the pub looking thoroughly dejected. A bloke sitting near him said: 'You look really miserable, mate. What's the matter?' 'It's awful,' he replied. 'I had everything a man could ever want – a gorgeous woman who couldn't live without me, a big detached house, loads of money and a

Mercedes coupé.' 'What happened?' asked the bloke. 'I'll tell you what happened, mate,' he said. 'Without any warning whatsoever, my wife walked in.'

The hard-living, hard-drinking football manager visited the police-station and asked if he could have a word with the thief who had broken into his house the previous night. 'Why do you want to do that?' asked the sergeant. 'I wanted to see if he would tell me how he managed to get in without waking the wife,' he replied.

The local club sent its captain along as the sole judge to the sheepdog trials in Cumberland. He gave the first dog life imprisonment, the second a fine of £200 and the third a suspended sentence for two years.

Mary, a steward, was a good girl and had been told not to accept lifts from strange men. One day as she was waiting at the bus stop, a car pulled up and the lone driver said: 'Would you like a lift?' She said: 'No, thank you. I live in a bungalow.'

The soccer star and his attractive girlfriend were planning to get married and he was describing his financial situation. He asked: 'Do you think you'll be able to live on my wages?' She said: 'Oh, yes, but what will you live on?'

Then there was the streaker who distracted the crowd at a charity match at St James's Park. Fortunately she was caught by the bouncers and ejected.

In Glasgow last week a Celtic supporter collapsed from starvation after spending a month on the back seat of a pay-as-you-leave bus.

Then there was the supporter who was imprisoned in

Dartmoor because of his beliefs. He believed the watchman was fast asleep.

> When the chairman asked his wife why she thought it was time they had her mother down for a few days she replied: 'Because she's sick to death of being up in the attic for so long.'

The footballer asked his mate: 'Is it better to have loved a short girl than never to have loved a tall?'

> Then there was the ground steward who was charged with attacking a fan with a razor but was acquitted because he hadn't plugged it in.

There was the young football apprentice who, when he went away to the club for the first time, was told by his mam to put a clean pair of underpants on every day. By the end of the week he couldn't get his football shorts on.

> The father was watching the football match, oblivious to anything else, while his wife was being driven demented by their little son, Dennis. She said to her husband: 'Will you speak to Dennis?' When there was no response, she shouted at him: 'Will you speak to Dennis?' The father turned his head slowly, and said: 'Hello, Dennis!'

Proverb: 'He who laughs last is a football steward who hasn't seen the joke.'

> Toast to a retiring footballer: 'May you die in bed at 95 years old, shot by a jealous husband.'

A toast to active footballers: 'Here's to our girlfriends and wives – may they never meet.'

> The football steward, returning drunk from the pub, was trying to fit his key into a lamppost. A friendly

policeman said: 'I don't think there's anybody in tonight.' 'There must be,' said the drunk. 'There's a light on upstairs.'

The henpecked footballer informed the man at the bar that his wife had eloped with his best friend. 'What's his name then?' 'Don't know,' replied the footballer. 'I've never met him.'

His idea of a balanced diet was a pint in both hands.

Doctor: 'I don't like the look of your husband.'
Player's wife: 'Me neither, Doc – but he's good to the children.'

The vain star went to the dentist and told him he was worried because all his teeth were going yellow. 'What should I do?' asked the footballer. 'Wear a brown tie,' advised the dentist.

He had given almost all his money to sick animals but hadn't known they were sick when he backed them.

The old footballer had to have an operation. The

doctor was trying to console him: 'Don't worry, a few weeks after amputating your legs, we'll have you on your feet again.'

The Sunderland policeman was trying to stop a would-be suicide from jumping off the bridge into the Wear. 'Look,' he said as the man stood on the parapet. 'Think of Sunderland, who've just made it to the Premier League. You're going to have a great year.' 'But I'm a Newcastle supporter,' said the man. 'Well then – jump, you b*****!'

A star manager had been under stress, and his psychiatrist had told him to get away and have a good holiday. He later received a postcard from Spain. It read: 'Having a wonderful time. Why?'

The same psychiatrist received a barely decipherable card from another of his footballing patients who was an alcoholic. This one read: 'Having a great time. Where the hell am I?'

The steward asked his wife: 'Do you believe it is possible to communicate with the dead?' 'Yes,' she said. 'I can hear you distinctly.'

The star took his wife for a meal and they had to wait . . . and wait. 'Excuse me,' he asked the head waiter, 'but did that fellow who took the order leave any family?'

And another time: 'Are you sure you're the waiter I gave my order to?' 'And what makes you ask?' enquired the waiter. 'It's just that I expected a much older man.'

The steward's wife was going to give birth imminently. He telephoned the ambulance and the operator asked: 'Is this her first child?' 'No – this is her husband,' he replied.

The football star had been suffering for a while with

pains in the stomach, so the club sent him to see a specialist. After extensive tests, the consultant said to him: 'I find this quite unbelievable, but I have to tell you that you're pregnant.' 'You're mad!' said the footballer. 'I can't be.' 'But you are,' said the specialist, 'and it's the first time in history. You'll be the talk of Harley Street.' 'Never mind Harley Street,' replied the star. 'I'll be the talk of our street as well – I'm not even married.'

Tommy, the football manager, had just died and was not even buried. The ambitious Trainer went to see the chairman. 'Mr Chairman,' he asked, 'I was wondering if you would have any objection to me taking Tommy's place?' 'Not at all,' said the chairman. 'I have no objection if the undertaker hasn't.'

A well-known footballer got into a taxi on the night after the PFA dinner and asked to be taken to the Grosvenor Park Hotel. 'You are at the Grosvenor Park Hotel,' said the taxi driver. The football star got out, handed him £20, and said: 'Next time, don't drive so fast.'

The football star took a girl he had met at the night club back to his digs, where he invited her up to his room. The girl asked him: 'If I go up to your room, do you promise to be good?' He said: 'Good? I promise to be fantastic.'

He's not a bad footballer, and they reckon he has sex nearly every night of the week – nearly on Tuesday . . . nearly on Wednesday . . .

There was the murderer who was considered unfit to plead when the judge discovered he was a Halifax Town season ticket holder.

Alex Ferguson asked to see Andy Cole the Monday after a match, and Ladbroke's were ready to take bets on Cole missing the meeting.

Sticker on the back of Third Division footballer's car, clearly put out by hearing what Premier League players were earning: 'Why can't I be rich instead of well-hung?'

Kevin Keegan sent Terry McDermott out to buy Flowers on Valentine's Day, and Terry ended up on a train to Blackburn.

Celtic Park has been broken into and the entire contents of the trophy room stolen. Police are believed to be looking for a man with a green carpet.

Question: 'Why, during the 1995-96 season, were West Ham like Pampers?'

Answer: 'P*** at the front and s*** at the back.'

The seven dwarfs went off to watch Wolves in a Cup match, and Snow White was getting really worried because it was getting very late and they had not returned. At last she heard one voice chanting: 'Hi Ho, Hi Ho, It's off to Wembley we go.'

'Ah well,' she said. 'At least Dopey's home.'

The parish priest was very proud of the football medals and cups he had won as a young man which he kept in a cabinet in his living-room. One night, on returning to the presbytery after taking a service, he found a thuggish burglar breaking into his cabinet. 'Please return what you have taken. You know Jesus and I are watching you,' said the priest. 'Stuff you and Jesus,' replied the thief. The priest turned around and there behind him sat a 12-stone

Rottweiler. 'Jesus,' he said, 'take his bloody legs off.'
On the chairman's farm two cows were looking over the
fence, and one said to the other: 'What do you make of
this mad cow disease?' The other one said: 'Nothing to do
with me – I'm a duck!'

> The same chairman had two fish in a tank. The little
> one turned to the big one and said: 'Hey – do you
> know how to drive this thing?'

Two crocodiles went into a pub in Glasgow which was
owned by an ex-Rangers player, and ordered two pints
and two packets of crisps. When they'd had them, the
barman went over to where they were sitting and asked:

'Beer OK, lads?'

'Fine,' they replied.

'Crisps OK?' he asked.

'Fine,' they said.

'Then why the long faces?' he asked.

The football star went into the sweet shop in the High
Street which had a notice in the window which said:
'Condoms – Fitted by Hand.' There stood the most
beautiful of girls. 'Excuse me,' he said nervously, 'But are
you the one who fits the condoms by hand?' 'Indeed I
am,' she panted. 'Well,' he continued, 'Would you mind
washing your hands – I'd like a quarter of mint imperials,
please.'

> 'Remember,' said the football steward, 'A dog is not
> only for Christmas – there should be plenty left for
> Boxing Day and the day after.'

First fan: 'They're a load of turkeys this team we're playing today, aren't they?'

Second fan: 'What do you mean?'

First fan: 'Well, they're going to get stuffed, aren't
they?'

First player: 'Are you having the family for Christmas?'

Second player: 'Nah! This year we're having a turkey!'

Steward: 'I always like to see the family coming at Christmas. It gives you the chance to get the door locked and hide behind the settee.'

Then there was the player with a drink problem who leaned across the bar and said to the landlord: 'Really, I'm a man wi' very simple tastes. Gi' me a bottle of vodka, a tin of biscuits and a dog.' 'Why the dog?' asked the landlord. 'Hell mon, someone has got ta eat the biscuits,' replied the player.

First footballer: 'Our chairman has been married three times.'

Second footballer: 'God, he must like wedding cake!'

Manager's wife: 'I thought you were going to play golf with the chairman.'

Manager: 'Would you play with someone who cheats, moans all the time and won't buy a drink?'

Manager's wife: 'I certainly would not.'

Manager: 'Well, the chairman won't either!'

9
Surely, It Cannot Be True

Introduction

Perhaps it is the same in every sport. But, undoubtedly, if you are looking for evidence of extremes of fanaticism, the abandonment of all that is rational and sheer pigheadedness in the face of adversity, then you need look no further than football.

Fanatics and Fanaticism

Newspapers and magazines thrive on relating stories that are at once both entirely true and totally unbelievable. What follows is but a brief selection:

'I knew a man who used to wear his full Hamilton Academicals kit – hat, scarf, headband, wristband, shorts, socks – when he listened in to wireless reports of his team. He would sing and chant, shout abuse and encouragement at the appropriate moments and even went so far as to buy from his wife a cup of Bovril and a meat pie at half-time.' (*Observer.*)

'An 11-year-old boy used his glass eye and spare to play football when a neighbour confiscated his tennis ball. He broke both his glass eyes. He is to be given another eye under the Health Service.'(*Daily Mail.*)

    'Football is well worth the entrance fee because it requires loyalty on the part of club supporters, and if a man is loyal to his club, he is apt to become loyal to his wife, his boss and his country.' (*Birmingham Mail.*)

The behaviour of spectators at some Rugby matches has declined because the wrong sort of people go, just as now a lot of wrong people play. Rugby used to be played only at better class schools. To attempt to lump Rugby, the game, and the spectators with the thousands of layabouts at the soccer grounds is quite useless, as it is to compare the amateur game with the professional, with its wages, absurd transfer fees and now, God help us, talks of strikes.' (Letter in the *Daily Mirror.*)

    'In St Paul's Church, Kingston Hill, Surrey, yesterday, footballers' shirts were draped on the pews and corner posts, and flags stood in the aisle and miniature goal posts hung on the walls for a footballers' service. The vicar, Canon A. Wellesley Orr, opened his sermon with short blasts on a referee's whistle.' (*Daily Mail.*)

    'Mr Barclay says in his parish magazine: "I know a 'live church' in South London where a football service is held. The local football club members attend in their jerseys and miniature goal posts are erected over the pulpit. When the vicar has preached for ten minutes someone blows a whistle and shouts half-time."' (*Daily Mirror.*)

    'I have a friend who firmly believes that the Virgin appeared to him and called out in a loud voice: "Up the Reds!"'(*Bury Evening Chronicle.*)

'Teachers in Liverpool have noticed that pupils are depressed after the city's soccer teams have lost a match. Now a team of psychologists from Liverpool University is going to question 200 boys in eight secondary schools. A research psychologist, Mr Kevin Fleisch, who is running the survey, said yesterday: "It is worrying to think what happens at Easter time, when GCSE examinations are going on at the same time as critical League and Cup matches."'(*Guardian.*)

> 'Meanwhile, Cup fever in the town has reached a climax. Example: A Bournemouth supporter died yesterday. By lunchtime four people had called asking to buy his ticket.' (*News Chronicle.*)

'He and his wife have six children. Their favourite treat is to be taken to tea at the Ritz. "It's cheaper than the cinema and it's the only place I know in London where they

can run about. There's room for them to play football in
the corridors," says Mr Buchan.' (*Sunday Express.*)

> 'Mr— was a member of Coventry supporters' club.
> Mr Gilbert Beyfus, QC for Mrs— "Did he discuss
> football intelligently?" "To tell the truth, I used to
> get him a cushion and he went to sleep."'(Report in
> *News Chronicle.*)

'My husband is a jolly good sort, one of those very hearty
men. He wears corduroys, smokes a pipe, and talks about
nothing but beer and football from the start of the season
onwards. My nerves won't stand much more of it.' (A
wife at Tottenham Police Court – *Daily Mail.*)

> At least one spouse got her eventual revenge: 'I once
> heard of a woman who had her husband, a Chelsea
> supporter, cremated and his ashes put in an egg
> timer. She said he had never worked for her in his
> life, so he might as well do something now that he
> was dead.' (Letter in *Daily Mirror.*)

. . . And Away From Football . . .

'Will the supporter who borrowed the donkey from
Scarborough Sands please return as season has started.'
(*Yorkshire Evening Post.*)

> And in the same category . . .
>
> 'Will the person who borrowed the two ferrets a
> month ago and borrowed another on Tuesday night,
> with a string of onions, return one ferret – they can
> keep the onions!' (Advert in *Kent & Sussex Courier.*)

'A Piper Aeroplane, making an emergency landing on a
golf course at Boca Raton in Florida was forced to veer
away from the fairway when four golfers failed to notice
the operation. "Everything would have been OK if these

damned golfers had moved out of the way," said Scott Slinko, who was on board with a pupil. As it was, the plane hit a palm tree and crumpled. Irv Brown, one of the golfers, was unphased: "Concentration – that's the name of the game. One of the benefits of playing football!"'

'No one in England will be peevish at the passing of the Ashes. We have been beaten by a much better team. Oddly enough, and to the permanent bewilderment of foreigners, that is an experience in which Englishmen still find a keen enjoyment.' (*Evening News.*)

The Intellectually Challenged

Some claim that footballers and their fans are 'thicker than mourners at a brewers' wake'. Nowadays, in the age of political rectitude, they would be 'intellectually challenged', and the following would tend to support that description:

'Please could you settle an argument I have been having with my wife. An acquaintance has recently adopted two Chinese baby boys, and his one desire is that they should play football, hopefully professionally. I maintain that this will never happen because in China football has never been popular, and they will have great difficulty in understanding English. My wife says I am speaking nonsense.' (Letter to the *Evening Gazette.*)

'England manager, Don Revie, had a champagne breakfast in Harrogate today – and spelt out his recipe to get the country out of its mess. "The country is in a terrible state and it is only the people who can put it right by hard work and dedication," he said at a reception in the Majestic Hotel. "We have to work a lot harder if we are to stop inflation.

We have to put in a lot more hours and a lot more effort. I shall do what I can on the football side."' (*The Times.*)

'Sport. Learn the principles and necessary skills in becoming a professional footballer. One day course.' (*Evening Gazette.*)
  'Radio Merseyside, assuming difficulty with the spelling of fullback Stig Bjornebye, gave prizes to listeners who could spell his name. They hadn't counted on the entrants who had difficulty spelling "Stig".' (*Herald.*)
'Football fans got a shock when, after the match between Ipswich and Norwich, they flocked to a Norfolk pub advertising topless bar staff – the staff were all men.' (*Sunday Mirror.*)

  'It never fails to amaze me, while watching soccer in wet weather, that no one has ever thought of giving the players a cloth to wipe the ball at throw-ins.' (Letter in *Daily Mirror.*)

A woman, married to a professional footballer, was informing fellow dinner guests that, as a young girl, before she was married, she was very innocent and naive. She said: 'I didn't even know what a homosexual was until I met my husband.'

The Gamblers
Bobby Thompson, the Geordie comedian, used to tell the story of when he answered a knock on the door.
  Bobby: 'What di ye want?'
  Caller: 'I'm from Littlewoods, Sir.'
  Bobby: 'Great! Me treble chance must have come up.

Come in, Bonny Lad.'

Caller: 'Actually, Sir, I've come to take the three-piece suite back.'

Gambling, particularly on the Pools, has always been an integral part of the football fan's life.

> 'For my Pools coupon I have used numbers formed from those on the hymn board at Church. I have had five minor dividends. I put part of my winnings in the collection plate.' (Letter in *Daily Herald.*)

'A chronic gambler who backed winning teams every time he prayed in Church for help to clear his debts was so impressed by the power of prayer that he has become a Roman Catholic Priest.' (*Daily Telegraph.*)

> '. . . betting shops should be called Off-the-Course Racing Commissions Acceptance Establishments. They should be conducted with tone, and have uniformed attendants and a light catering service.' (Letter in the *Daily Herald.*)

'The other day I went out to post an important business letter, and, being anxious that it should reach its destination by a certain time, asked a postman who happened to be standing by what chance there was. His reply was: "Is it to Littlewoods?" I asked what difference that made. He replied: "Pools have priority."' (*Manchester Guardian.*)

> 'When I have filled in my soccer coupon I lay it on a plate and sprinkle a little nutmeg powder on it. Then I leave it for 24 hours before posting it.' (Letter in the *News of the World.*)

'It was stated that, after the match, the three men were playing pitch and toss in the street when the street lamps were switched off at 11.40 p.m. To enable them to carry on the game they went to a telephone box, took the directory, and set fire to the pages.' (*Sunday Dispatch.*)

The Violent

Violence and thuggery, on and off the pitch, have always been features of the game. Overwhelming police presence, closed-circuit TV and the convoys of fluorescently-clad stewards now control the terraces, while on the field of play, instant video playbacks and card-flashing officials have ensured that, at least in the top Divisions, cynical and pre-meditated assaults are rare . . . but still exist.

'Having been a supporter of Exeter City from 1929 until moving to the Isle of Wight last October, I deplore the growth of soccer violence. I cannot see the issuing of identity cards providing a solution, and in my view the punishment of these hooligans should be more severe. For a first offence, a heavy fine should be imposed, and if the offender is brought before the magistrate a second time, the label "F.A. THUG" should be branded on his forehead.' (Letter in *Portsmouth Evening News.*)

'The judge told five youths: "If this were an earlier century, and I had the powers of long ago, I would order you to spend all the Saturday afternoons of the whole season locked in the stocks outside the gates of QPR club, where you would be looked upon by all decent supporters with the contempt you deserve."'(*Daily Telegraph.*)

'The changing-room brawl after a hockey and net-ball tournament between girls from two Luton schools ended with one girl being taken to hospital with bruising and another being stabbed with a needle. Others were kicked and punched and yesterday education chiefs ordered an inquiry into the fight. (Derby matches have always been the source of extreme behaviour. The banned girls said, more reminiscent of soccer, that they had only "done it for kicks.")' (*Daily Express.*)

'Every time a well-known footballer scored a goal, a man from the Council went round to his house to collect the mortgage arrears. "We used to watch for when he scored, because we knew he would be on a bonus that week," said Mr John Hayes, a deputy clerk to Nottinghamshire County Council, at a meeting of the council's Finance Committee yesterday.' (*The Times.*)

'A youth who stabbed a man in the face with a piece of broken glass following a football match was sent to a detention centre for three months at Durham Crown Court yesterday. And after sentencing him, Judge Alistair Sharp told the teenager to use his fists and fight like an Englishman in future.' (*Northern Echo.*)

'At the court following the Junior School football match, the mother said she was not very abusive, but she did call Mr— "a monkey-faced, button-eyed old git".' (*Liverpool Echo.*)

'Deaf viewers are to protest about the language of two footballers during a row shown on BBC's Match of the Day. Although the words could not be distinguished by most viewers, the deaf lip-read the exchange.' (*Daily Telegraph.*)

'It is because of unnecessary cruelty to worms that I would also suggest the prohibition of all games on grass. I once saw a beautiful worm unnecessarily killed by a football player's boot, and no doubt death by violence must be caused to millions of these useful creatures by the pursuit of balls.' (Letter in *Western Mail.*)

'Meads was kicked on the head, and had to have three stitches put in the cut. Kirkpatrick broke his nose early in the match. Villepreux played most of the game with two ribs broken. Many others were hurt. Some of the injuries were deliberately inflicted. These deeds made unpleasant watching. But, taken as a whole, this was not a game that got out of hand.'(*Guardian.*) (Rugby – supposedly a hooligans' game played by gentlemen, whereas football is a gentleman's game played by hooligans.)

'Constable— said: "I approached the men who were throwing bottles into the crowd. I drew my baton and struck all three. This had a quietening effect."' (*Manchester Guardian.*)

'Surely the government must now see that the only way to stop something like the shooting of three policemen happening again is to take drastic action. Here are my suggestions to stop such things – (1) Give murderers a trial in public in a football stadium and televise it. (2) No jury. (3) No defence, and lastly, execute murderers in public.' (*Newcastle Evening Chronicle.*)

'I have an idea to stop footballers and spectators from fighting during the match. When they start fighting, the National Anthem should be played over the loudspeakers. They would then have to stop and stand to attention.' (Letter in *Bristol Evening Post.*)

'The magistrate, Sir John Cameron, told McCallum: "Fortunately violence on the golf course is not very prevalent. I am not going to take as serious a view as if this had occurred on a football ground."' (*Daily Mail.*)

'A 30-year-old man accused of murdering a woman in his flat at Moss Side was said in Manchester today to have a "main passion in life – football". Mr F. J. Beezley, for the Director of Public Prosecutions, said: "Having left this unfortunate lady under the bed, he seems to have gone about to football matches quite happily, although he does say the matter was on his conscience."' (*Manchester*

Evening Chronicle.)

> 'To commemorate Southampton's victory in the FA
> Cup, the City Council is to plant a new rose garden
> to replace the one trampled by fans as they welcomed
> the Saints home.' (*Sunday Express.*)

When England played Georgia in the World Cup match
in November 1996, a guide book on that country gave
this piece of information: 'You will be able to take your
handguns into your rooms, but semi-automatics must be
handed in at reception.'

> 'SIR – Last Saturday I took a group of boarders at
> the prep. school where I am a housemaster to a foot-
> ball match between Maidenhead United and Ruislip
> Manor.
>
> 'On the way to the game the boys were asking me
> how I chose their Saturday night video. I told them
> that I take note of the film's classification and try to
> avoid bad language, violence and nudity.
>
> 'We stood behind one of the goals; in the first
> minute the goalkeeper dropped the ball and uttered
> an expletive that echoed around the ground.
>
> 'In the fifth minute, the right-winger was scythed
> to the ground by a vicious tackle that left him
> writhing in agony. However, I felt pretty sure that
> my third "video worry" would not occur – then
> halfway through the second half, a streaker danced
> across the pitch.'

'But, sir, I thought you said . . .

PHILIP CARR,

  Windsor, Berks'

  (*The Times.*)

> Shout from the crowd at an inter-college football

match at Cambridge between Trinity Hall and Jesus
College: 'Come on, Hall – you can nail Jesus!'
From a parent on the touchline during a junior schoolboy
match in the North-East: 'Come on, Our Lady of the
Rosary – get stuck in!'
    BBC Radio report following football riots in
Columbia: 'Police fired rubber bullocks – er, sorry –
bullets.'

And What of Violence in Other Sports?

'The hunt involved was the Norwich Staghounds. Lt Col
Brian Gooch, Joint Master, said last night that the stag
was one of those bred for the sport and returned to its
paddock unharmed. "No stag is ever hunted more than
three times in a single season. The hound caught on the
railings was unhurt. I would have no part in anything
involving cruelty to animals."'(*Daily Telegraph.*)

    'Mr N. Ridley (C., Cirencester and Tewkesbury)
said: "I have no objection to animals and birds being
shot when they are going to take food or water or
going to roost, but I think there is something
unpleasant about the way in which they are often
ensnared and shot at when making love."'
(*Guardian.*)

'Nearly every night scrap metal worker, D— F—, took
his young bride through a couple of rounds of boxing
before they went to bed. D—, 32, is keen on boxing. His
20-year-old wife, M—, is not and she has not been feeling
very well lately. Now – after three weeks of marriage –
M— is back home with mother. "My husband doesn't
want a wife; he wants a moving punch-bag," she said yesterday.' (*People.*)

'One of the many things I like about Stracey as a world champion fighter is that he recognizes and realizes how ruthless his job must be. He wasn't above hitting Lewis low, or after the bell.' (Frank McGee in the *Daily Mirror*.)

'During the last six months I have knocked over no fewer than four cyclists. On each occasion the cyclist was entirely to blame. In future I shall let them take the consequences of their own folly, and make no effort to avoid them.' (Letter in the *Sun*.)

'So long as ... school cricket is played with a soft ball, there will be juvenile crime.'(Letter in *John Bull*.)

The Deceitful

A nineteen-year-old unemployed man was remanded on £950 bail by Marlborough Street magistrates, London, yesterday, accused of obtaining £30 by deception. He was said to have placed newspaper advertisements offering "Cup Final seats for sale". People who responded were sent small wooden stools with "Cup Final" written on them.' (*Sunday Times*.)

'Wimbledon ticket spivs are up in arms over "unfair" fines. They claim that they are being put out of business by excessive court penalties. "We realize the police have got a job to do, but so have we, and a £5 fine every couple of days suited us fine. But this is going to unfair extremes." (*Evening News.*)

The Sexually Challenged

'Cup Final ticket wanted, cash, or miniature life-like nude rubber doll of Phyllis Dixey, the music hall artist, in exchange.'(Advert in *Exchange and Mart.*)

'A 20-year-old man, who admitted indecently exposing himself and asked for seven similar offences to be considered, was told by a magistrate to go and join a football club.' (*Watford Evening Echo.*)

'A ten-year-old boy, whose mother, carrying a supermarket bag, took him to join a tennis club, was told he would be better advised to find a football team to play for.'

'Sunday football will be played at Dulverton, Somerset, to stop boys whistling at girls.' (*Daily Mail.*)

'There's a superstition in football that once a player marries he loses his form. That wouldn't happen to me. With Molly by my side I would play better than ever.' (*People.*)

'It was the last straw when a group of naked footballers charged into the netball girls' tea-making session in the Sports pavilion. Captain A. P. Cross said at yesterday's meeting of Tongham Parish Council, near Aldershot: "At times you get 40 young girls, and 50 men in the pavilion. With people running about in the nude, it doesn't help girls making tea."' (*Daily Mail.*)

'The Wolves' defeat of Spartak was a very good effort,

but it was with something approaching horror that I read
the English players kissed each other after each goal was
scored.' (Letter in the *Daily Mail.*)

'Players of Tudor Rose, junior team of Chelsea FC,
are to have lectures on sex education next month as
part of their grooming as potential professional footballers.' (*Star.*)

'Gentleman, 40, desires lady friend: must like boxing,
wrestling, football, etc.' (Advert in *Manchester Evening
News.*)

'My girlfriend and I were in love and were thinking
about getting engaged. Then her father bought her a
season ticket for Bournemouth for her birthday and
she has not seemed the same since.'(Letter in the
Woman's Mirror.)

'The wives of six Luton Town footballers had their hair
set in champagne yesterday – because their local hairdresser believes it is not fair that their husbands should
get all the glamour.' (*News Chronicle.*)

'Man offers proposal to any woman with ticket for
Leeds United *v* Sheffield United game. Must send
photograph (of ticket).'(Advert in the *Yorkshire
Evening Post*, 1990.)

In the Middlesbrough Sunday League, in the early 1970s,
'Tygmat Academicals' was playing the 'Newmarket
Hotel' when one of the Academicals players committed a
bad foul. The cries immediately went up: 'Jack Matthews,
what on earth are you doing?' 'Calm yourself down, Jack
Matthews!' 'Not again, Jack Matthews!' The player was
booked, and the game resumed. After the final whistle,
one of the spectators asked a Tygmat player why Jack
Matthews' name had been given, when it was Eddie

Watson who had committed the foul. 'I didn't even know that Jack played football,' he added. 'He doesn't!' said the player. 'But we only have 13 in our squad, and we can't afford to lose anybody through suspensions. So we signed Jack on and, if anyone has to be booked, it's him – and then we all club together to pay the fine!'

And What of Other Sports?

'Mrs Soper said: "Mixed health clubs are all right for a place like London, but Rugby is a respectable town."' (*Sunday Mirror*.)

'I am a shy, retiring sort of a chap, keen on sport but not a great success at parties. The girls all flock round a man I know who can waggle his ears. How is it done? Or can anyone suggest an equally successful party trick?' Wallflower, Manchester. (*Daily Sketch.*)

'A 30-year-old housewife – accused of stealing two tins of meat from a supermarket – told Leamington magistrates that she had "never been the same" since she saw a man running about in the nude. "I have been under sedatives from my doctor ever since," she said.' (*Leamington Morning News.*)

'Mixed bathing is permitted in the Council swimming baths at Bradford-on-Avon (Wilts) only if the bathers are related.' (*News Chronicle.*)

'I don't think it is at all polite the way bowlers rub the ball all over themselves at cricket.' (Letter in the *Manchester Evening News.*)

'Bachelor, 33, 5ft. 6in., would like to meet girl/girls interested in messing about in boats; state other interests.'(Advert in *London Weekly Advertiser.*)

The 'Detached From Reality' Brigade

'When I watch modern soccer players, long-haired and emotional as a lot of hysterical women, kissing each other when they score a goal, it reminds me of an incident on the polo ground at Secunderabad in 1922. I was lucky enough to score the goal that won the cup, and started waving my stick in the way that a Zulu used to wave his assegai during a battle. The Second in Command of my Regiment quietly called me over, as captain of the team, and impressively said: "You should remember there are losers."A lesson I never forgot! When he died a couple of years ago, I sent that incident to his vicar in a Berkshire village as my tribute to a great English sportsman. The vicar read it out at the funeral service.' (Letter in *Daily Telegraph.*)

'I do not like wasting time when I am watching TV on my own. I like to do something else at the same time. I do foot, finger and eye exercises. I shrug my shoulders and roll my head round and round. During the World Cup, whenever the players took a corner or there was an injury I went down on my back to do a few tummy exercises and circle my legs round in the air.'(Letter in the *Daily Herald.*)

'Since the present government came in we have won the World Cup and the Eurovision Song Contest. That should silence the knockers.'(Letter in the *Daily Mirror.*)

'Play croquet and enjoy it, but do not teach it to children. Let them cut their teeth on football and cricket, or other gentlemanly games, and when they have proved themselves good losers introduce them to croquet, so they can learn to fend for themselves in the cut and thrust of life.'(Letter in *Daily Telegraph.*)

And What of Other Sports?

'Mrs Thatcher said: "I can't understand all the fuss about student grants. Carol managed to save out of hers. Of course, we paid for her skiing holidays."'(*Sun.*)

'Sir Charles, in these hard times, is an unostentatious motorist. He has the Fiat for getting about in, and an Aston Martin for going to the country at the weekend. He does, of course, also have an office aeroplane and a yacht for holidays.' (*Drive Magazine.*)

'In the winter he shoots, but it is something of an agony because he is very fond of birds and finds it hard to justify the idea of shooting them for sport. Luckily, he says, he doesn't have much time to think about it.'(Profile of Jocelyn Stevens in the *Sunday Times.*)

'English country gentlemen often hunt birds and no one objected when Sheikh Zaid Ben Sultan, ruler of Abu Dhabi, decided to try his hand at the sport at his

luxurious English country mansion. What distressed
neighbours was that he used a machine gun.'
(*Newsweek.*)

'I have one hope. The young prince is attending a school
whose theme is manliness. I say it would take a man to get
up and say: "No, father, I am not coming out with you
murdering animals. I am going to send a subscription to
the League Against Cruel Sports instead."' (Report in
Daily Telegraph.)

> 'Where so many people are mistaken is in supposing
> that the royal palate is exotic – that the Queen break-
> fasts on caviar, lunches on lark's tongues, and dines
> on filleted porcupine. In point of fact, her tastes are
> quite simple. She is not fond of any shellfish, but has
> a weakness for game and venison, particularly if it is
> shot by a member of the royal circle. As she has said:
> "It tastes so much better then."' (*Today.*)

'The Mayor said he was a great animal lover, and he
detested people who were cruel to animals. "It is bad
enough with children, but when it comes to dumb animals
it is terrible," he said.'(*Dorset County Chronicle.*)

> 'We want more autocrats. I am an autocrat, because
> by birth, breeding and intelligence I am fitted to
> lead.' (Mr Austin Hopkinson, MP, in the *Daily
> Mail.*)

'I am convinced that if a fox could vote, he would vote
Tory.' (Letter in the *Sussex Express and County Herald.*)

> 'Fox-hunting Lady Anne Fitzalan-Howard, 21-year-
> old daughter of the Duke of Norfolk, has a date in
> the church hall near her father's castle on Friday
> with the local branch of the British Union for the

Abolition of Vivisection. Wondering how Lady Anne reconciles her support for this cause with her own love of fox-hunting, I phoned her. Angrily she said: "There is no connection. One is sport and the other is downright cruelty."' (*Sunday Dispatch.*)

"'I've ridden cows all my life," she told me. "They make a marvellous ride and they're good jumpers: hedges, four-bar gates, the lot. I always wanted to ride one to hounds, but my people wouldn't let me."' (*News Chronicle.*)

'He (the Duke of Norfolk) hunts regularly on blood-stock horses of his own choosing and breeding, and once showed a surprising sense of humour by flicking a pat of butter on to a screen at a dinner party.' (*Cavalcade.*)

'Sir Gordon Richards, former champion jockey, and now successful racehorse trainer, was off to Barbados. "There is nothing we can do about the economic situation," he said. "We're all in it together."' (*Scottish Daily Express.*)

'I personally own a bull terrier, and would say here and now that I have far more in common with my dog and any horse than I have with ninety-nine and three quarters of the people I meet.' (Letter in the *Daily Express.*)

'Had Hitler and Mussolini been cricketers, I do not think we should have had all this trouble that is going on in Europe today.' (Sir Francis Lacey.)

'The great moment came when the umpire, W. A. J. West, one of the most famous umpires of all times, could not be found for the group. "Where's West?" we asked. "He's gone west," swiftly retorted Mr Stocks, maintaining the highest traditions of Uppingham humour.' (*Daily Mail.*)

'Racial characteristics heavily handicap the Japanese Rugby Union Football team at present touring the United Kingdom. The lack of weight in the scrummage and height in the line-out suggest that it would be more in keeping with the British sense of justice and fair play if the players selected, especially at forward, in the teams playing our guests were limited in weight and height more nearly to the weight and height of their Japanese opponents.' (Letter in *Daily Telegraph.*)

'Every Sunday the papers come out with the same story of "rough charging". I can just imagine the reception a rugger player would get if he asked for a hacked shin to be sponged! I was crocked for life in a sportsman's game, and I'm proud of it.' (Letter in the *Daily Express.*)

'Mr Wilf Young, secretary of the School's Amateur Boxing Association, said last night that Etonian boxers would never have been short of opponents if they had been prepared to fight boys from comprehensive schools.' (*Daily Telegraph.*)

'When the field went away, nuns tucked up their skirts and scampered after hounds, horses – and the fox. And last night, at the Sacred Heart convent, in Woldingham, Surrey, the Deputy Headmistress, Mother Shanley, said delightedly: "It was a delightful day. We actually made a kill in the convent grounds!"' (*Daily Express.*)

'Worthing Motor Club are thinking of using a petrol shortage rally. It would be exactly the same as a normal motor rally except that the cars would stay parked in the same place the whole time. Drivers would be given route instructions, would run out to their cars at one minute intervals and then sit in them and work out where they would have gone.' (*Sussex Evening Argus.*)

'A young couple I know have taken their tortoise with them on a motorcycle holiday tour. He has his own box on the back of the machine. I wish more tortoise owners would take such care of their pets at holiday time.' (Letter in the *Daily Mirror.*)

And Some Things You Didn't Know ...

'England players are on £22,000 bonus if they win the World Cup. West Germany, who are fourth favourites, are on £2 a day spending money, plus ten stamped picture postcards of the Derbyshire Peak district.' (*People.*)

'The ground at Sheffield yesterday was frost-bound and though liberally treated with sand, 16,000 spectators were soon laughing at the antics of the players.' (*Sunday Sun.*)

'My old uncle has an unusual pulse beat – sixty to the
minute. Without the help of a clock, he can time accu-
rately eggs boiling for three minutes; rounds of boxing
during broadcasts; the two minutes' silence on Armistice
Day; exposure periods for our cameras; and the interval
at half-time football matches.' (Letter in *Illustrated.*)

> 'L—, aged 32, a football steward, of Hampreston,
> Dorset, was sentenced to nine months' imprison-
> ment for stealing two balls, three tracksuits and com-
> mitting bigamy.' (*News of the World.*)

'Educated, aristocratic, 28, ambitious, chess, croquet and
soccer player, fly fisherman, Bisley medalist, musical;
seeks position in politics.' (Advert in *The Times.*)

Footballers have featured in hundreds of hit songs over
the years – from Paul McCartney's hymn of praise for a
German striker – 'Mueller Kintyre' – to Peter, Paul and
Mary's song to stir the mind of a five-year-old: 'Clough,
the Magic Dragon'.

Here we go:

'Moore than I can say'

'Howe's Party'

'Wichita Lynam'

'If Hughes Knew Suzie Like I Know Suzie'

'Brown-eyed Hansen Man'

'Itsy Bitsy, Teeny Weeny, Yellow Paul Kerr Dot Glen
Keeley'

'Can't Buy Me Ndlovu' (The Beatles)

John Lennon's prophetic song about the Nottingham
Forest and England fullback: 'Give Pearce A Chance'

Roy 'Chubby' Brown's curious song about a former

Manchester City manager, of whom he had obviously never heard: 'Who the f*** is Allison?'

'Dedicated Follower of Fashanu' (The Kinks)

And four Number 1 hits with strong football associations:

'Ferry 'cross the Mersey'
'You'll Never Walk Alone'
'Back Home'
'World in Motion'

And What of Other Sports?

'There is something specially clean and wholesome about boating men of which one is not so conscious among other athletes.' (*Sunday Times.*)

'Duncan Sandys was born to command. He was educated at Eton and Oxford where he studied some, worked his golf handicap down to seven, and was given an Indian servant by his father for his 21st birthday.' (*Newsweek.*)

'I was intrigued by your note on the glass-blower's "Frigging" in last October's issue. This must surely be the origin of the expression, "frigging about", meaning doodling or wasting one's time. I thought it an expression peculiar to Pembrokeshire, but recently I heard a Yorkshireman from Hull use it and I have never heard that Pembrokeshire had any special connection with the glass-making industry.' (Letter in *Town and Country.*)

'Cemetery superintendent and groundsman, Frank Maule, is delighted with his farewell present from his employers. He has been given a grave space.' (*Daily Mail.*)

'For 40 years Jim Mandy earned a living in vaudeville,

letting people swing a 10 lb. sledgehammer at a 50 lb. rock balanced on his head. He thinks that one day there might be a new demand for this form of entertainment. So, just in case, he keeps training by beating his bald head with blocks of wood every morning.' (*Reynolds News.*)

> 'Shyness does queer things to people … I had an uncle who used invariably to enter a room full of company walking on his hands, or on all fours, barking like a dog.'

'WELFARE STATE BLAMED FOR HEAVIER JOCKEYS' (Headline in the *Scotsman.*)

> 'Winter explains why horses are nearly always gelded before they are sent into a steeple chasing career. "All these colts think about is women. Once they're cut it alters their whole character. They become much kinder. They are more generous to you. You couldn't race a horse with his testicles in. If he hit them on a fence he'd be so careful afterwards he'd be no use at all."' (*Sunday Times.*)

'The Bible is the inspiration of Louis. He always reads it before entering the ring, and then, according to one of his seconds: "All fortified and everything, he just wades in and knocks the other guy's head off."' (*Daily Express.*)

> 'Perhaps it will be some comfort to his wife that at the time he crashed he was travelling faster than any man has ever travelled on a motorcycle before.' (Writer in the *Sunday Express.*)

'Herr Walter Funk, the German Finance Minister, is not the same Walter Funk who fought Pat MacAllister at Nottingham Victoria Baths.' (*Nottingham Evening News.*)

'Crossed in love, Nicholas Steel-Jessop, 20-year-old insurance clerk, of Needham Market, Suffolk, put on a top hat and frock coat and rode 85 miles to London on a penny-farthing. He said: "When I was jilted, it made me feel an awful failure. The ride restored my confidence."' (*Daily Express.*)

'Every room in a £687,000 motel-cum-leisure centre to be built at Southport, Lancs., will be carpeted with artificial turf so golfing guests can practise in privacy.' (*Sunday Mirror.*)

'For two hours the committee of a golf club in south-east England debated whether women players might be allowed to wear trousers on the Links. Their decision was: "Trousers may be worn by women golfers on the course, but must be taken off on entering the clubhouse."' (*Daily Mirror.*)

'Fylde's baths manager, Mr Noel O'Shea, plans to solve the disappearing swimsuit problem by asking for a shoe or a piece of underclothing from those who can't afford the £5 deposit.' (*Lancashire Evening Post.*)

'Opening their home has meant sacrifices for the Wellesleys: in 1973 the Duke built a magnificent mosaic-clad pool in the conservatory, but now it's out of bounds to them on public days.' (*Radio Times.*)

'He had sold dozens of pairs of these swimming trunks made of a new plastic material before someone discovered it was soluble in water.' (Southport *Guardian.*)

'A council has refused clay pigeon shooting enthusiasts permission to use land at Ribchester, Lancashire, after a nearby nudist club complained that members have been peppered by stray pellets.' (*Daily Express.*)

'For Hire for the Season. Seaside or Tour. The World's Ugliest Woman. 18 stone. 31 years old. 1 tooth. Face full of wrinkles like a prune. Charming personality.' (Advert in *World's Fair*.)

'Greyhound for Sale, eats anything. Fond of children.' (Advert in the *Hayes News*.)

'He has always been a man to bear misfortune with stoical endurance. A racehorse owner for the past twenty years, he had his first winner – Goblin – only three weeks ago.' (*Sunday Telegraph*.)

'There are few *Vogue* readers who have never harboured a slinking desire to be thrown across the saddle of a plunging white stallion, galloped to a palmy oasis and stuffed with dates in a striped silk prison by swarthy warriors.' (*Vogue*.)

How many times have you watched your team miss a sitter and yelled: 'GORDON BENNETT!'? – Well, Gordon Bennett was a Scotsman whose family emigrated to America, where his father founded, and became editor of the *New York Herald*. He became editor, and reputedly spent more than $30 million on extraordinary ventures. According to one story, when he was in Paris entertaining the Paris editor of the *New York Herald*, he couldn't get a table, so he bought the whole restaurant. Afterwards, he gave the restaurant to the waiter on condition that chips would always be on the menu and his table would always be available to him. So whenever you hear anything exceptional, you say: 'Gordon Bennett!'.

'Football's European Championship was the work of Frenchman, Henri Delaunay. The very first game was between the Irish Republic and Czechoslovakia which took place in April 1959. In the finals in 1960, the USSR beat Yugoslavia 2–1 after extra time.'

'Three young men are going to run all the way from Southampton to New York – around and around the deck of the Europa – as a demonstration for World peace.' (*Evening Standard.*)

'From Surrey, there is the story of the man who planned to go to Haydock Races at the weekend, and on the Wednesday, Thursday and Friday nights, he dreamed of the number seven. He thought that the supernatural was trying to get through to him with a message. When he went to the Races on the Saturday, he put everything he had on horse number 7 in the seventh race – and it came in seventh.'

Notice on the rear window of a car in Woodstock: 'So you think I'm a bad driver. You should see me putt.'

From the quarterly newsletter of a Devonshire equestrian club: 'Col— said he could not abide sloppiness: girls who rode to hounds should ride dressed properly or not at all.'

The Superior Sport Brigade

'The British cyclists finished eleventh in 100km road team trial. Their performance was particularly commendable since a man shot himself through the head not 20 yards away from where the British were assembling before the start of the race.' (*Guardian.*)

'A high degree of skill and intelligence are required (for croquet) and therefore it is not going to attract the lower income groups.' (Croquet Association chairman quoted in *The Times.*)

'I would like to have a go at the World Record for having a ferret down your trousers. I have two ferrets and would put both down. I believe I could put one of my ferrets down for a whole month and I wouldn't even know that it was there.' (Letter in the *People*.)

'We must preserve the Boat Race in these days of the hydrogen bomb. Otherwise life becomes intolerable.' (From the *Listener*.)

'Tornado would train girl to ride wall-of-death; good knitter preferable.' (Advert in *Southend Standard*.)

And Cricket . . .

There still do exist pockets of aficionados who believe that cricket is a spiritual experience which embodies all that is good, fair and honourable in this tormented world. To them, the smack of leather on willow, the fragrance of

new-mown grass and soft summer days recall memories
of their uncomplicated youth when the world was a better
place. It was then the Empire held sway, cricket flannels
had such razor sharp creases that you were in danger of
losing your parts if you crossed your legs, and afternoon
teas of triangular sandwiches, clotted-cream and straw-
berry scones were washed down with Earl Grey tea in
bone china cups and matching saucers. However, that
small band of romantics is rapidly dwindling as Atherton
picks up dirt and Illingworth slags off Malcolm. The
members of the MCC, who wear their ties as proudly as
any D-day veteran, still encapsulate those days of yore,
and long may they do so. They will empathize with the
following:

'Johnson, at 29 a fine batsman and an off-spinner not
far off the Test arena himself, seems eminently suitable.
He is a thoughtful and intelligent cricketer who must have
made many followers of Test cricket less suspicious of the
products of the London School of Economics.' (*Daily
Telegraph.*)

'His abiding interest in cricket continues, and when,
to the delight of the spectators, he hit two sixes in the
match his eleven played against the touring MCC
team at Auckland in 1961, it was perhaps the apogee
of his career as Governor General.' (Obituary of
Viscount Cobham in *The Times.*)

'There have been various occasions since he became an
England cricketer when Greig has overplayed his hand.
What has to be remembered, of course, is that he is an
Englishman not by birth or upbringing, but only by adop-
tion. It is not the same thing as being English through and
through.' (*The Times.*)

'The suggestion that Lord's cricket ground be used as a greyhound racing track in winter is almost sacrilegious. You might as well suggest that Westminster Abbey be used as a cinema when a service is not being held.' (*Sunday Express.*)

'The parson of a village where a friend of mine lives was perturbed at the persistent shortage of rain. Cattle and roots were suffering; the outlook was gloomy. He decided to pray for rain at morning service the next Sunday. Then a troublesome thought struck him. "No," he told my friend, "not next Sunday; I shall put it off till the Sunday after. I'm not going to do anything to spoil the Test Match."'

'The Headmistress of Godolphin, Miss C. R. Ash, was of the opinion that the School Certificate for girls was only valuable if taken in their stride. She said that one of her best cricketers went entirely off her bowling last summer because of examination worries.' (*News Chronicle.*)

'When Frank Groves, of Talbot Terrace, Leeds, was summoned at Great Yarmouth Police Court today for failing to conform with a traffic sign, the managing director of his firm wrote to the Bench: "May I respectfully ask you to remember what Yorkshire did for England in the last Test Match?"' (*Cambridge Daily News.*)

'. . . the whole English cricket-loving public, which, so far as Test matches at any rate are concerned, includes almost every man and literate male child, and the more responsibly-minded women as well.' (*Evening Standard.*)

'Mr Justice Oliver told Manchester Assizes today that a ball hit for six which soared out of a suburban cricket ground and struck a woman on the head could not be regarded as a nuisance.' (*Yorkshire Evening Post.*)

'It's a funny kind of month, October. For the really keen cricket fan, it's when you discover that your wife left you in May.' (Denis Norden.)